THE PRIESTS

"The evidence of the beauty and joy of life is always present, even in the physical world, as imperfect as it is. Even in the jungle we could find it. Even in darkest Africa we could find evidence of God's light and love and beauty. It's in the people, it's in the country. It's not that difficult to find."
—Albert Schweitzer

"Even though we are less barbaric than we were two thousand years ago, it is very difficult for enlightened beings to incarnate in the world today."   —Yogananda

"It is assumed that the wealthy have become wealthy only because they have exploited the masses. Of course nothing could be further from the truth, but it is the way the masses often think nowadays. It is just envy."   —Andrew Carnegie

"The good leader serves as a conscience for the people and warns them of the consequences of their demands and behavior. He must be the mouthpiece of the public will, not the tail which drags along behind everything else."
—Sir Winston Churchill

OTHER BOOKS BY
ROBERT R. LEICHTMAN, M.D.

The Psychic Perspective
The Inner Side of Life
The Hidden Side of Science
The Dynamics of Creativity
The Destiny of America

FROM HEAVEN TO EARTH:

THE PRIESTS OF GOD

BY ROBERT R. LEICHTMAN, M.D.

The Fourth In A Series

ARIEL PRESS
Atlanta, Georgia

This book is made possible by a gift
to the Publications Fund of Light
from Judy Dean and Bill Mueller

THE PRIESTS OF GOD
Copyright © 1980, 1981, 1982, & 1997 by Light

All Rights Reserved. No part of this book may be used or reproduced in any manner whatsoever without written permission, except in the case of brief quotations embodied in articles and reviews. Printed in the United States of America. Direct inquiries to: Ariel Press, P.O. Box 1387, Alpharetta, GA 30239. No royalties are paid on this book.

ISBN 0-89804-084-1

TABLE OF CONTENTS

A Brief Introduction — page 7
The Priests of God — page 11
Schweitzer Returns — page 15
Yogananda Returns — page 74
Carnegie Returns — page 138
Churchill Returns — page 201
Glossary — page 262
From Heaven To Earth — page 271

A BRIEF INTRODUCTION

The Priests of God is the fourth of six books in a unique series of books by Dr. Robert Leichtman called *From Heaven to Earth*. Each book in this series contains the transcript of four interviews, conducted mediumistically, between Dr. Leichtman and the spirit of a well-known leader or genius.

The interviews began in 1973. They were first published, in 1979 and 1980, as a series of twelve books, each book containing one complete interview with the spirit of an outstanding psychic or medium—people such as Edgar Cayce, Arthur Ford, and Madame Blavatsky.

The popularity of the first series of interviews encouraged Dr. Leichtman to embark on a second set of twelve. This time, however, he decided to broaden the scope of the interviews so that it would embrace the whole domain of creativity, genius, and leadership. As a result, he interviewed such people as Albert Schweitzer, Mark Twain, and Albert Einstein. These interviews were conducted in 1979 and 1980 and published in 1981 and 1982.

Public acceptance of these interviews has remained strong ever since they were first published. But it has proven awkward to keep 24 individual books in print, so we have decided to reissue all 24 interviews in a new format—six books each containing four interviews.

The 24 interviews divided naturally into six groups, so that each book in the new format focuses on one specific theme of the work of bringing heaven to earth. The four interviews in this volume, for instance, all deal with service to God and humanity. Albert Schweitzer embodied the ideals of sacrifice and service in his outstanding work ministering to the sick in Africa. Yogananda was one of the great spiritual "missionaries" of our time, bringing the hidden wisdom of the East to the attention of the spiritually hungry in the West. Andrew Carnegie demonstrated that big business can be an important venue for spiritual service, too—and set the keynote for the growth of philanthropy for the last one hundred years. Sir Winston Churchill took the lead in rallying the forces of light and goodwill against the greatest political threat to humanity in thousands of years.

The other five volumes in the new format are thematically grouped in much the same way:

The Inner Side of Life—interviews with C.W. Leadbeater, H.P. Blavatsky, Cheiro, and Sigmund Freud and Carl Jung.

The Psychic Perspective—interviews with Edgar Cayce, Eileen Garrett, Arthur Ford, and Stewart Edward White.

The Hidden Side of Science—interviews with Nikola Tesla, Luther Burbank, Sir Oliver Lodge, and Albert Einstein.

The Dynamics of Creativity—interviews with William Shakespeare, Mark Twain, Rembrandt, and Richard Wagner.

The Destiny of America—interviews with Thomas Jefferson, Benjamin Franklin, Abraham Lincoln, and a group interview with seven key people from America's history—Alexander Hamilton, Jefferson, Franklin, the two Roosevelts, Harry Truman, and George Washington.

As the title *From Heaven to Earth* suggests, the purpose of these interviews is to acquaint readers with the current thinking of these outstanding individuals, even though they have left their physical bodies and now work on the inner dimensions of reality. Many new ideas about psychic phenomena, spiritual growth, government, art, service, and civilization are set forth in the conversations—as well as a new revelation of the relation between heaven and earth. The interviews are not just academic discussions of the historical accomplishments of these people; they probe new frontiers of the human mind. Each is a thoughtful, witty, and lively exchange of ideas.

It is not the intent of this series to document the existence of life after death—or the effectiveness of mediumship in contacting the spirits of those who have left their physical bodies. Nor is it necessary, for these matters have been scientifically proven many times over in other writings—indeed, in many of the books written by the people interviewed in these books. The doubting reader will find ample proof in the works of Sir Oliver Lodge, Stewart Edward White, Eileen Garrett, Madame Blavatsky, Arthur Ford, and C.W. Leadbeater—as well as the many books about Edgar Cayce. Instead, the interviews in *From Heaven to Earth* are offered as a way of demonstrating that we need not be content with just an echo of great geniuses who have lived and died; their voices can literally be heard again. Their spirits and ideas can actually return to earth. Heaven is not some faraway place inaccessible to mortals. It can easily be contacted by competent psychics and mediums who have correctly trained themselves. And such contact can produce insight and new ideas of great importance.

A more complete introduction to the interviews is contained in volume one, The Psychic Perspective, *in conjunction with the interview with Edgar Cayce. In it, the nature of the mediumistic trance, the origins of this project, and the value of creative genius are all discussed in detail. For information on ordering this book, or the entire series, please see page 271 in this volume.*

A second introduction, which originally prefaced the interview with Albert Schweitzer—the first book published in the second set of interviews—is included in this fourth volume. It describes the theme of "the priests of God."

—Carl Japikse
ARIEL PRESS

THE PRIESTS OF GOD

The ultimate reason why we strive to contact the kingdom of heaven is to become an agent of God's light, illuminating the darkness wherever it exists and spiritualizing civilization and the earth through all that we do. It is not enough to be a devotee of an abstract God, Who sits on a throne somewhere apart from humanity. Nor is it sufficient to sing hymns of praise and confess our sins. The enlightened person does more; he worships God by serving His evolutionary plans. He becomes a steward of life here on earth, and by example, leads others to do the same. Frequently, he is not even perceived by the masses as a servant or worshipper of God, because his field of endeavor is not within the traditional scope of religion; yet he knows heaven, loves God, and serves the Plan.

Such a person could truly be called a *priest of God,* not in the conventional sense of a somber ecclesiastic garbed in black, but as an agent of light who practices the presence of God in everything he does. Eventually, we are all meant to become priests of God in this sense, and should strive toward that goal. Although this destiny is still a future one for most of us, nonetheless there have always been true priests of God with us, serving heaven, leading humanity, and healing the imperfections of earth. Indeed, many of the greatest servants of God mankind has ever known have walked this earth, touching heaven, within the last three centuries.

As this thought occurred to me, I knew I had found the purpose of the second set of interviews—to demonstrate how contemporary priests of God have revealed divine wisdom, love, and talent as they worked to enrich civilization and culture in all its many facets—in government, the arts, literature, music, science, medicine, industry, philosophy, religion, and education.

Armed with this thought, I began to consider the qualifications I should look for in choosing the spirits to interview. To my mind, the priest of God is a person who is able to find God in the midst of everyday life and, by the power, inspiration, and refinement of his talent and understanding, manifest something divine in his work. He brings heaven to earth—not just to worship it and reveal it, *but to use it to transform the world!* He does not necessarily conduct services in churches or temples, but renders service where it is needed, to teach and enlighten, to beautify, to lead in times of crisis, to help harness physical resources for human use, and to heal both individuals and society.

Having outlined these criteria in my mind, the choices emerged quite rapidly. I immediately thought of the Dutch artist Rembrandt van Rijn, who was surely a priest of the paintbrush. In music, many choices could have been made, but the composer Richard Wagner stood out clearly as a high priest of spiritual purpose. Who is not swept into a vision of heaven in listening to his operas?

I chose Mark Twain in literature. As priests of leadership, I selected Sir Winston Churchill, who led not just England but all of civilized humanity through the crisis of World War II, and Abraham Lincoln, who healed a badly divided nation with charity and patience. Benjamin Franklin could certainly be thought of as a priest of leadership, too, but I believe it even more appropriate to recognize him for his contributions to diplomacy and philosophy.

Albert Einstein was an easy choice as a priest of science, a man who used his mind as his primary scientific instrument. Also from the world of science, I selected Luther Burbank, the horticultural wizard. In industry, I thought of Andrew Carnegie, who built a fortune in steel and then set a model for enlightened philanthropy, using his wealth to fund public libraries throughout the nation and support other worthwhile charities and public projects.

I also wanted to interview representative priests of enlightened service. In this category, I chose Dr. Albert Schweitzer, whose hospital in Africa became a symbol of unselfish Christian service, and Paramahansa Yogananda, the Hindu mystic who brought many of the spiritual teachings of India to America and helped inspire new interest in this country in the life of spirit.

Each of these great individuals richly deserves the title "priest of God." Not only did they work with brilliance and genius in their chosen fields, which is significant enough, but they also were healers of society. Only Dr. Schweitzer treated broken physical bodies, but all of them healed, to some extent, the broken aspirations, the diseases, and the confusion of humanity as a whole. Churchill healed by stopping the aggression of fascism. Mark Twain healed with his pen; his literary masterpieces, so often regarded today as stories for youth, actually served to enlighten the American public to a new sensitivity regarding racial discrimination and the value of human individuality. Wagner and Rembrandt healed ugliness. Carnegie worked to heal, by example and by contribution, the intense materialism of the past century. Burbank, Einstein, and Yogananda healed ignorance. Franklin and Lincoln were two of the prime contributors to the health of America as a nation.

All qualify as priests of God in another way, too— through their work, they brought a fresh revelation of God's light and love to meet our modern needs. They did not just recycle old approaches to living; they *innovated,* in profound and spiritual ways. Einstein's new ideas in physics have stretched the minds of many an individual who has sought to comprehend them. Yogananda and Schweitzer touched thousands of people with a higher quality of God's love than they had ever encountered before. Lincoln and Franklin lifted the concepts of community and brotherhood to new levels of nobility.

As I began conducting the interviews, I came to appreciate how appropriate the concept of "priests of God" actually is. Although all of these individuals are well-known to history, I discovered that we really know very little about their true humanity and scope of character. History all too often traps itself in the mundane details of the lives of great people, striving for "objectivity" but forgetting that the subjective elements of genius are even more interesting. As a result, we tend to miss the fact that some people go far beyond the common motives and activities of ordinary people, and strive to reach a higher level of achievement. I was delighted to find, however, that all the spirits I had tapped were quite eager to talk about the spiritual impulses which drove them in their work—indeed, sometimes drove them to sacrifice their well-being, their fortunes, and their health. They also talked candidly about the inspiration which guided them, the dedication and love that kept them going, and their views on the dignity and nobility of mankind. That, after all, is what is truly important about each of these gentlemen—not the details of their work and lives.

ALBERT SCHWEITZER RETURNS

Perhaps the best way to describe the life and work of Albert Schweitzer is to liken it to a finely cut diamond, sparkling in brilliant sunlight. Schweitzer was a man of multiple facets—not a jack of all trades, but a genius of the highest order. His greatest and most enduring fame, of course, comes from his work as a medical missionary in equatorial Africa. There, he built and equipped a hospital from his own income, and devoted the final fifty years of his life to treating the medical needs of the natives. But it is also important to realize that Albert Schweitzer was *already* a famous individual before he decided to become a doctor and go to Africa. He held a university chair in theology, and his book, *The Quest for the Historical Jesus,* had established him as a world figure in his field. He was also recognized as one of the leading interpreters of his time of the music of Johann Sebastian Bach, and was in popular demand for organ concerts. To renounce such recognition and pursue an entirely new career—and in a God-forbidding place such as the African jungle of 1915—surely must have struck Schweitzer's contemporaries as sheer madness. But diamonds are of special merit; they are of a higher quality than emeralds or pearls or other precious gems. So was Schweitzer. It is not credible to believe that *his* genius and love were just another accident in time and space. His lifetime and accomplishments are obviously the consequence of enormous talent, dedication, wisdom, and hard work. He was, indeed, *more* than a diamond—he was a diamond sparkling in brilliant sunlight. He was a man who revealed, through all that he did, the powerful presence of God within him.

The renunciation of comfort, position, and fame was actually a very logical step for Schweitzer to take. While other theologians were content to preach and discuss religious concepts, Schweitzer firmly believed that religion should be honored in one's daily activities and duties. Unless charity, love, faith, and goodwill are brought to life in a meaningful way in our own self-expression, they are dead—for us. And yet, as Schweitzer observed, these qualities of consciousness are far too frequently left unexpressed.

In his day as well as our own, for example, the concept of charity was often reduced to the intimidation and manipulation of people to donate money, time, and effort as a means of expiating guilty feelings about the imperfections of the world. Charitable work was often left to the direction of people who were more puffed up with righteousness or smugness, than motivated by a genuine sense of love and caring. Moreover, far too many people involved in service plodded through their work with boredom, resentment, and a confused sense of duty, rather than cheerfulness and a willingness to help.

In his service in Africa, however, Dr. Schweitzer set an example of caring and dedication which richly deserves to be considered the work of a priest of God. In his patient, gentle way, he demonstrated what genuine love is, and the purpose it serves. For him, love was not just another four-letter word to be used in lectures and sermons to intimidate others into being more guilty or contrite. It was a powerful force within himself—and within every human being—which helped him view all of life as a noble creation of a loving God. Love helped him be aware of the magnificence of God, and His presence in all things; it drew him into communion with the creative and healing potential in all life forms. Love motivated him to act with kindness and wisdom, and to be an agent of its benevolence and greatness in all that he did. Love gave him the vision to see the needs of people, and supported him as he sought to relieve their distress. Love lifted him up so he could comprehend the inner dimension of life; it enabled him to endure in spite of the misery he confronted every day. Love revealed to him the beauty in all things—and led him to enter into oneness with God's great love for His entire creation.

It should be little wonder, then, that Dr. Schweitzer turned to a desolate and forgotten area of the planet to initiate his medical mission. Where else was there a greater need for intelligent and compassionate service? Where else was there a less civilized, more harsh country in which to work? Where else was there a greater opportunity to demonstrate the healing and transforming power of divine love?

The obstacles he had to overcome to perform this service were formidable. When he and his wife Hélène arrived in Lambaréné, in what is now the African nation of Gabon, they did not step into someone else's shoes. They had to build a hospital with their own hands, teach the natives the value of medical care, overcome the superstitions and fears of the local tribes, and work, at least in the beginning, with very little support.

During World War I, Schweitzer was sent to France as a prisoner of war—because he happened to be born German. That interrupted his missionary service, but gave him a chance to write. After the war, however, he returned to Lambaréné and reconstructed the hospital. At the time of his death in 1965, the hospital had grown to the point of being able to care for 350 patients, plus their relatives. A nearby leper colony Schweitzer had also founded cared for 150 patients.

For this work "on behalf of the Brotherhood of Nations," and his writings, Dr. Schweitzer was awarded the Nobel Peace Prize in 1952.

To my mind, Schweitzer's work in Africa illustrates three important features of genuine service. First, it must be motivated by a sincere love and regard for all of life—what he called "the reverence for life." We do not serve only those whom we like and those who will like us in return, or repay us. We serve where there is a need. Second, an individual who would serve should have the capacity to serve cheerfully, without a martyr complex and without selfish motives for doing so. The service should be seen as a way of honoring the life of the spirit, not as a terrible duty to be performed to a chorus of moaning and groaning.

And third, we must not treat the people we serve with condescension or "holier than thou" smugness. Dr. Schweitzer served because he cared about the welfare of the people he sought to help. He saw them as children of God with needs to be met—not as savage natives or stupid heathens to be converted.

In this regard, it seems to me that Dr. Schweitzer's service was not limited to the tiny compound of Lambaréné. The direct beneficiaries of his loving care were the African citizens of Gabon, but indirectly, the whole of Western civilization profited. Dr. Schweitzer returned to Europe numerous times, giving concert and lecture tours to raise money for his mission. As he did, he helped educate thousands of Westerners to look beyond their personal needs and help support the work of Christian charity wherever it might be focused.

I am also deeply impressed by what Dr. Schweitzer gave up in order to perform this service. He could have made much more money, directly touched the lives of more people, and enjoyed himself far more if he had pursued his musical gifts as a full-time career. His expertise and interest in music were such that he became a world authority on the reconstruction of ancient organs—even while working in Africa! Certainly it would have been an easy rationalization to make, especially after being taken prisoner of war, to abandon the hospital in Africa and pursue more comfortable activities. But he did not. He returned again and again to Africa and worked to add to his hospital and staff. Even as an aged man, he continued to render excellent health care to the people of Lambaréné. I doubt that the temptation to abandon his work ever entered Dr. Schweitzer's mind, however. The type of service he performed, honestly motivated by spiritual love, tends to be an activity which is pursued without doubts, rationalizations, or hesitations. The personality that is dominated by the love of the innermost spirit automatically acts as an agent of goodwill to do those things which serve the one life. In this regard, the service of an enlightened individual is just as natural as the reflexive blinking of our eyes when we are surprised by a loud noise.

Those who knew Dr. Schweitzer well often tell of his quiet and thoughtful patience and gentleness. As tired as he might be, for example, he would still sit down to answer his mail, knowing how important the letters could be to those receiving them. As exhausted as he might be, he always had time for visitors as well as patients.

In the interview that follows, Dr. Schweitzer talks extensively about what was obviously one of his favorite themes—the nature of loving service. He comments on his idea of resignation or renunciation, removing it from the usual context of self-annihilation and placing it in the more dignified, enlightened perspective of discovering the inner life of spirit, our individual connection with God. Repeatedly, he encourages us to make the effort to establish these inner links with spirit.

I also inquired about his philosophy of "reverence for life," which he wrote about extensively in his later books, especially his *Philosophy of Civilization* and *Out of My Life and Thought*. He comments that love alone is not enough to guarantee effective service; it must be activated by the will to do good works. As he puts it, it must become the *will to love* and the *will to life*.

In answer to questions, Dr. Schweitzer also comments on perceptions he made in his writings regarding the problems of pessimism and skepticism in world thought, as well as the nature of evil. This highly thoughtful man has some very strong convictions about these subjects—and about the responsibility of each human being to learn to think for himself or herself. That, he suggests, is the only way to fully eliminate one's vulnerability to evil. His comments are worth careful evaluation and reflection.

At one point in the interview, he cried, as he thought about the disease and hardship of life in Africa—and the obstacles Africa must still overcome in reaching full status as a member of the world community. I was deeply impressed by the maturity of this man's compassion and tenderness. Indeed, throughout the whole interview, the room was charged with a special quality of reverence. At times, as he was speaking, he focused on specific elements of the quality of love, and the magnetic charge in the room intensified even more. Then, as he withdrew at the end of the session, he gave a silent benediction, which left us uplifted for the rest of the day.

As I understand it, that was the kind of person he was in the flesh as well. Like Jesus, he revealed the nature of spiritual love in all that he did—in what he said and wrote, through his acts, and by his attitudes and approach to life. The power of love was with him as he spoke; it filled him as he wrote. Indeed, I would highly recommend any of his later writings.

In the interview, Dr. Schweitzer appears through the mediumship of my good friend, David Kendrick Johnson. David was the medium for almost all of the interviews in the first series; he is a very gifted artist and psychic. Also participating in the interview was my colleague, Carl Japikse.

Leichtman: I'd like to start by discussing with you your philosophy of "reverence for life." Can you describe how that approach to living evolved? What events or steps in reasoning led you to this reverence for life?

Schweitzer: I suppose the most important factor is that I

was—and am—natively religious. I am a spiritual person at heart. As a child growing up, I began examining a lot of the precepts and beliefs that were taught; and, in careful reading of the Bible, I came to the realization that these were not just ideas to accept and believe, but they also had to be practiced every day, in my attitudes and acts. So, I started practicing them, and that became, gradually, my "reverence for life."

Leichtman: You spent a long time in religious studies, and wrote several books on the lives of Jesus and Paul. As I looked into this, it became apparent that your thinking about Biblical concepts went through a tremendous evolution. Early on, you seemed to take a rather literal view of the life of Jesus and what He taught. Later on, your perspective seemed to become more of what I would call the "rational mystic." How did that evolution occur?

Schweitzer: A true mystic is always rational.

Leichtman: I should hope so.

Schweitzer: As you know, mysticism in not anti-intellectual. The impressions of the true mystic are just as rational as they are heartfelt. And to answer your question, I had a number of intuitive impressions about Jesus that gradually influenced my perspective. I guess you could say I had a vision of Him which changed my thinking drastically.

Leichtman: You had a vision of Him which changed your life?

Schweitzer: Yes—not in the sense of seeing an image of Him, but I did have a profound insight into His all-encompassing love and dedication. After that, I knew for sure He is a living presence of great importance. It is impossible to question His significance after an experience of that intensity. And it's probably also impossible *not* to have reverence for life after this kind of experience. Reverence for life is a very important aspect of Christianity. As you are wont to say, man has been put here to be God's steward on earth. I sincerely believe that.

Leichtman: In your early books, such as *The Search for the*

Historical Jesus, you wrote of the kingdom of heaven as a supernatural kingdom to be experienced after death and the resurrection of the body. At that point, you apparently had not evolved the philosophy of life you held later on. How much of the difference between your early and later thinking is the result of the fact that the clergy of that day seemed unimaginative and literal-minded?

Schweitzer: A good deal of it. I had to accept some of the ideas of the clergy simply because I was monitored in my writing efforts.

Leichtman: Yes—as I remember it from your biographies, the mission society that sent you to Africa could accept you as a doctor but not as a minister, because your ideas were a bit too "radical" for them.

Schweitzer: That's true.

Leichtman: Well, many people in Christianity and other religions talk a great deal about "love," but never seem to express much love in their lives. You, by contrast, seemed impelled to demonstrate Christian charity.

Schweitzer: Yes, and I'll tell you why. The statement in the Bible, "By their acts ye shall know them," struck me as very important. To demonstrate love seemed far more significant than talking about it. It was an imperative to me. But it was sincere; I didn't expect to get a lot of "credit points" from my peers for being a loving person.

Leichtman: What was your attitude toward the clergy and philosophers of that day—your peers—who talked and talked about love but didn't really treat their fellow man with much affection, let alone love? How did you handle that paradox, that sanctimony? Did it embitter you or depress you?

Schweitzer: No—I did my best to demonstrate my views about love and reverence as vital aspects of religion, and tried to help them see that they were off the path a bit. You also have to remember that many people enter the ministry not because they are religious, but because it enables them to exercise a certain power over people they would not have otherwise.

Unfortunately, that is a *very* common reason why people enter the ministry.

Leichtman: Yes, I'm aware of that. Well, why did you choose to go to Africa, of all places, to demonstrate the power of love? Why didn't you do your work in Europe, where life and circumstances would have been more comfortable and familiar?

Schweitzer: Well, for one thing, there was a greater need in Africa, and love responds best to a genuine need. The need itself drew me, in a way. Another factor was that I wanted to test myself a bit.

Leichtman: Well, you certainly did that.

[Laughter.]

Schweitzer: I should say so! It became apparent very quickly after I arrived that the clinical standards of Europe were just not going to work in the jungle. We found we had to be willing to sacrifice some of those clinical standards in order to make the people comfortable. Otherwise, they would not have come: they would not have been able to relate to a European-type hospital setting. They would have been frightened. Now, that was a real test, but we worked out ways so that the families could stay with the patient, as often as possible.

You know, I wish modern hospitals in Europe and America were more like that, permitting the family to stay with the patient. A hospital can be very frightening and depressing, and that can impede the process of getting well.

Leichtman: Wasn't there also a problem of superstition, which made it more desirable to let the family stay with the patient?

Schweitzer: Oh, yes. Some of the people, for example, would only eat food that had been cooked by their wife or a family member. Of course, that wasn't just superstition—they were also afraid of being poisoned by other patients! We solved a lot of these problems by providing dormitories for the patients and their families—a space in which they could build a hut and live in it together.

Leichtman: I want to return for a minute to our discussion of philosophy. During your life, you were impressed by and wrote about the problems of skepticism and pessimism in world philosophy and religion. Do you still see these as major problems?

Schweitzer: Absolutely—and they are both deadly to religion and philosophy. Pessimism and skepticism are really outpicturings of the blight of materialism, which blinds us to an inner view of life, so that all we can see are the difficulties of physical life and emotional impoverishment. The pessimist and skeptic are so busy being pessimistic and skeptical that they are unable to perceive spiritual values.

We live in an imperfect world. There's a lot wrong with society and with people—and it's discouraging. I would certainly be sympathetic with any intelligent person who does, from time to time, entertain pessimistic thoughts and feelings about his life, work, and society. When you read in books that God is love and hear people talk about how wonderful it is that God has designed the world and loves us, it is sometimes very challenging to your faith and intelligence to accept these ideas at face value, when there is so much disease, distress, pain, and misery in the world. Some doubt, skepticism, and pessimism is probably rational, because the problems to be solved are not easy ones. But what is absolutely irrational is the assumption that the problems *are all there is,* that the world is somehow dead or corrupt. It is irrational to assume we're doomed, that life is doomed, and society is doomed—that life is hell and is never going to get any better.

This is the great advantage that the people who find meaning in life and value in their religion, whatever it is, have over the pessimists and skeptics. They know there's something more than the problems and misery. This is particularly true in Christianity, and also in Judaism. We are supposed to look to God as a source of salvation—not salvation from fire and hell, but salvation from this blight of pessimism, depression, and misery.

Japikse: Salvation from our own negative attitudes.

Schweitzer: Yes, and from the attitudes of those around you. Bear in mind that I probably saw more misery, grief, and sickness in my lifetime than most people would see if they lived five hundred years. And when you confront that kind of misery, you can either kill yourself with agony and frustration and depression, or you can try, as best you can, to correct things and make life better. You try to be healing, soothing, and reassuring. And as you do, you align yourself with the forces of the world that are healing, soothing, and reassuring themselves. Pretty soon, you come to know that there *are* hidden resources of light and love, dignity and nobility in yourself, in other people, and in all creation.

As you continue to work with these forces, as your ally, they become very real to you. They prove their existence to you as you reach out for them—to get through another day, to rise above your fatigue, to conquer your pessimism, or to be helpful in the world, in whatever way you have the opportunity to do so. The misery, pessimism, and depression never go away entirely, but they eventually threaten you less, because you become absolutely convinced that your real identity, your real source of life and help, is the great universal force called God. This force is God's power, wisdom, love, and nobility all wrapped up together, permeating all life.

My point is this: the objective world is sometimes pretty miserable, sometimes very beautiful. But it is *designed* to be beautiful, lovely, and healthy—and *we* are designed to know that and appreciate it. And we have a duty to help others see this, too. We have the duty to work with God's wisdom and love to help make the world a better place in which to live and to be a healing influence in whatever we do in life, whether we are raising children or tending the sick or teaching school or working in a factory. We can all take on God's life as an ally in our daily life. In the beginning, we do this in order to find relief from our discontent, but eventually we do it to be more helpful in the world.

Japikse: How much of this pessimism and skepticism is a result of our own struggles with difficulty and grief, and how much is the result of contamination of theology and philosophy with ideas that focus us on doom, hell, and despair?

Leichtman: Yes, hasn't the church in particular been a major contributor to pessimism and skepticism?

Schweitzer: Of course it has. That's why the church is so attractive to those people who lust for the power to manipulate others. Think of it in this way: if you were brought up in a family filled with apathy, fear, depression, or discouragement, it would be very hard for you to overcome that conditioning. And it would be twice as difficult if you were also being told in church, with enthusiasm and in great detail, that you were born in sin, living in sin, sure to die in sin, and therefore going to hell.

There are agents of doom and gloom everywhere in society, and these people often attract quite a following. Human nature still contains a lot of fear and pettiness, and these charismatic individuals often prey on that ignorance and fear in society. At times, they become very influential. It's a terrible problem, and I don't have any great remedy for it, except this. Every person has an obligation to think for himself and to realize that no matter how rotten life may seem, or how much others may make of the hardships of living, there is also beauty in life. There is still love, affection, and goodwill in human nature. There are still moments in our life which fill us with joy and contentment. No one is without these moments, not even the Hitlers of the world.

So, each of us has a choice in this regard—a choice of whether we will feed on misery and hardship, or on the things of life which delight us and fill us with beauty, happiness, and peace.

The evidence of the beauty and joy of life is always present, even in the physical world, as imperfect as it is. Even in the jungle we could find it. Even in darkest Africa we could find evidence of God's light and love and beauty. It's in the people, it's in the country. It's not that difficult to find. But to find it, you must realize that the prophets of doom are wrong—dead wrong. And they ought to be ignored. As more people do this, they will fill the churches of the prophets of doom with emptiness—with the most lovely emptiness you can imagine. And that's just what the prophets of doom deserve.

Leichtman: Emptiness?

Schweitzer: Emptiness!

Leichtman: Is there a special responsibility on the part of those people who seek to serve humanity and God to guard against being pessimistic while they serve? Teachers, for example, have a marvelous opportunity to convey the healthy attitudes toward life you have described, but often just end up regurgitating the philosophy of pessimism.

Schweitzer: Well, I think your question answers itself. There is no doubt that we have an obligation to keep our misery to ourselves. It's a case of good manners and common sense; if you have a cold, you don't rush down to the store or restaurant and sneeze on everyone. So why would anyone want to sneeze the germs and viruses of his pessimism, anger, or fear on to anyone else?

Now, I'm very much aware that many good parents, teachers, and counselors feel the necessity of warning their children, students, or patients of their naïveté and preparing them for the fact that the world is not a perfect place. That's not pessimism—that's just being realistic. But if they then go on and broadcast a message which basically indicates that there is no hope, no future, and that everyone is just as mean, hostile, and depressed as they are, then that's nonsense.

Actually, I suppose that's worse than sneezing—it's more the psychological equivalent of spreading the bubonic plague. Pessimism can be terribly infectious—and so can defeatism, cynicism, and anger. These are infectious plagues raging throughout society. Everyone ought to be aware of these plagues and protect himself from them—and from those people who carry them. This is a very serious problem, as serious as the

Black Death of the Middle Ages. It's literally wiping out the useful lives of millions of people.

Leichtman: Yes, I know exactly what you mean—and I hope our readers won't be tempted just to dismiss it as a clever metaphor. You are not really using this as a metaphor at all, are you?

Schweitzer: No, I'm talking about something quite real. The plague of pessimism is just as real as trees and rocks and mountains. The forces of doubt, cynicism, despair, and anger probably do more to harm people than the pollution of the air and water and earth does, or an ailment such as tuberculosis.

Leichtman: Well, what can we do about it? What's the treatment?

Schweitzer: I've already pretty much described the treatment on an individual level: each person has to come to grips, all by himself, with his God and the inherent beauty and benevolence of life. I guess we could carry our analogy of sickness a step further; if you were physically ill, one way of restoring good health would be to get plenty of fresh air, sunshine, a good diet, and rest. The same is true in overcoming the plague of pessimism. Getting fresh air would mean getting away from people who are prophets of doom and pessimism, people who constantly try to drag you down to their level of pettiness, fear, and anger. The sunshine would be the light of the spirit, our inner light of wisdom and love. If everyone would learn to bathe in that, every day, that alone would solve a majority of ills in society. Getting a good diet would mean feeding yourself with good ideas, noble aspirations, confidence, and optimism. And plenty of rest would mean that we should stop exercising the bad thoughts, the pessimism, and the anger which make us miserable.

It's been my observation that people persist in evil because they are afraid to take the responsibility to do something better. They go on being evil because it has become a habit. So, to fully treat this problem, on a societal level, people must be taught that they do have a responsibility to function morally.

That's not an easy assignment, but it can be demonstrated. And, it is hoped, the demonstration will inspire the right people.

Leichtman: Since you just mentioned the word "evil," perhaps we'd better define it before going any further. How would you define it?

Schweitzer: Well, it's not quite what most people think it is. Evil does exist in the world, but not in the form of an individualized devil who tries to tempt us or hold us back. It is constructed out of the individual and collective ignorance, pettiness, apathy, fear, and anger of the human race.

Leichtman: Can you explain how that happens?

Schweitzer: Quite simply, there are a lot of people who do not yet understand that they are spiritual beings. They become annoyed at the circumstances of their lives, and start to hate life, or fear it, or just sink into despair and apathy. They deny their spiritual heritage, and that's evil. And as they are generating their hatred, fear, and anger, they in fact create energies we would call "evil."

I somewhat object to the term "evil," because it has so many terrible connotations. I would rather just say that there exists human pettiness and ignorance. There is sickness in the mind and heart, as well as the body, of many people. But it is all correctable. It can all be healed. When we look at evil from this perspective, we can see that it is possible to conquer it individually. We can find within us the sources of goodwill, peace, courage, and strength that we need to combat our individual ignorance, fear, anger, or pessimism. And, whether or not we think of ourselves as religious, it is the duty of each of us to find this capacity within ourselves and use it. We must not surrender to the negativity in our lives.

Japikse: Well, many people interpret what the Bible says about evil quite literally, that there is a devil. After all, Matthew reports that Jesus faced three temptations from the devil, who appeared to Him and spoke to Him. And when Jesus said, "Get thee behind me, Satan," the devil cowered and went away. Is that the way it happened? Many people believe it is, but you seem to be implying that Jesus was perhaps confronting something more subtle than a gross and deformed caricature of evil.

Schweitzer: Most of the major events of the life of Jesus, as recorded in the Bible, actually did happen as described, or in close approximation. But some of the stories are also symbolic. The life of Jesus, as told in the Gospels, is really meant to represent the Odyssey of every spiritual aspirant. Jesus the man had to confront, quite painfully, every element of His own human pettiness, fear, and anger, and conquer it, until it was completely extinguished. He also had to conquer the same elements in His friends, His family, His enemies, and, to some extent, in mass consciousness. This is also something every spiritual aspirant must do—he has to learn to handle the pettiness, anger, and fear in mass consciousness. We can't just live out our lives quietly, cleaning up our own act, and believing merrily, for the rest of our lives, that we have done our work and now are saved.

Leichtman: We don't just ascend to seventh heaven and stay there?

[Laughter.]

Schweitzer: No one does that, not even the Masters. That would be like assuming that a ten-year-old who took a bath and scrubbed up completely would never have to take another bath the rest of his life. *[Laughter.]* It's a silly idea. You have to work very hard to spiritualize the personality, so that your wisdom, compassion, goodwill, and courage dominate every element of your human nature and life expression. And as you work to do this, you will find that negative elements within yourself and within mass consciousness come to the surface, to create difficulty for you, in the form of temptation.

That's the sort of temptation Jesus was facing in the story in the Bible. He was facing the demonic elements within mass consciousness—a battle or temptation which is far more difficult to handle than when you are dealing with your personal pettiness alone. Of course, the spiritual aspirant does tend to deal with both levels of temptation—personal and collective—at the same time. After all, the collective anger of humanity feeds your own personal anger. So, as you begin to conquer your own anger, you also begin to immunize yourself and separate yourself from the collective anger of the masses. But it is the ultimate temptation of confronting the pettiness and ignorance of mass consciousness that the story in the Bible symbolically describes.

Of course, at clairvoyant levels, the collective anger, vindictiveness, and lust within mass consciousness frequently appear in dream-like images. These dream images or symbols can have a lot of power to them, and can appear to you in your dreams or meditations or moments of crisis. They are actually more commonly felt than seen. But Jesus was an excellent clairvoyant, and so He would be able to see these dream images of the evil of mass consciousness. He could speak to the dream image, and the dream image could speak to Him. That doesn't mean Satan is real—but he does exist at one level of perception as a dream symbol representing the evil of mass consciousness.

I don't want to get too esoteric here, but more people ought to realize that every human being has a subconscious, and every subconscious knows how to dream and create dream images. You don't have to be trained to do this—it's automatic. You're born with this dreaming mechanism. And mass consciousness is really the subconscious of the whole human race. So it is possible, in dreams and at other times, to encounter symbols of mass consciousness that can be quite powerful. They aren't real, but they can seem real when you dream them. Jesus was confronting some of these dream symbols from the subconscious of the human race.

Japikse: Based on what you just said, it seems to me that we should each be very careful how we use our imaginations and subconscious thoughts. It doesn't sound as though it would be very healthy to go around emphasizing our images of pettiness, anger, and the like. I'm thinking in particular about the fundamentalists who rant and rage about Satan and condemn just about everyone to hell.

Schweitzer: The people who rant and rave about the devil are feeding the problem, by building up the dream image of Satan. They are summoning the devil—and whether they love it or hate it doesn't make any difference. They are feeding it. And in some ways, they create devilish qualities and forces—which is, of course, completely unChristian.

Jesus did not appear on earth to warn us that the devil is going to get us. He came to say and demonstrate by His love and wisdom that God is here to help you—not that the devil is going to get you, but that God is here to help you. If you share your life and burdens with Him, you will find that help. And that's the message Jesus gave, over and over again, through what He said and how He lived His life.

Leichtman: I think it can be said that your life demonstrated that same message, too. Your life story is a very rich example of true Christian charity and humility. It is people like you who enrich humanity and teach us to be loving, in spite of great obstacles. But weren't you depressed at times?

Schweitzer: Oh God, yes. The amount of human misery I saw in Africa was immense. By and large, the Africans still are in a state of misery. We knew we could only treat a fraction of the problem. We could only help those we could reach—and that was depressing.

Leichtman: I asked that because some people seem to think that to be a proper Christian, you must always be gleefully cheerful.

Schweitzer: A proper Christian regards the world as it is and responds appropriately. Certainly, when Christ saw misery, He often cried.

Leichtman: Yes.

Schweitzer: And then, if it was appropriate, He healed the person. A true Christian would respond to whatever conditions presented themselves, knowing that every circumstance is an opportunity to do God's work.

Leichtman: I take it the same maxim would apply to a good Jew, or a good Buddhist, or a good Moslem.

Schweitzer: Yes. The theme of loving service is universal.

Leichtman: In your writings, you also talked about the idea that everyone must ultimately find his or her own spirituality through "resignation."

Schweitzer: Yes—this is part of developing a proper relationship with God. Resignation is the act of giving yourself over to the work of God.

Leichtman: Just what is it you are resigning from?

Schweitzer: From the self-centered belief that "I am the only important person in the world." This is a very arrogant attitude.

Leichtman: Yes. The popular phrase for it is "looking out for number one."

Schweitzer: You also have to resign from the notion that it is possible to create your own personal reality, and that God has little or no influence in your life. That just isn't so, and if you believe that it is, then life will give you abundant experiences to prove you're wrong.

By resignation, I'm referring to the attitude which Jesus demonstrated over and over again: by myself, I can't do much, but with the Father, I can do all things. It's a resignation from personal egotism, from delusion and ignorance, and from despair and misery. It starts with the realization that you as an individual are important, you have responsibilities and make a difference in the world, but if you are ever going to be something significant, you will have to align yourself with your spirit. You will have to accept your spirit and work with it. That means resigning some of your arrogance, ignorance, and pettiness—and embracing a greater dimension of life, the God within you.

And that doesn't mean treating the personality as though it were nothing. I'm talking about beginning to see the personality in its true perspective, as a vehicle for spirit, rather than a thing that exists all by itself, all for itself.

Leichtman: In your writings, you mentioned that other people take a different view of resignation. Some Easterners, for example, go through the steps of resignation but end up being apathetic and withdrawn from the world—which you certainly were not.

Schweitzer: That attitude is not appropriate in the Western world, as you well know. It is completely inappropriate.

Leichtman: I do know that, but some people don't seem to get the message.

Schweitzer: Our role in the West, and especially in Christianity, is to go about our worldly duties, doing the things that need to be done. Now, that doesn't happen very often, but there are some people who heed the ideal.

Leichtman: Some people say, however, that the physical world is just an illusion. If you get caught up in it, you delay your spiritual progress. If you try to help out, it's just an ego trip, so let it go. What would you say to that?

Schweitzer: I'm sorry, would you repeat the question? There's a rather large audience of spirits in the room, and I was distracted by a comment that was being made over here. I don't know if you've noticed the crowd or not [clairvoyantly].

Leichtman: Yes, if it gets any larger, we're going to have to charge admission. *[Laughter].*

Japikse: A little manna from heaven.

Leichtman: And they can't touch our chocolate chip cookies, either. They may sniff, but not chew. Did you have chocolate chip cookies in Africa?

Schweitzer: No.

Leichtman: It must have been a truly impoverished, primitive life without chocolate chip cookies. *[Laughter.]*

Japikse: Talk about sacrifice! A true test of Christian dedication. *[Guffawing.]*

Leichtman: Well, to return to my question. There are some people who say yes, you should be resigned from the world— in the sense of ignoring it, because it doesn't amount to anything. It's just an illusion. Any effort to get caught up in that illusion would simply delay your spiritual progress. This is what I call spiritual nihilism. What do you think about it?

Schweitzer: It is an attempt to live a lie. It is not the duty of a Christian to ignore the world. The healthy Christian goes about the world doing whatever is needed to make it a better place, to help his fellow man. Sitting and meditating all day long, which I assume is what you are talking about, doesn't do any good at all. Unless meditation is accompanied by the effort to be useful in the world, it can actually cause the personality to become disconnected from the spirit. The person would eventually die and that would be the end of that—except that he would have to come right back and try again, until he learned the purposes of living in the physical plane.

Leichtman: You obviously see the physical plane, then, as an integral part of God's creation—

Schweitzer: Oh, yes!

Leichtman: Deserving our full and loving attention.

Schweitzer: I wonder how people can convince themselves otherwise.

Leichtman [laughing]: They have to work very hard at it. Well, from what you've been saying, it seems to me that you found the antidote to pessimism and nihilism in your philosophy of affirming life. This affirmation or reverence of life was obviously something that profoundly guided you every day. How can other people find or touch this realization?

Schweitzer: It comes by integrating the healthiness of your inner life with the circumstances and work to be done in your outer life.

Leichtman: Can you give some examples of that?

Schweitzer: Well, in working with my patients, for instance, I knew that whenever a cure actually occurred it was because I was holding something of the love of God in my inner life and focusing it into my work. The power of that love, focused through my daily activities, was the healing force, as much as anything else.

Leichtman: I will want to come back to that topic of

nonphysical healing, but what other ways could an average person put his attention on the inner life as he goes about his daily work?

Schweitzer: A simple opportunity for the woman who's a wife or mother is to go about her daily tasks bathed in the realization that she is a focus for the love of God, and so she radiates that love throughout the house. Many women do this quite successfully—in fact, it's more common than many people believe. These women are not necessarily able to carry on a brilliant conversation; they may not be strikingly beautiful. But they seize the opportunities available to them to express the love of God.

Leichtman: What kind of opportunities do the executive, the office worker, or the sales clerk have to do this?

Schweitzer: Well, the executive could focus love—I'm using this one aspect of God to make it simpler to talk about, but there are other aspects of the inner life—by letting his employees know that he is grateful for the work they do. He could express his appreciation every time someone does extra work, or does a job especially well, and he could take care not to fuss inappropriately about shortcomings in the performance of a job. The person working in the office can learn to love what he is doing and do the best job he can.

Leichtman: You're talking about doing something more than just being nice, aren't you?

Schweitzer: I'm talking about rising above the personality and contacting something of the inner life of the spirit, and then expressing that in your daily activities. Some people do assume that being nice is the same as being spiritual, but that's not usually the case. Niceness is generally just an expression of the pleasant elements of the personality. The life of spirit is something more.

If you really want to bring through the spirit, I would suggest a very simple technique. You should examine your life, your lifestyle, your friends, and the experiences of your life, and find as much as you can that is beautiful or noble or worthy of praise. Then, you should be deeply thankful that at least a fragment of God's kindness or goodness or nobility or beauty exists within you or your life experience. The evidence of this might be the kindnesses a co-worker has shown you, or the fact that your children are sometimes delightful and sweet, or the fact that you have done an exceptionally fine piece of work. But whatever it is, you should appreciate it, because it is good. You should thank God that this goodness exists, that this much of the inner life is being expressed, and it touches you. And it's marvelous.

At that point, you should also be thankful that something exists within the universe which makes this possible. And wouldn't it be great if this Something could dominate our lives, our experiences, our memories, and our future? If you practice this kind of thankfulness, you will actually begin to tap the hidden current of love behind all creation, all events, and all people. Just in talking about it now, I am tapping that current. It's very real for me—and it was very real for me much of my adult life in the physical plane.

Once you plug into this dimension of creation, everything else begins to come with it—guidance, power, courage, strength, healing, a glimpse of nobility, and even a glimpse of perfection. You get caught up in a state of mind and feeling that alters your whole perspective about yourself, your work, and the other people you know. For me, this is a complete formula for finding God within life and within ourselves—and for using it in daily life.

Japikse: Yet doesn't one have to do more than just believe in this current of love? You say you are tapping into it right now, and did so during your life as Albert Schweitzer. But I imagine there are a lot of readers who have never had this experience.

Schweitzer: That's why the practice of thankfulness is so important. Belief and faith are important—I don't want to say anything that would tarnish the value of right faith and right belief. But it is through thankfulness and praise that you begin to discover the inner presence of the God you propose to believe in. The only way you can link yourself to the power, love, and wisdom of God is by finding aspects of these qualities within yourself—within your mind and within your heart. And the easiest way to do that is by being thankful for whatever you can find that is worthy of being praised.

Now, this is really very easy to do. Even a child can do it—in fact, even a cat or a dog can be thankful. And so can every adult. Which means that every adult has the ability to focus something of God's will or God's plan into his life.

Leichtman: I think those are very important statements for people to muse about.

Now, in addition to love, you wrote about the *will to love* and the *will to life,* which go beyond just loving people through your work. Could you define the will to love and the will to life in practical terms as well? The reason I'm asking is that there are so many people who think they can substitute emotional mushiness and sentimentality for spiritual love.

Schweitzer: Mushiness and sentimentality tend to indicate negative traits of emotional behavior, not love. They clutter up the emotions. No truly religious person would want to indulge in either mushiness or sentimentality: they are inappropriate to the life of spirit. A person who does this needs to be shown how to refocus on his inner life.

Now, to comment on the will to love and the will to life, the will to love, I suppose, is the power to act in a loving way. It is the power to do things which make you helpful and useful in the world, and that is categorically and dynamically different from love itself.

The person who never rises above sentimentality shortchanges himself, by thinking that's all there is. It's a whole lot better than being angry or miserable, I'll grant you, but it's certainly not all that love is meant to be.

You can sit in your bedroom or meditation room or cave or chapel and just love the world, but that may not be terribly helpful in dealing with very real human needs in society—or even your own family. People have to act; they have to do things. We live in the physical world and there are physical needs which have to be attended to, in physical ways. We have to use our hands and feet and mouths and typewriters and tape recorders. The will to love, then, is the power to act in a loving way. It's more than just love, and I wish more people would appreciate that. We are not doing our spiritual duty unless we ground our love in loving and healing activities. Now, the will to life is a bit greater than the will to love, because life is more than just love. The will to life involves the expression of all aspects of one's livingness, and that would include the expression of talent, wisdom, intelligence, and life's purpose. It's quite different from the will to love. I'm tuning into it right now and am summoning these energies. It's qualitatively a different experience—a different vibration, if you will. In mundane terms, I suppose you would say the will to life is the impulse to use whatever you have in the way of talent or goodwill or good ideas to honor your opportunities and duties in life.

Japikse: When you say you are tuning into the will to love or the will to life, what do you mean? Where are these things located? Are you tuning into Mars, where there is a special repository of divine qualities, or how are you doing this?

Schweitzer: No, I'm tuning into the higher dimensions of my own self.

Japikse: By that, do you mean your own self, as opposed to the medium's self?

Schweitzer: Yes. But he has them, too.

Japikse: Sure.

Schweitzer: You find them within you. You can find them within every human being, but you have to rise to a dimension of spirit which Jesus poetically referred to as the kingdom of heaven. And the kingdom of heaven really is within. I don't know how people can miss the significance and implications of that message. It's so abundantly clear to me. The kingdom of heaven is an intense personal experience for me; it eradicates all doubt or cynicism about this topic.

I find it very frustrating that I can't go around giving this inner knowledge to others. Of course, this is the limitation on all teachers, gurus, and priests, and anyone else who is trying to talk about the kingdom of heaven and God's love and will. All of these things exist within each one of us, but none of them can ever be demonstrated with machines or gadgets. People can't take photographs of me and prove that the kingdom of heaven exists within me, and yet it's there. It's the most real thing that I experience. And it's the most real thing anyone else can experience, too. But that's the point: each person must find it for himself or herself. Each person must prove it to himself or herself through his or her own experience; each person has to individualize and internalize this life of God. You can't get it out of a book. You can't get it by listening to me. I can only say that it does exist. It's marvelous. You can discover it, too, by following these steps.

It's not within your subconscious, or your pineal gland, or your solar plexus. It's within the dimension of your spirit. Everyone has one. So look for it there—in the essence of your own greatness and humanity, nobility and wisdom. No matter how long it takes or how difficult it may be, looking for it is exceedingly worthwhile.

Leichtman: How often, in your moments of fatigue and discouragement, did you feel that you were somehow being sustained or driven by a supernatural or transpersonal force?

Schweitzer: I felt that I was moved by that transpersonal force most of the time.

Leichtman: Would that kind of awareness be one way of sensing the meaning of the will to love or the will to life—that there really is something within you that emanates from beyond your own personal desires and capacities?

Schweitzer: Certainly. Our most significant discoveries about life generally don't come in visions or while reading religious tracts; they come in simple insights gained in the midst of our daily activities. They come while we try to act in loving and kind ways.

Leichtman: Can we comment more on the idea of reverence for life? You wrote extensively about the need, in this regard, for every intelligent person to develop a system of rational ethics. How should the average person go about that? I take it from reading about you that you were rather against the notion of people allowing others to impose their dogma on them, accepting it as a matter of faith.

Schweitzer: Yes, this is the danger of unintelligent, blind belief. Now, I'm not trying to encourage cynicism and skepticism, which perpetuate ignorance as much as blind belief. Both extremes are antispiritual—they indicate that the person is surrendering his obligation to think. He's trying to avoid his responsibility to make critical decisions about his life. I'm talking about the decisions of ethics, of how he hopes to act. I'm talking about answering questions such as: "What do I stand for?" "What do I accept as right in my life?" "What do I cherish as my ideals for living?"

As children, we naturally imitate the ethics of those who are very close to us, but as we become adults we must begin to revise our ethics in order to honor our own individuality and intelligence. We must become discerning about what is going on in life and make decisions and choices of our own.

Obviously, every person is going to make a lot of mistakes, but part of developing a code of ethics is being willing to make those mistakes, and learn from them. Any mistakes we may happen to make can be changed in due time. But at least they are *our* mistakes, and not someone else's we are just copying.

It's absolutely essential to do this for ourselves. If we are to avoid being passive victims of mass consciousness and the manipulations of other people, we must exercise our responsibility to think for ourselves. We must honor our duty to challenge, in gentle ways, the status quo, mass thought, and mass attitude. And we can do this without becoming arrogant or a rabble rouser. We can do it rationally, intelligently, and gently.

The basis for our ethics is meant to be our spiritual

guidance. Our personal ethics are meant to reflect the spiritual wisdom and natural laws of the cosmos.

Leichtman: Well, what does that mean? I know some people who could take that last statement you made and interpret spiritual guidance to be whatever they feel they want to do.

Schweitzer: That's absolute nonsense. That's no basis for ethical living.

Leichtman: Well, what would you tell these people?

Schweitzer: I would tell them to ask themselves how they would want to be treated by life and by people—and then ask themselves, can I behave that way myself? Can I treat other people the way I would like them to treat me? If not, then they'd better revise their expectations of how others should treat them—or vice versa.

Leichtman: It sounds like the Golden Rule.

Schweitzer: It is. And it's an excellent criterion for refining your ethics. Another good guideline to use is the notion that God gave me my life. He also gave you your life. So, in a sense, we are both something of God, and in that light, we should treat each other ethically and with respect. We should not try to cheat each other, because we would be cheating God, and therefore ourself, because we are of God.

Now, I won't pretend that it can't be a real problem to try to understand how to act in specific circumstances. But that's the value of ethics—it gives us a framework for acting.

Ultimately, you become aware that there is an underlying, absolute truth to living—and that absolute truth is the life of God. Now, that's a long way from the notion of "doing anything you want." And it's also a long way from the rebellious attitude of, "No, I'm not going to listen to what anyone wants me to do—even God."

Part of the confusion surrounding ethics is a result of this. There's a natural tendency to let others make your decisions for you—and also a natural tendency to resist outside influences. Both of these tendencies are dangerous and must be outgrown. We must learn to think for ourselves. From time to time there may be unusual people that we admire and respect, and we may want to imitate them. Perhaps their advice is good for us, and so we accept it. But we have to be very selective in doing that, and make sure we have thoroughly evaluated it for ourselves.

Japikse: What you seem to be advocating here is not a collection of rules about what to do or what not to do, but a set of very active, living principles that can be applied to the circumstances of life. Is that a fair conclusion?

Schweitzer: I think so. Ethics have no use unless we can apply them to our lives. At times, of course, we may only be able to apply them in part. Our ethics are meant to be ideals for acting in life—if we could honestly do our very best, this is how we would like to treat others, and how we would like them to treat us. But even though we are often able to carry out these ethics, some days it's just not possible. We're tired or grumpy or have just gone through some tragedy. The fact that elements of our pettiness occasionally take over does not reduce the value of our ethics. So, within this context, yes, ethics are meant to be very active, living principles. If you simply sat around on a stump and speculated on what *could* be done and what other people *ought* to be doing, that would be nothing more than an exercise in sophistry and sanctimony.

The pursuit of a spiritualized set of ethics is really the effort to find God within you. You are trying to internalize God in your personality, in your life. You are trying to internalize your religion, by making conscious choices of your own. You hope that these choices are governed by your highest intelligence, and not by expediency, or by inflammatory articles in the newspaper, or the latest news on TV. As a general rule, they'll probably be consistent with the commonly-accepted ethics of religion, and sane, intelligent living. What I'm saying is that the pursuit of ethics is not going to make you an iconoclast, a hermit, an anti-establishment hippie. The rational development of ethics leads you back to God.

Japikse: Most people seem to think of God as something static, yet you seem to be implying that God is very active.

Schweitzer: Quite active, yes. And abundantly available, too, I might say.

Leichtman: This seems to be a point where you differed from the standard philosophy and theology of your day. The philosophers and theologians of your time tended to see God, and many still do, as the abstract, invisible essence of life.

Schweitzer: Who was somewhere up in the sky.

Leichtman: Yes—remote, aloof, unavailable, and perhaps indifferent.

Schweitzer: Well, life just does not work that way. I think of God as being everywhere. I have had this proven to myself on many occasions. When I can cover myself with God's love and then heal someone, I have proof.

Leichtman: Yes, I understand. You are thinking of God as a very active, vital force in the midst of daily life.

Schweitzer: And He is always right there—before you, within you, and everywhere around you.

Japikse: It seemed to me in reading about you that you considered the realization of the active nature of God to be almost a prerequisite of spiritual resignation. A lot of people resign themselves or sacrifice themselves, but without having that kind of commitment to an active expression of the life of God.

Schweitzer: Yes, and without that dedication, it's obviously a false resignation.

Japikse: They are resigning to something other than God.

Schweitzer: They are going through the motions of a formula they really don't understand, in the hopes of becoming immediately more aware. But a false resignation does not bring an expansion of consciousness. It might bring the semblance of growth, but it would only last a short while.

Leichtman: What about the people who try to find God by entering a passive, mentally numb state of mind?

Schweitzer: That doesn't work, either. It's a type of false resignation, because you have to work actively and earnestly. You have to express the love and wisdom of God to find the love and wisdom of God.

Leichtman: You mean you can't just "be," as they say, and find God?

Schweitzer: That's right.

Leichtman: You seemed to promote an almost revolutionary concept for theologians: that we should not accept our religious beliefs simply on the basis of faith. We need to look for the evidence which will add understanding to our belief.

Schweitzer: I remember having the awareness quite early in life that the concepts taught by theologians now are not the ideas Christ intended to teach. He worked very hard to attain His gifts of spirit—and He worked hard to use them in a mature, loving way.

The major obligation of religion in the West is to help people find an element of God in themselves and in their lives. Religion should provide instruction in how to do this and assist people in healing those aspects of their lives which need a touch of the divine—a touch of guidance, inspiration, love or whatever. Churches should do this for society as a whole, too, at least to some extent.

And here's something interesting to think about: the reason that many theologians have become political—and it really is appropriate for them—is that they have tried to find God and have failed, for one reason or another.

Religion runs into problems when it starts imposing rules and regulations, instead of inspiring people to discover the kingdom of heaven within themselves. That substitutes faith in dogma for faith in the Christ, faith in the benevolence of life itself. And it gradually distorts the emphasis of the church and its theology, from spiritual to political. As a result, an occasional individual may be attracted to the ministry for the wrong reasons—for the comfort of a powerful position in the community and the opportunity to control people, rather than help them. It's unfortunate that this occurs, but these people are fairly easy to spot. They do not have the basic reverence for life.

I think I've wandered off the topic somewhat.

Leichtman [chuckling]: You're allowed to do that. I was

asking, I suppose, about the anti-intellectual aspect of the modern church. There are some people, for example, who claim that all you have to do to be a properly spiritual person is read the Holy Scriptures and believe them. They advocate accepting spiritual values and ideals on faith alone, and regard intelligent inquiry as a sign of weakness of faith. Some of these people, for instance, would say that there is no need to bother to research the phenomena of life after death; you should accept this on faith alone.

Schweitzer: Well, I don't want to say anything that could be construed as anti-faith, because faith is important. But the proper Christian also understands that the mind is important, and must not be negated. The proper Christian doesn't just read the Scriptures and believe them; he thinks about them. Now, that doesn't mean that he questions whether they are right or not; it means he thinks about how this passage of Scripture can help him, in his daily life. What does it tell him about the inner life of God—and about expressing that inner life in his life?

The Scriptures were written to lead you to the kingdom of heaven, but you have to do your share of hard work, too. And that requires the active use of the mind and intellect.

Leichtman: Yes, it's a tremendous challenge to anyone's mind to approach subjects as profound and vast as God and mysticism and the nature of life. Where should one begin? How do we know we're making progress?

Schweitzer: Well, one sign that you're making progress is that the Scriptures begin to have greater meaning for you. They're not just something to believe anymore; they also have personal meaning and application to you. They come alive in your life, and help you improve the quality of your life and work. You become more aware of the beauty around you, and view the things that are ugly from a higher perspective. There are many signs of progress which can be observed, but most of them are very ordinary. Your attitudes toward the events of life become more mature; your dealings with others become more harmonious. Your work becomes more inspired. Your reverence for life deepens.

Now, as for where to begin, I think I've already covered that. You begin by looking within, and finding the sparks of divinity already at work in your life. That's much more important than memorizing the Bible, so that you can quote chapter and verse better than anyone else, and win every argument. The Bible was not written for the purpose of hitting other people over the head with it—either figuratively or literally. *[Laughter.]* It was written to guide us and inspire us in our thinking. *It is meant to be thought about!* And if the person who memorizes the Bible would spend as much time thinking about it as he does committing it to memory, he would know a lot more than chapter and verse.

Leichtman: I'd like to talk some more about Africa, if we might. You obviously found great meaning in the work you did in Africa. How did that evolve over the many decades you lived and labored there?

Schweitzer: Well, the greatest source of meaning lay in the opportunities I had to help people. That started with helping the people become healthier, but it included a lot more, too. I was able to help them deal with their problems more intelligently and less superstitiously, for example. We were also able to help some of the young people become citizens of the twentieth century, and that was the beginning of something we hoped would continue. That would be the process of helping Africa become a citizen of the twentieth century. I suppose that would be one of the greater purposes of the work I tried to do.

Right now, there are many clumsy attempts going on to make Africa a fuller citizen of the twentieth century. Many of them won't work—especially the experiments in socialism. I don't see how people can advocate any style of socialism; it just won't work in the world.

Japikse: Why not?

Leichtman: Yes, why not?

Schweitzer: The citizen in a socialist country spends his

life living under someone else's authority and responsibility. He is not responsible for doing his own work or making his own way—the state is. And that is anti-spiritual. Socialism is anti-spiritual by nature, whether or not religion is banned, because it dehumanizes the individual. It dehumanizes society. All of life becomes a bureaucracy in a socialist country.

Leichtman: What about Marxism?

Schweitzer: I'm including Marxism as a brand of socialism, but I'm talking about more than just communism. I'm including the whole socialist movement. At one time, in Europe, some of the basic principles and ideals of socialism could have done some good—if they had been applied differently. But as it is now, socialism is so horribly dehumanizing that I don't think it is possible to rationally defend it.

Leichtman: What do you think will be the outcome of all this?

Schweitzer: By and large, Africa will become a democratic continent—eventually.

Leichtman: That must be a long ways in the future. I see no sign of it, as yet.

Schweitzer: It might make it by the next century. I don't really know when this will happen, but it is already beginning to occur—in very small ways, to be sure, but it is beginning. The Africans are beginning to realize that they want to be free to be the best people they can be. And they are being taught to think in that way by a few people here and there. Certainly, that's something we tried to teach the people who came to us. We tried to teach them the value of bettering their life and the value of helping one another.

Leichtman: Well, it only makes sense that if our Creator designed us to be free, within reason, to be helpful to one another, and to be proper stewards of the earth, then that intention should eventually have some influence on the nature of our governments and social institutions.

Schweitzer: Absolutely. And it has had its impact, perhaps more than many people realize. America would be one example. This country is more fortunate than most, in that you have the latitude to do your own work, to be a good person, and to be a helpful person. There may be times when it seems that you are helplessly bound in the regulations of government, but the system does have within it the mechanism to right itself eventually. And, I'm told, there is going to be some "house-cleaning" in your government that will really take. The citizens are tired of being ashamed of being Americans, and that apparently will be the impetus for some effective reforms.

Leichtman: Ah, so we don't have to move to Canada, after all. *[Laughter.]*

I had a professor in medical school who had worked with you in Africa. He was a red-faced, chubby Austrian named Zeller.

Schweitzer: Oh, yes, I remember him.

Leichtman: He was a very kind fellow, but very discouraged about his work in Africa, as if the vastness of the medical needs, and the primitive and superstitious nature of the natives, made the work almost impossible. His attitude was that his contribution was negligible.

Schweitzer: But the people he helped, he did help.

Leichtman: Of course.

Schweitzer: Well, it's important to keep that in focus. And it's also useful to have ways to renew yourself, so that you don't get overwhelmed by such attitudes. In my case, being able to play the organ served the purpose of reestablishing my perspective toward my work. Through the music I played, I was also able to do a little meditating, and that renewed me, too.

I was very discouraged the first few years I was in Africa. At one time or another, the fact that we could do so little was very discouraging to all of us. But I tried to handle it by simply thinking about the person I happened to be treating right then. I disciplined myself to think about helping him get well, and then I went on to the next. I found that much more effective than dwelling on all the masses of people who were sick in

Africa. Sometimes, you have to be pragmatic in order to preserve your sanity.

Leichtman: That would seem to be a good guideline for anyone seeking to serve God: to keep focused on the practical things we can do, instead of worrying about the vastness of human needs.

Japikse: To pursue the good we can do, and not the good we cannot do.

Schweitzer: I'd like to share a memory here. I remember being very depressed late one afternoon, so I went to a place on the grounds where I liked to walk at that time of the evening, if I had the time, because the shadows of the late sun through the leaves of the trees always fascinated me. And just as I turned the corner of the building to go there, to watch and wonder, I saw two little black children playing together, having such a good time. They were dancing and playing in the sunlight that I also loved so much. And I thought, isn't it wonderful that these two children, surrounded by all this misery, can have such a good time? And I immediately felt better. I kept the memory of that evening in my mind ever after that, so that whenever I became depressed, I could think about it and the joy of that particular moment of time. And that would refresh me and help me go on.

Leichtman: I suppose we all have to find these magical moments.

Schweitzer: What I was taken with was the absolute beauty of those two innocent children, and their playing, and the sunlight through the trees. I was thankful for being able to see such beauty, and that made me feel better.

Leichtman: I suppose that's what you meant when you said that the best evidence of God's love and God's beauty here on earth is found in ordinary moments.

Schweitzer: Yes.

Leichtman: Did your music also have that reassuring, inspiring effect on you?

Schweitzer: Of course. I loved the times I could get away

for a little while to play the organ. But I played music primarily because it was extremely enjoyable to me. I felt marvelous. And it did have a healing effect on me—and even on the other people in the compound. The organ could be heard almost everywhere in the compound, and it seemed to have a calming effect, even on the people who didn't understand the music. But that wasn't the reason why I played the music. I played because I found joy and beauty in it, and was delighted to give a sense of joy and beauty to those who might be listening.

I must confess that playing music was such a natural thing for me that I never even thought about why I was doing it. It's like eating; you don't have to have an intellectual reason for eating. You get hungry and you eat. There's no big mystery about it. It's a natural thing, and playing music was as natural to me as eating. I wish more people would appreciate that it's not always necessary to analyze everything they do and produce an elaborate set of reasons justifying it. Sometimes you do a helpful, healthy thing just because it's natural to do it; you would never think of not doing it. This is often especially true when the spirit dominates the personality. The personality starts doing things that are simply natural to the life of spirit.

In playing music, I found a sense of beauty and joy that lifted up my spirits. I was also very much aware at times that this sense spread to others listening to the music—even those who weren't paying attention to it. It was easiest to see the effect on children, but it sometimes even influenced the animals. So, I kept it up.

Of course, from my current perspective, I can see that music does have a healing impact. Certain kinds of good music—particularly Bach—have a tremendous tranquilizing and healing impact on the emotions, and to some extent, the mind. When the emotions are calm and the mind is focused on the lofty qualities of life, such as joy, goodwill, and beauty, then all healing channels are nourished. The healing qualities of music can have their most direct impact on the personality, but indirectly they can also heal the physical body.

Leichtman: You were a recognized authority on Bach. Of all composers, why did Bach seem to strike your fancy so much?

Schweitzer: When I was playing Bach, I found God in the midst of the music. It was a very real, joyous experience for me. I found God's love and peace and order and wholeness while playing Bach. I became consumed in my spirit. Now, I realize that not everyone who listens to Bach, or even plays Bach, has this same experience. But it is potentially there for everyone.

Japikse: Would you care to comment on specific qualities of spirit which might be focused through Bach's music?

Schweitzer: Well, I probably should leave a question of that nature to Richard Wagner [whose interview will appear later in Volume V of *From Heaven to Earth*].

Leichtman: Oh, we'll ask him, too, but you might have a better feel for Bach.

Schweitzer: Well, let's see. First, we'd better specify which Bach we're talking about. I will limit myself to Johann Sebastian Bach, and not his relatives. Now, Bach wrote in many different styles. But to give you a simple answer, the music of Bach tends to be very compatible with the theme of reverence for life and devotion to ideals, which I suppose is why I was in such harmony with it.

Whenever I played Bach, the music filled me with the awareness and conviction that there is something within every person, every animal, every plant, and every element of life that is utterly lovely and beautiful. I was filled with awe and reverence and devotion. Some aspects of Bach are more focused in joyfulness, but the overall effect of Bach's music tends to create a genuine sense of sympathy. There's a consoling, reassuring, mystical presence in his music.

Other aspects of Bach's music contain the kind of refinement you find in highly organized, carefully structured intelligence. There's a sense of refinement in Chopin's music, too, but it's different. In Bach, it is the refinement of a meticulously conceived plan—as though it were part of a divine engineering work connecting heaven with earth. It helps tune the listener into the intelligence and mind of God.

The curious thing is that these qualities of Bach will tend to draw an appropriate response even from people who do not understand the music.

Leichtman: That's not surprising. After all, music speaks directly to the subconscious.

I'd like to talk about Africa some more. What can you tell us about the types of illnesses you encountered there? Certainly, they would be quite different in Africa than what we are accustomed to here in the West. What special problems did you have in dealing with these illnesses?

Schweitzer: The problem of infections was a great deal more serious in Africa than it would be here. We lost a great number of people to some simple infections that don't even affect Westerners. We tried inoculating everyone who came to us to try to prevent these infections, but we didn't always have enough serum. Many of the people who came to us had wounds of one sort or another, but we were also able to spot other problems and correct them while they were staying with us.

Leichtman: You did a lot of surgery, too, didn't you?

Schweitzer: Yes. I would do more amputations in a year than I ever thought one doctor would see in a lifetime—and mind you I had to work in conditions that were somewhat less favorable than a modern hospital.

Leichtman: Why amputations?

Schweitzer: A person would get a cut on the foot, for instance, but by the time he had reached our hospital, it was so infected that the leg had to be removed. Gangrene was a big problem.

Leichtman: You recorded that there were many strangulated hernias, also.

Schweitzer: Yes.

Leichtman: Did you find much mental illness in "stress-free" Africa?

Schweitzer: Ohhh—particularly in women.

Leichtman: Really!

Schweitzer: Most of the time, we could do very little to help them.

Leichtman: How was the mental illness you saw in Africa different from what we deal with here?

Schweitzer: A lot of it was based on the fact that the typical African is very superstitious. I ran into a lot of people who thought they were possessed by a demon. Because they believed it, in effect, they were. It was very difficult to deal with those people. For one thing, just communicating with them could be quite a problem. But we tried everything—we even found a couple of witch doctors to help us deal with many of these patients. They would communicate more readily with the witch doctor. And the one we used the most was intelligent enough to know that I was trying to help these people, so he cooperated.

Leichtman: Was witchcraft a prevalent problem?

Schweitzer: It was almost universally practiced, in one form or another. I'm not saying that everyone was a witch doctor, but everyone at least had amulets somewhere on him. Many of the men would carry around medicine bags, very much like the American Indians.

Leichtman: Was this responsible for a significant amount of the mental illness you encountered—or was it just a harmless superstition most of the time?

Schweitzer: Well, some of the mental illness was caused by the sheer hardship of life in Africa, of course. Women would commonly get terribly depressed and become catatonic, simply because of the enormous burden they had to carry all the time. But, yes, superstition was a major factor—and certainly not harmless.

Superstition is a terrible problem in Africa and other underdeveloped areas where the culture is not especially advanced. Of course, superstition exists in some of the most sophisticated areas of Western civilization, too, but it takes a different form. Human nature tends to think in magical terms—we project our feelings and ideas and personalize the meaning of events. We will react to a simple event in which someone annoys us by magnifying its meaning to us—by assuming, for example, that this one event is proof of the individual's deep dislike for us. That's superstition—and we all tend to do this, from time to time.

When you are dealing with a more unsophisticated group of individuals, such as the natives of Africa, this kind of magical thinking becomes very active. The natural fears of these people and their lack of understanding combine to make superstition a very, very powerful force indeed. And while human nature has its beautiful side, it also has its ugly side, and an awful lot of anger, rage, defensiveness, and possessiveness gets expressed. And that's more threatening than the beautiful, so the average person tends to be more obsessed by it. Then, in Africa, you have to add another factor: that the simple survival involved in just getting through the day or growing up to adulthood tends to consume the bulk of a person's attention. If you're confronted on a daily basis by the raw, destructive forces of nature and the literal beasts of the jungle, it's not too surprising that sometimes you might have to confront nonphysical beasts. The African native often lives in a jungle of his fears and superstitions, as well as the physical jungle—a cultural and psychological environment of focused negativity, possessiveness, jealousy, fear, and so on. Because of the proclivity to magical thinking, these emotions tend to take on symbolic form, and terrible things are created in the collective feeling and traditions of the tribes.

I can look back on this problem and see it more clearly now. And, yes, these collective fears and angry forces can be used to harm people, when manipulated by evil people. It does happen.

The African tribesmen simply don't know any better. They live that way and they die that way. I'm not condemning them. But a good deal of illness was generated as a result of these problems. It was usually triggered by jealousy or fear between two people, or an argument between two families, caused by some social gaffe. It was very common to seek revenge by means of magic.

There wasn't much we could do about these illnesses, because they were more psychological than physical. We did try to reassure the patients that they were under our protection and had nothing to fear; we tried to immunize them from their own superstition and environment, but weren't terribly effective.

Leichtman: Well, these problems are difficult to treat even today, with our modern facilities and training. They must have been even more difficult for you in Africa. Let me move on to a different aspect of the medical work: what we today call faith healing or spiritual healing. Did you consider this a significant part of your work?

Schweitzer: Certainly. As I said earlier, it was my loving concern as much as my medical treatments that helped the men and women I treated become well—and I fully believed that during my lifetime, too. We tried to create an environment of health, an environment of love at the compound. Whenever possible, for example, we tried to give some of the people who came to us positions in the compound, in order to help them keep the quality of their life a little better than it had been. It also relieved us of some of the burdens of routine work. We didn't really pay them, but gave them a place to live and food to eat, and saw to it that the quality of their life improved.

What I am saying is that we didn't just treat them, we *cared* about them.

Leichtman: Did you ever go so far as to practice "laying on of hands"?

Schweitzer: Of course.

Leichtman: I bet you even prayed for your patients.

[Laughter.]

Schweitzer: Absolutely. I take my religion seriously—now, even more seriously than before.

Leichtman: Spiritual healing, laying on of hands, and that kind of thing are becoming very popular nowadays.

Schweitzer: Yes, but people ought to be very careful about seeking out this kind of healing.

Leichtman: Why is that?

Schweitzer: When you are being healed by laying on of hands, you are picking up elements of the consciousness of the person doing the healing. As you know, not all of the people who practice this kind of healing are virtuous and filled with the reverence for life. Some are not even particularly good people. If that's the case, then the "healer" would leave you with something very undesirable—something much worse than what you had to begin with.

Leichtman: Then that would be a "sicker" instead of a "healer." *[Groaning.]*

Is spiritual healing something that should be talked about and perhaps taught in medical schools?

Schweitzer: Definitely. And I'm delighted to see that more and more medical people are giving it more attention, and finding it to be helpful. Spiritual healing, after all, is a natural companion to the scientific techniques used by the average physician in his daily practice. It doesn't replace them, but neither should medicine replace the spiritual side of healing. They ought to complement each other.

Frankly, I would be very concerned about anyone entering the profession of medicine, psychology, or nursing who rejected the concept of spiritual healing. I'm not saying doctors and nurses should necessarily practice laying on of hands, but I think it is stunning if they reject the possibility of spiritual healing. It is always the spirit that does the healing. Medicine is a set of practices which augment that healing process. Every physician, psychologist, and nurse ought to understand that he or she is only able to act with full effectiveness when cooperating with the spirit of the patient.

Spiritual healing is not the exclusive property of grim-faced clerics, after all. Deep within each person is a healing force which every health professional needs to understand is his ally. It is there to be summoned, and applied. It can be fed by our own reverence and appreciation of it. It can be nurtured by our prayers. *These* are the practices of spiritual healing.

Japikse: From these remarks, and the comments you made earlier about superstition, it would seem to me that spiritual healing is really the direct antithesis of superstition. Superstition can only occur in the absence of spirit, whereas spiritual healing calls in the presence of spirit. I mention this because many people seem to think of spiritual healing as superstition.

Schweitzer: Yes, I think you have a valid point. The basic power of superstition is fear and ignorance; its net effect is to destroy. In spiritual healing, however, you are dealing with different forces, in a different dimension, with a different purpose, and different results. The only thing the two have in common is that both require a certain measure of belief. But what doctor, nurse, or psychologist would ever want to be destructive to his patient? That is not compatible with good medicine or psychology. But it is the net result of superstition. So, in that sense, it is the exact opposite of spiritual healing.

Leichtman: You seem to be suggesting that the essential ingredient of healing is the quality of the healer's consciousness—his or her reverence for life.

Schweitzer: Yes.

Leichtman: Which is not really something you would learn, let's say, in a weekend course on "How to Become a Happy Healer."

Schweitzer: You can't obtain a reverence for life from someone else. You have to cultivate it within yourself. That means going through the careful, step-by-step training a mystic would go through. That starts with the long process of getting to know yourself, as the Greeks taught it. I'm not talking about getting to know your hang-ups, your feelings, and your wishes, although you will have to learn to control them. I'm talking about getting to know your spirit, your wisdom, your love, and your potential. I'm talking about getting to know the healing force within you—and the ultimate truth about who you are.

As you do this, you'll develop some of the gifts that will

let you operate more fully at inner levels—gifts like clairvoyance and psychic ability. But you must not confuse these gifts of the inner life with the inner life itself. People who stop searching for the ultimate truth about themselves after they develop a bit of psychic ability or clairvoyance are letting themselves get stuck on the wrong level. Being clairvoyant or psychic is no guarantee of an ability to heal. That comes by being able to touch the healing force within you.

Leichtman: What would you recommend to someone interested in contacting this healing force? Will reading books help, or meditating, or what?

Schweitzer: Reading the right books could be useful, yes. There's a lot of good information about the nature of the healing force, for example, in the little book the two of you wrote, *The Way To Health*. Meditation can be helpful, too. But just reading books and meditating is not the whole story.

Leichtman: What else should be done?

Schweitzer: Primarily, practicing what we've been discussing throughout this entire interview. That is, reaching inward and knowing that there are divine elements within you, within the patient, and within the universe that can help you do your work as a doctor, a nurse, or a psychologist. You are not alone in wanting to help this person; you are not alone in caring about his or her well-being. And so, you focus your own deep concern for the well-being of your patient, and work with the confidence that there are other, greater forces of caring and healing being focused through your individual concern and efforts.

Now, that may not seem as spectacular as some of the techniques taught in the weekend seminars, but it's the real key to spiritual healing. The capacity to love and nurture the health of your patients is the single most important feature of all healing.

Japikse: That sounds like something that would take a whole lifetime to cultivate.

Schweitzer: Well, it does grow and mature slowly—step

by step. There is no such thing as instant enlightenment.
Leichtman: Yes, and I think that's something your own life demonstrated very nicely. Your maturity and understanding seemed to evolve, become richer, and acquire more meaning as you went from experience to experience. And that greater maturity was reflected in your writings.

Schweitzer: That's the way life is. If you are a person who expects to attain instant enlightenment, you are probably also a person who will stop after making very little progress, and just stay there, believing that you've accomplished what you set out to do. You've gained your instant's worth, and so you stop. But if I was going to name the worst sin I could think of, that would be it.

Leichtman: What would be it?

Schweitzer: To stop growing. To stop enriching your life and your thinking.

Leichtman: Well, you certainly were not guilty of that sin. I would hope some of our readers will be inspired to pick up your life story and study it, because it's an excellent example of what we're talking about here. You would involve yourself in extremely intense work, either in Africa or in your concert and lecture tours of Europe, but then there were also periods in your life when you had a little more time to yourself. It's obvious to me that it was during the periods of intense involvement that you really grew; the quiet times of reading and meditation served more to consolidate the meaning of recent activities and to prepare you for new growth.

Schweitzer: I think that's basically true. From the perspective of the inner life, all experiences of daily living are opportunities to grow, to serve, to love. They all contribute to what you do. Meditating is important, but it doesn't do the whole job. One has to act in the world.

Leichtman: Is this what you mean, then, by the idea of Christian service to our fellow man—that there is something enriching about the work of service in addition to knowing you are helping someone else?

Schweitzer: Absolutely. When you are engaged in proper works of service, you always receive more than you give. That's the marvelous aspect of love: you are always enriched by expressing it, never impoverished. You get back more than you give. Both the giver and the one who receives the gift therefore benefit.

Leichtman: To my mind, this is one of the most central ingredients of the Christian religion, when properly understood—the need to work in service, to help one another. That concept isn't as strong in other major religions, is it? Did you find, for example, many Hindu or Moslem missionaries or hospitals?

Schweitzer: I wasn't aware of any; there may not have been any in all Africa. But I really don't know.

Leichtman: The Christian religion has sponsored many hospitals and orphanages throughout the centuries, but I don't recall that being a major concern in other religions, except Judaism.

Schweitzer: Judaism, of course, is the foundation on which Christianity was built. No, I doubt that there were any Moslem or Hindu hospitals.

Leichtman: What do you think of the holistic health movement in medicine today?

Schweitzer: It's a marvelous idea, an idea whose time has come. There's some nonsense associated with it, of course, but that's always the case when any good idea gets started.

Leichtman: Do you have any specific warning or advice as to what to look for?

Schweitzer: Results. *[Laughter.]*

Leichtman: Can you be more specific?

Schweitzer: If an unorthodox treatment works, then go ahead and use it. If it doesn't, then try something else that does.

Leichtman: That would seem to be an effective way of measuring almost anything.

Schweitzer: If it were used, it would quickly eliminate a lot of the silly ideas that have been coming up. By and large, however, the people who are behind the current movement are sensible enough to do this.

Leichtman: Yes, they are. Well, to continue this line of thought, from your current perspective, what would you like to see people in medicine do next?

Schweitzer: Become more aware, in their training and their practice, of how much the quality of their concern for the patient does actually contribute to the healing process. Many health professionals, unfortunately, never really love their patients enough. And when that happens, it cuts the heart out of our profession.

The extreme, of course, is the doctor who gets all wrapped up in his investments and his luxuries, and his office becomes a money mill. That kind of doctor should not be in practice—or, at least, he should reevaluate the meaning of his practice. But that's probably a good idea for all health professionals, not just the ones at the ridiculous extreme. We should all be in the habit of reevaluating the meaning of our practice, on a regular basis. Because that's the only way we can increase the usefulness of what we do. And, as much as possible, we should reevaluate how we can be more caring, more loving.

Leichtman: Yes. What do you think about the movement to teach patients the value of controlling their own attitudes toward health, and assuming responsibility for it?

Schweitzer: That's an idea of major importance to medicine. It certainly deserves attention—patients need to become aware of the healing force within them, even more so than doctors. And not just become aware of it, but learn to cooperate with it.

Leichtman: Do you have any other advice for the medical profession?

Schweitzer: Medicine should be doing ten times more good for people than it is now. For one thing, I would like to see more emphasis put on the new trend to approach healing in terms of a medicine of wellness and a psychology of wellness.

The emphasis should be on promoting healthiness, not on sickness.

Leichtman: Yes.

Schweitzer: And training patients to be healthy.

Leichtman: That expands the concept of healing, so that you don't have to be sick in order to get better.

Schweitzer: I'm glad you said that.

Leichtman: Well, I wasn't the first.

Schweitzer: But in the context of our conversation, it was very apt.

Leichtman: It's very obvious to me, from the writings you left behind and the way you conducted your life, that healing meant far more to you than simply caring for sick or diseased people. It involved an improvement or uplifting of consciousness, not just in individuals, but potentially in society, religion, government, and the world as a whole. What should be done to further this work of healing society?

Schweitzer: More people have to follow the injunction given us by Jesus, to find the kingdom of heaven within. We must start dealing with reality, both at inner and outer levels. And that means being active at both levels. The inner life must be expressed through active service in the outer world, and everything we do in the outer world should be guided and inspired by our inner life.

I suppose the real key to healing society is the idea behind the title you chose for this series of interviews, *From Heaven to Earth*. As we discover the hidden life of God within ourselves and within society, and bring it into expression in our lives collectively, we heal society. As we bring heaven to earth, and build new awareness of the kingdom of heaven among the peoples of the earth, we heal society.

Ideally, the churches should take the lead in this endeavor, but I am realistic. They probably won't. They are sometimes so busy *following* those who have come and gone that they have little time left to *lead* those who are here. So, the movement to help people discover the kingdom of heaven within them is probably better off separated from the organized church, at the moment.

The early Christians taught each other how to discover the hidden life of God within, but that aspect of the teaching has largely dropped out of the church. It's a very bad thing that it was dropped; that kind of teaching ought to be part of the work of the church. It was stopped for political reasons, I believe.

Leichtman: Let me go back to music again, which was obviously one of your great loves in life. You gave concert tours, wrote books, and even made recordings. I have the impression that the music was more interesting to you, and certainly more fun, than your missionary work.

Schweitzer: Yes. Of course, in doing all that, I was earning money to help support the clinic. And, it was self-healing, too.

Leichtman: If you had had your druthers, what would have been the most enjoyable way to spend your career?

Schweitzer: Essentially, I *did* have my druthers. I did what I really wanted to do.

Japikse: Was that because being a missionary "felt good," or because you had a real dedication to that work?

Schweitzer: Well, of course, it was because I had a real dedication—very much so. When the opportunity came, I thought, "Ah-ha, that's what I want to do." And even when I was depressed by the nature of my work, that work was still what I wanted to do. I had thought it through; it was a strong conviction with me.

Japikse: Well, we have both observed people who make a big show of performing "service" to mankind, but the service they choose is really not a service at all, it's just a thinly-disguised gratification of their own emotional desires.

Leichtman: Yes, they are camouflaging their selfishness as service. But it is quite clear that you were performing genuine service. You were not just doing what you really enjoyed. You undoubtedly enjoyed what you did, just as we enjoy what we do, but your purpose in doing it was not just to satisfy your emotions or ego.

Schweitzer: That's true. I did what I wanted to do, but the "want" was based on a conviction about the value of service, not emotional gratification. I thought it was the most useful way to live my life.

It was determined by the values I held—the value of being able to do some good, the value of being a proper Christian.

Leichtman: Would those values be best described as feelings, thoughts, or a dedication?

Schweitzer: Values involve all three—they involve your whole being. They originate in spirit, but they aren't worth much unless your personality and your feelings embrace them, too. When a man gets in the proper perspective with God, the choices of what he is going to do with his life become obvious. And they are the right choices.

Leichtman: Of the three most significant areas of your life, your music, your philosophy, and your medical practice, which was the most difficult?

Schweitzer: The medicine, of course, but I don't want to sound like I was a martyr. Much of the time, the hardship was a beautiful experience, and a satisfying and fulfilling experience, in its way. I was able to overcome my fatigue and limitations and keep on working.

I never considered myself a martyr, because I always had great help from the spirit. The work of service is never easy—or it wouldn't be true service. This is part of service; you have to cast yourself in a role where the personality alone cannot do the work required. To achieve your goals, you have to call forth the life of the spirit. And as you do, you bring more of heaven to earth.

Once you realize this about service, it does become a joyous experience—even the hardships. As Jesus said, "My yoke is easy, my burden is light." That is a very profound statement.

Leichtman: Some people might say that the combination

of music, philosophy, and medicine was rather odd. Was there a unifying theme which connected them for you, or were they simply three distinct activities?

Schweitzer: There was a common denominator, but I'm not sure I can easily explain what it was. Let me put it this way. Each of these was an expression of the best within me—and the best expression I could make.

Japikse: When you say, "an expression of the best within you," what exactly do you mean? Some people would just assume it was the best way you could show yourself off.

Schweitzer: No, I wasn't trying to show myself off. I accepted duty as a value, and I felt I had a duty to express the talent I had in those three areas. I owed myself the expression of those three facets of my personality.

Leichtman: You owed it to your personality or to your spirit?

Schweitzer: To my spirit, of course.

Leichtman: In other words, this self-expression was a way of honoring your spiritual duty.

Schweitzer: Yes. And so, the common denominator of these three expressions would be *me*. Not me the personality, but me the spirit. They all became the same thing to me, because each was an opportunity to contribute something of my spirit to life.

Let me add this, too. By expressing myself in these three ways, I honored God. I looked for God's love, and I found His beauty and wisdom, too. I found God's music, God's ethics, and God's healing power. That's why I say these three expressions all became the same expression to me.

And this is true for many people, I think. They seek God and suddenly have a major breakthrough, leading to a new appreciation of every aspect of their life.

Japikse: If I might play the devil's advocate a moment, a little while ago you said that the marvelous thing about service is that the one who serves always receives back more than he gives. And we've just been talking about self-expression. I can easily imagine some readers might misconstrue these statements as advocating selfishness.

Schweitzer: Well, a certain measure of what I might call "enlightened selfishness" is necessary in order to live life in the physical plane. I'm not talking about ordinary selfishness, however.

Japikse: Is there perhaps a less confusing way to describe this "enlightened selfishness"?

Schweitzer: Enlightened selfishness can be thought of in terms of living your life in a responsible way—making sure that you support yourself, educate yourself, and do what you can to enrich human life. It would include what we've been talking about today—reaching inward for the truth.

The ordinary variety of selfishness, however, tends to be just the opposite. It rejects responsibility for one's own life, and demands indulgence and pampering from others. They can both be called "selfish," because they are "of the self," but the difference is great. The person who rejects responsibility is very sick of mind.

Japikse: Would it perhaps be better to label this "enlightened selfishness" as a love of selfhood—or a love of the God within?

Schweitzer: In general, yes, but it is also useful for people to take the apparent contradiction of the phrase "enlightened selfishness" and toy with it in their minds until they understand *how* it means "the love of the God within." Keep in mind, in this context, that the word "ego" generally is used in a negative sense, but the word means, very simply, "I am." Now, some people would give the phrase "I am" a negative connotation, but I don't at all.

Before you can serve, or love, or heal, you have to be able to express "I am." You must be able to be selfish in an enlightened manner. The goal of humanity, after all, is not to eliminate selfishness, but to enlighten it. And it is important for individuals to have the desire to learn as much as they can in a lifetime, to experience as much as they can in a lifetime, and to reach inward and find God and then turn outward and honor Him through self-expression.

It's important for people to wake up, suddenly one morning, and discover that they have a lovely, gorgeous continent within them, that's just begging to be explored. That's an awakening from ordinary selfishness into enlightened selfishness.

Japikse: What would you say is the proper motivation for service?

Schweitzer: The need to be useful. That sounds a little egotistical, but it is necessary to live life being needed and being useful.

Japikse: No, I don't think that sounds egotistical, because it implies that you have something worthwhile to offer, and you are giving it freely. You are not just going around spreading your good intentions.

Schweitzer: The line from the Bible that I quoted before, "By their acts ye shall know them," applies again here. The person who is serving with the wrong motivation will be exposed by the quality of his service. But the true Christian will be motivated by his concern for his fellow man.

Japikse: Yes. Well, having spent your life in service, what advice would you give to others who would serve, but are not sure where to start?

Leichtman: Should they all rush off to Africa to do missionary work?

Schweitzer: Not at all. There are plenty of opportunities to serve in the context of your own environment and circumstances. The place to start, of course, is wherever there is a need that can be met by a talent or gift you can contribute. So, start by looking for legitimate needs in your own family and work, and then evaluate your capacities—the capacities of your spirit, too—to meet those needs.

If you don't have the talents or gifts to meet a specific need, but feel especially drawn to serving in that area, then take the time to carefully train yourself so you can.

Japikse: Yes, I believe that's what you did—you did not actually start studying medicine until after you had decided to serve as a doctor. Are there glamours that people, especially Christians, develop about the value of service which end up interfering with the true purposes of service?

Schweitzer: I'm sorry, I'm not sure I understand how you are using the word "glamour."

Japikse: It's not a common usage of it. I'm referring to illusions or fascinations that people, especially Christians, might develop about service.

Schweitzer: I suppose you're referring to the fact that many people view service as a way of chalking up "brownie points" or "credit" in heaven. In fact, many of them believe that the more unpleasant or uncomfortable they are while serving, the more "brownie points" they'll get. But it doesn't work that way—that is an illusion. In terms of service, doing the right thing for the wrong reasons is simply wrong. It doesn't qualify as service.

Japikse: In your writings, you described a certain fatigue in civilization. We talked about pessimism and depression earlier, but this is a little different, as though you had the impression that this fatigue was stressing civilization. Is this fatigue still present, and if so, how does it affect modern civilization?

Schweitzer: Yes, the fatigue is still present. It is like a cancer in society. It can be seen among people who are not willing to take responsibility for their acts and thoughts, and in the governments which cater to them. It can also be seen in governments that refuse to let the people take this responsibility and tell them, "Oh, no, you aren't supposed to think for yourself. We'll think for you."

Japikse: What is required to revitalize society and civilization?

Schweitzer: For people to take responsibility for their own lives and actions.

Japikse: Does that have its correspondence in terms of civilization and large groups of people, too?

Schweitzer: The American civilization would be a good example of that, yes. It is designed to let people take responsibility for themselves, but many Americans have refused to take it. They have not made the choice—and you *do* have to make a choice.

Leichtman: Very good. Before we finish, I want to ask you what activities occupy your time now. How do you keep yourself busy?

Schweitzer: I continue to be concerned with the reverence for life, both here and in the physical world. I'm active with a large group of people who are involved in service to the world, each on his own plane; I try to show them what it means to be helpful in the world, what it means to love God and His creation, and what it means to find God—and that it is really the most utterly simple and rational and natural event of life. Finding God should be even more simple and natural than breathing, because we are designed to be loving and caring individuals. We are designed to be helpful.

But the impulse to help can be polluted by our desire for attention and self-aggrandizement; we can get fuzzy in our understanding of what is helpful and what is not. So I am helping people who want to serve to straighten out their understanding of the reverence for life and how to apply it. I am helping these people purify some of their feelings and intentions.

I am also active in some areas of medicine, by assisting those who are dedicated to being a healing influence on their patients. I'm even active in some of the research being done into the use of sound in healing.

I don't mean to imply that I'm working with a scientist who's making a gadget that will be released soon and heal millions of people. Sometimes the sound that heals is your own reassuring voice, saying, "There, there. I understand what you're going through, and I know it's difficult, but we can help you manage this with reasonable comfort." It's not the sound of someone singing or screaming.

Japikse: Gee, I thought you were in heaven chanting the sacred names of God all day long. *[Laughter.]*

Schweitzer: No. The only way we sound the name of God is by doing His will and serving His creation. That really is the only dance there is, to use a well-worn phrase. It's the only activity that counts. On the inner side of life, of course, a chant is a form of dance. "Chanting"—and I'm not talking about physically chanting—makes matter vibrate in a certain pattern so that it begins to dance up and down, in a sense, and rearrange itself in new patterns. That's why I used the term "dance."

Isn't that fascinating?

Japikse: Oh, yes.

Schweitzer: Well, I haven't said anything really useful.

Leichtman: No, but it makes a nice chant.

[Laughter.]

Japikse: When you say you are active helping people, what do you mean? I know what you mean, but some of our readers may not. How can you, as a spook, help someone in physical form?

Schweitzer: Well, I didn't mean to imply that everyone I help is physical.

Japikse: Sure.

Schweitzer: When I was in the physical, there was a large group of spirits I worked with, and I continue to work as part of this group. We help one another focus certain qualities of energy, and then send them on to the physical world. In fact, this is the work of many groups "up here." We summon aspects of God's wisdom or love and then project them to certain areas of the world, or groups, or specific people. There has always been, and still is, an urgent need for compassion, caring, tenderness, and gentleness in the world. We try to help meet that need.

Sometimes, we bring people into our little group and they learn from us by watching us, and by absorbing our frequency of energy. Some of these are people who are incarnate. They visit us during the hours of their sleep, travel with us on our rounds, and pick up some of our qualities of thought and consciousness, I guess by osmosis. At other times, we try to feed and sustain the goodwill and good intentions of individuals who have a capacity for reverence for life. We don't do their work for them, but we do help energize their good ideas and intentions and help nourish their love for the world and for their fellow man.

Leichtman: Can you tell us more about this group you work with?

Schweitzer: What would you like to know?

Japikse: Is it organized in any way, or just—

Schweitzer: In our state, organization is unnecessary. We all see the common goal clearly.

Japikse: Isn't there structure to the work?

Schweitzer: Oh, there is structure to the work, but we work in a state of harmony that would be impossible on the physical plane at the present time, except among rare individuals. We are very much in tune with each other, and we don't have to waste a lot of time discussing what we are going to do, because we each know what it is we have to do.

Leichtman: No committee meetings?

Schweitzer: We don't need them.

Leichtman: No political bickerings to see who runs the show? *[Laughter.]*

Schweitzer: There would be no place for that.

Japikse: Does everyone on your side of the veil work together in such perfect harmony?

Schweitzer: Oh, I was talking about the specific group I belong to.

If I may, I'd like to close with this thought. In physical life, I was a healer of sick bodies and minds. I did other things, but that was one of the major roles I played. And what I did in my work in Africa I now do on a larger scale. It's the same type of work, but now I'm working more to be a healing influence on certain segments of society and mass consciousness. I am actually dealing with almost the same forces and energies I dealt with in the physical—it's the same frame of mind. I'm still very much aware of the nobility and greatness that God has created within every person, and I'm still very much aware that you nurture this seed of greatness with love. So, in a very real sense, I'm continuing the same work I did in the physical.

I hope that more people will join me, too—not in my work, but in the realization of what it means to nurture the seed of life with love. I hope they will join me in finding their own unique connection with God within themselves, in finding that His love is also their love, and in finding that they, in union with God, can become healers in their own lives and their own circumstances.

That's the message I had the honor to deliver to the world. I talked about it a bit, I wrote about it a bit, but I think it's the service I performed that really delivered the message. That's always the case: it's what anyone is actually able to achieve that becomes the message of his or her life.

What I did, everyone can do. And I hope one day everyone is able to do as well as I did, or better. That's what we are designed to do, after all—we are designed to be vehicles of God's wisdom and love. That was my message as Albert Schweitzer—and it still is.

It hasn't changed a bit.

YOGANANDA RETURNS

The activity of bringing the love and wisdom and power of heaven to earth is an ongoing process. It happens every day in every part of the world. The belief that it is an unusual activity which could only happen in ancient times and in some special "promised land," as many religious fanatics insist, is utterly absurd. The manifestation of heaven on earth is meant to be a daily phenomenon, a natural happening in life.

In fact, considering the wide diversity of cultures and civilizations on the planet earth, it is reasonable to expect that each of the major societies throughout the world has had its role to play—a unique and specialized role—in the overall effort of humanity to bring heaven to earth. Only as we become aware of the major contributions made by each culture, in religion, philosophy, the arts, government, and science, do we begin to appreciate the full scope of the divine masterwork here on earth.

Unfortunately, we in the West often limit our understanding of God tremendously, by ignoring many of the fine contributions to religious philosophy and spiritual practices made by other cultures, especially the East. We tend to dismiss the rich traditions of Hinduism and Buddhism, for example, yet in many ways, these spiritual practices are far more highly refined than those of the West—certainly in terms of the expression of devotion, the use of meditation, and an understanding of esoteric principles. They deserve a greater measure of appreciation and acceptance.

For most of this century, there has been an effort to bring some of the major practices and insights of the East to the West, so that they might take seed and grow. This is not an easy task, however, for the whole milieu of culture in the East is considerably different from what we are accustomed to here in the West. The teachings of the East cannot be translated literally into English, or they tend to sound absurd; they must be transposed into the proper context. Then they come alive and make sense.

The problem is that not all of the teachers and gurus who have made the pilgrimage to the West are equally skilled in transposing their teachings. In fact, many just are not interested. They teach exactly as they have been taught, demanding that their students totally adopt the ways of the East and forgo the lifestyle they grew up in. Such teachers, however, do not represent the best of the Eastern traditions.

Probably the teacher who has done the best job of bringing the spiritual life of the East to the attention of the West is Paramahansa Yogananda. Born in India in 1893, he dedicated himself to the spiritual life at a very early age, studying in the ashram of Sri Yukteswar while also pursuing more conventional studies in school. He grew quickly into spiritual adulthood; in 1920, he was chosen to represent India as a delegate to the International Congress of Religious Liberals in Boston. This was the beginning of his ministry in America, which lasted until his death in 1952.

For the first ten years, Yogananda traveled extensively throughout America, lecturing to large crowds. In the early 1930's, he began to refocus his efforts, spending more of his time teaching smaller groups at the headquarters of the Self-Realization Fellowship, which he founded, in California. There he wrote his most famous work, *The Autobiography of a Yogi*, and labored to establish the roots of the spiritual tradition he had brought to America.

The facts of Yogananda's career, however, do not really tell us much about his greatest contribution. Yogananda was truly a man of God, an individual human being who radiated a pure and refined quality of devotion. In a very real sense, he could be called a *priest of divine love*. In him, love was the genuine article—not the sentimental goo or blissful niceness so common among superficial aspirants, nor the fanatic militancy which poisons so many "born again Christians." Yogananda was *filled* with divine love; he did not have to make the effort to be kind, for he was kind by nature. He did not have to struggle to be compassionate, for he had perfected compassion. He did not have to pretend to care for people, for it was part of his very being to care. He did not have to put on a show of patience and tolerance, for that was his life. Yogananda was filled with love because he had devoted himself entirely to loving God. He knew God intimately and revealed it through all that he did. Indeed, he would often stop in mid-lecture, caught up in his inspiration, and carry on a loving, moving conversation with God.

My admiration for Yogananda as a person and as a spiritual teacher is based on a number of factors. I view him as a leader in the necessary work of integrating the East and the West. At a time when the average Westerner associated Eastern spiritual men with cave-dwelling ascetics, nearly naked beggars, and fakirs who slept on beds of nails, Yogananda demonstrated what the spiritual life actually involves. He was dignified, cultured, enlightened, friendly, and comprehensible. He came to the West out of love for God, not personal ambition. He presented his message with respect and love for the people who listened to him. Today we are virtually deluged by emissaries from the East struggling for converts and attention, but few come anywhere close to the example set by Yogananda. Most rely on charisma, not love, on ritual, not understanding. Some are even openly greedy.

But I would not limit Yogananda's example to the way the teachings of the East ought to be presented. There is much that people of all religious persuasions can learn from him concerning an individual's relationship with God. While many Christians and Jews talk of love, yet conduct their lives with competitiveness, jealousy, and argumentativeness, Yogananda demonstrated a capacity to recognize and love the presence of God wherever it manifested, in Christian, Jew, Hindu, Buddhist, or Moslem. While many Westerners take their spiritual practices no further than brief prayers, the reading of scripture, and attending church, Yogananda taught that God is found through constant devotion to Him in all that we do. While Western religious leaders tend to presume that their traditions and practices are the only acceptable way to God, Yogananda taught the far more sensible principle that God is found by loving Him and serving Him, and that can be done in any constructive religious format.

It is wise to keep in mind that when Ralph Waldo Emerson suggested in a lecture in the middle of the nineteenth century that we all can and should have a personal experience with the God within us, he was accused of a shocking heresy. In many ways, the West knows very little about God or divine love, and we owe it to ourselves to listen and learn when someone such as Yogananda appears.

I would encourage both those who are familiar with the Eastern spiritual traditions and those who are not to take a fresh look at the life and teachings of Yogananda. Those who know something of the East will find in Yogananda a balance and intelligence which is frequently missing in other representatives of Hindu and Buddhist doctrines. Over and over again in the interview which follows, Yogananda stresses that no meditative technique is an end in itself, be it the asanas of hatha yoga, breathing exercises, mumbling a mantra into mindlessness, dancing around in a circle, or fasting. Some of these practices have value, he says, when performed in the context of a dominant and all-consuming love of God and reverence for life, but they mean nothing by themselves.

It is this latter ingredient, the love of God, which Yogananda demonstrated so well—and which is so often lost on the boat when the East comes to the West. And yet it is the heart of the East, and when it is lost, the practices themselves become nothing but clanging cymbals, the futile gestures of a fanaticism which buries its advocates in materialism.

Those who are not acquainted with the spiritual traditions of the East will find in Yogananda a rich source of information and possibly some new revelations. His *Autobiography of a Yogi* is possibly the best guide to the wonders of the East that has yet been published. It is not just an account of his life, but a marvelous tour of India and its holy men and women, their practices, and their beliefs. It also presents some of the key achievements of the spiritual tradition of the East. The most significant would be:

The East has long been a model of tolerance and patience, aware that God is the supreme force in all of creation. The West, by contrast, tends to be out of harmony with many of the rhythms of divine life.

The East is far more aware of the inner workings of consciousness and the invisible nature of God than the West. It was perfectly natural for Yogananda, for example, to pray to great souls that he revered, both from the East and the West, and to communicate intuitively with them, even though they had died.

The East has learned more about the process of purifying and spiritualizing the emotions than the West.

The East is comfortable with using divine forces for practical benefit and accepts what we would regard as "miracles" as natural occurrences of life. All too often in the West, unfortunately, any attempt to use God in a time of need is condemned as evil. In the East, however, spiritual healing, psychic feats, out-of-body travel, and contact with invisible forces and entities are considered healthy and normal.

Naturally, the topic both Yogananda and I were most interested in discussing in the interview was the integration of East and West. In many regards, I am concerned that the integration is not proceeding as effectively as it might, in large part due to the thoughtless and sometimes silly ways that Westerners approach Eastern practices. There is not that much actual *integration* of ideas and techniques; they are either accepted or rejected without adaptation or modification.

In commenting on this problem, Yogananda stresses that eventually integration will require far more than just *bringing* the East to the West. There is a distinct mentality and way of life here which demands something different than what works in the East. The practices and philosophy of the East are good starting points, but they must be developed into something new and appropriate for the West.

The interview covers a wide range of topics, from meditation to devotion to the philosophy of teaching. Often, to illustrate a point he was making, Yogananda would simply tune in to the appropriate divine quality and flood the room with it. His presence was a powerful one, definitely overshadowing that of the medium.

For those not already familiar with Yogananda's work and the Eastern traditions, a few definitions may be helpful. Several references are made, for example, to kriya yoga, a spiritual technique taught by Yogananda during his career. The technique of kriya yoga involves the concentrated focus on a simple breathing exercise. But as Yogananda explains, it is not the technique which counts. What is important is practicing kriya yoga in a framework of constant devotion to God. That is the real spiritual practice.

Indeed, many people in this country know very little about yoga. To them, yoga is the practice of certain physical exercises. That, however, is hatha yoga, the least significant of all the yogas. The word "yoga" means "union with God," and describes a large classification of various spiritual practices. There is, for example, bhakti yoga, which is the yoga of love and devotion; jnana yoga, which is the yoga of wisdom; karma yoga, which might be called the practice of the presence of God; and raja yoga, the yoga of the mind. As Yogananda mentions in the interview, each type of yoga presents techniques for a certain level of personal development.

We also talk a great deal about the use of mantras, since they have been so popularly associated with meditative practice in this country. As Yogananda points out, using a mantra is not a meditative practice at all—just an introductory procedure.

Near the end of the interview, Yogananda states that he is still active, busy directing divine forces to humanity and in being a helpful influence to those he worked with when he was on the earth. In this way, he is keeping up an ancient Eastern tradition of spiritual teachers continuing to assist their followers on earth after they pass beyond the physical plane themselves. Although most Westerners little suspect it, this ongoing assistance is common in our tradition, too. Unfortunately, ignorant superstition keeps the average person from realizing the help which is offered to him.

The medium for this interview was Paul Winters. I am joined in asking questions by my colleague, Carl Japikse. Mr. Japikse's wife Rose also sat in on the conversation.

Yogananda: It will take me a minute to get adjusted here. While I'm doing this, maybe I can describe what's going on. It feels as though I am trying to throw a very small dart through a tiny pinpoint. The pinpoint, of course, is the vehicle through which I am talking [the medium].

Leichtman: Well, I hope you have good aim. *[Laughter.]*

Yogananda: So far, so good, but it is a very intricate path that the dart must be thrown through.

Leichtman: I know, and I don't want any of your darts landing over here. *[More laughter.]*

Yogananda: No problem.

Leichtman: I have a big astral—I'm liable to get hit. *[Guffawing.]*

Yogananda: If you're lucky, you will be. I've brought my very best set of darts with me today.

Leichtman: Oh, good.

Yogananda: Before we get into questions, I would like to address the issue of whether or not I am the real Yogananda or just a thought-form in the mind of the medium, for the benefit of those who will be reading this interview and possibly have doubts. I will say this: the vehicle which is sitting here before the three of you and speaking to you is not Yogananda. It is a vehicle which I, Yogananda, have borrowed for the purpose of communicating with you and participating in this series, but it is no more me than the tape recorder on the table is me or the typewriter which will transcribe my comments is me. The ideas and thoughts that I will be communicating through this medium, however, and which will be recorded on tape and transcribed by typewriter, are the ideas and thoughts of Yogananda.

For the benefit of those who have studied my works and perhaps even knew me, I want to say that the style of speaking and expressions I will be using in this interview are not representative of the way I talked during my physical incarnation. I am only able to use the words and expressions which are available to the personality of this medium. I would hope that the reader would appreciate that for the duration of this interview, my inner essence is expressing itself through a physical personality, just as it expressed itself through the personality of Yogananda. Because of this medium's skill, I will be able to get my ideas and thoughts through quite successfully, but not in the same "packaging" that my friends and students are accustomed to.

Leichtman: Yes, those are the standard limitations of any communication through a medium. But how can the reader reasonably satisfy the question of whether or not you are Yogananda, if you do not particularly sound like him?

Yogananda: There are two ways. The first is by experiencing the quality of the consciousness which is presently associated with the medium, and recognizing it as that of Yogananda. However, that is an experience available only to those of you who are gathered here in the room.

Leichtman: Yes.

For the record, I would say that I am certainly experiencing a very high level of energy here which is not the normal state of consciousness of the medium. My impression is that I am communicating with an individual who is able to act at the buddhic level [see glossary]. And I am clairvoyantly perceiving certain forms which are suggestive of the presence of Yogananda, although I would hardly claim that these perceptions *alone* are conclusive.

Yogananda: The second way of satisfying, beyond reasonable doubt, that I am Yogananda is to evaluate the merit of what I say. If it is consistent with my thought and teachings, that should be sufficient. Of course, I do not intend just to rehash my teachings; I hope to be able to add something to them.

That is the experiment we are undertaking today, is it not?

Leichtman: Absolutely.

Yogananda: That's why I came, in any event.

Leichtman: Does this mean that you are not going to tell us the name of the puppy dog you had when you were a boy?

[Laughter.]

Yogananda: Yes.

Leichtman: Aha—he forgot. *[Giggling.]* I mention that because a lot of people seem to demand that kind of evidential trivia before they will accept the validity of mediumistic communication. But it has always seemed to me that such trivial "facts" are easily pulled out of the ethers and do not prove a thing.

Yogananda: That's right. And if it were the intent of this interview to engage in such trivialities, I wouldn't be here! And I doubt that any of the other people involved in this series would be very much interested, either.

Leichtman: Yes. Our purpose is not to prove the validity of mediumship, but rather to demonstrate its real potential. And to help a new generation of humans to become better acquainted with such outstanding people as yourself.

Yogananda: That's very kind of you. I hope I will be able

to comment on the work I did and perhaps indicate the larger goals it is leading toward.

Leichtman: Very good. Well, just before this session began, we were discussing the fact that you were one of the leading lights in the process of integrating Eastern spiritual traditions with the West. Would you say that was one of the major themes of your work as Yogananda?

Yogananda: I would say it is one of the major goals of the work of humanity, and I was glad to be able to contribute to it. I am referring now to the interaction and integration of the differing cultures and spiritual traditions within humanity. The ultimate goal of humanity is to express the divine will of God as a single, unified whole. This cannot occur, however, until there is an understanding and appreciation of the different elements in human civilization—until the different traditions of the human family are honored yet molded into one.

Of course, the two major traditions which have developed are the Eastern and the Western—one being very old—the Eastern mystic tradition—and one being relatively young—the Western scientific tradition. Both of these, with their differences and positive contributions, must eventually come together to form one humanity, one expression of God.

If this is sounding at all disjointed, I am still getting settled in here. I hope it will get a little easier as I become more acquainted with the medium.

Leichtman: Well, the integration of East and West is a very important subject, and I hope we can discuss it thoroughly. But before we get into the heart of it, let me needle you a bit. Some people would say that cities on the west coast, like San Francisco and Los Angeles, have virtually become suburbs of Tibet. They are almost overpopulated with hordes of teachers from the East who have brought with them their customs and techniques, but have made no effort to *integrate* those traditions with the customs and needs of the West. They are just teaching Americans to be Eastern-style mystics. I'm not sure that's to our advantage.

Yogananda: In the early stages of integration, it must be expected that certain, doctrinaire individuals will lose sight of, or perhaps never quite grasp, the larger perspective they are participating in. They fail to see that the goal is the intermingling of the two traditions. Instead, they become very rigid in their attitudes and unable or unwilling to adapt what they know so it will be appropriate for people with a different background. They feel it must be taught exactly as they learned it.

It is very easy to forget that there are spiritual techniques and then there are the individuals who use the spiritual techniques. Often, it is necessary for a teacher to alter or modify the techniques he teaches so they will be more useful to those he is teaching. Unfortunately, this basic principle is sometimes lost in the process of bringing Eastern techniques to the West. It is important to remember that the Western individual has been brought up in a different cultural setting than the Easterner, with a different kind of physical vehicle and different subtle bodies as well.

Leichtman: That cuts both ways, doesn't it? The West has sent to India some of our most fire-breathing fundamentalist Christian ministers, who certainly do not represent the best of our tradition or thinking. They just make God look petty and angry.

Yogananda: Of course.

Leichtman: But the same thing happens in reverse, too. India has sent us some of her "fundamentalist" gurus, if I can call them that, who set to work teaching us fundamentalist Hindu practices and rituals. And they make God look stupid. And yet, Americans do not seem to be able to recognize that they are dealing with what I would regard as a debased version of Hinduism—or Buddhism, when that is the case. To me, much of what is being taught over here would be considered quite inadequate in the East, yet it is glorified by some in the West as the ultimate.

Yogananda: Well, one way to help people get over this hurdle is to teach them that underlying the technique or dogma of any system, whether it is of the West or the East, is each person's inner being and the love of God. Questions may arise from time to time about techniques and doctrine, but we can *always* rely on the love of God to be the pillar which gives us the basis for looking at the various techniques and systems set forth, and choosing what is best. Getting to know this love of God, and learning that an individual's devotion to it is always returned in much greater magnitude, is the starting place of all spiritual growth. Unfortunately, many people manage to get themselves all tangled up in the dogma and techniques and writings of a particular system, and lose sight of the goal, which is to become one with God.

Leichtman: It seems to me that Easterners have a much better understanding of that goal—union with God—than we do in the West, but that quite often in the East the emphasis is placed on union with the most transcendent elements of God. As a result, there is almost a deliberate neglect of union with the elements of God which are expressing themselves through the physical plane—the divine ideal which is manifesting through physical forms. The Hindu and Buddhist often become "other worldly" and neglect the physical plane and the needs of civilization.

Yogananda: This is true, and it is indicative of the differences between the two traditions, and the need for integrating them—each learning from the other and striving for something better than what we already have. For the sake of this interview, I think it will be acceptable to make some simplifications which would be inappropriate in other contexts. If we think of the whole planet as being a single entity, then the spiritual tradition of the East represents the entity's development of understanding and unity with God, and the spiritual tradition of the West represents that entity's development of divine talents, creativity, and productivity.

Now, that's a gross oversimplification, but we can expand on it as we go along.

Leichtman: I don't think enough people in either the East

or the West recognize that the West's preoccupation with the physical plane is a legitimate spiritual activity.

Yogananda: Well, it is. And the combination of East and West should eventually produce an entity, the human race, which is involved in both, not just union with God but also the expression of that union in physical manifestation. That is the contribution of the talent and learning of the West. And while both of these traditions, the East and the West, have been developed and are very successful in their own right, now is the time—over the next several centuries—for the people of this planet to look toward uniting and combining their talents and knowledge.

Leichtman: You seem to be implying that there is a different dharma and karma for both the East and the West, by which I mean a different spiritual duty and a different set of lessons to be learned. Would it be useful to talk about these lessons, as a basis for then exploring how the integration of East and West should occur?

Yogananda: As long as we think of it as a division of mankind's spiritual inheritance, rather than opposite extremes, sure.

Leichtman: Of course.

Yogananda: In that context, then, the major distinction I would draw is that the Eastern tradition is very personal and in a sense self-centered. The goal of living the spiritual path is primarily to struggle back to union with God.

Leichtman: From earth to heaven.

Yogananda: Yes. It can be likened to an individual walking up a flight of stairs. He sees the light at the top of the stairs and struggles toward it. The Western individual, by contrast, is less interested in the struggle to get up the stairs; he would rather find an elevator which would take him to the top of the stairs immediately, where he could grab the light. It is at that point, however that his struggle begins, as he endeavors to bring it back down the stairs. He preoccupies himself with bringing heaven to earth, whereas the Easterner focuses himself on lifting earth to heaven. Need I say more on that?

Leichtman: That sounds as though you are suggesting that the Western emphasis on scientific discovery, the life of service, and the need to be active in the physical world are all appropriate spiritual practices in the West. Given a person with right intention and right motives, a lifetime devoted to teaching, psychology, science, or some other field of contribution could well be a noble expression of his or her spirituality and worship of God.

Yogananda: Why, absolutely. This is the ultimate goal of evolution—to express the love and wisdom of God in everyday life. It is not enough just to know this love and wisdom; we should be striving to make them manifest on the physical plane as quickly as possible. Which means it would not be practical to have an entire planet of people caught up in bliss and rapture all day long—or all that spiritual, either. It is important to plow the fields, too, if I may use that phrase symbolically. The combination of these two activities—the quest for God and plowing the fields—is what will lead to the fruition of the will of God on the planet Earth.

Leichtman: Isn't there still the assumption in mass consciousness, though, that the person who plows the fields, or works in the factory, or teaches, or serves humanity's needs in some other fashion is not quite in touch with the love and wisdom of God? And when he finally sees the light and actively pursues spiritual interests, he will then perforce withdraw into a life of introspection and contemplation? That's a fallacy, of course, but one that seems to be rooted rather deeply in mass consciousness.

Yogananda: Well, it's not appropriate for the West, even though it is rather common in the East. But this kind of misunderstanding is typical of the confusion which can occur when elements of two different lifestyles come together. The merger of two different spiritual traditions can be expected to take quite a while and be fraught with many misunderstandings, especially in the beginning. At this stage, the pendulum is sweeping from one extreme to the other, and this accounts for some of the mistakes being made and the willingness of some people to totally reject their former way of life in favor of being completely absorbed into a new set of traditions—new to them. It would be nice if we could find the point of balance right away and instantly blend the best of the West with the best of the East—and a few teachers may be able to do that. But the vast majority of people cannot. For them, the pendulum needs more time, and must swing back and forth repeatedly. It is in this way that the integration will occur.

Japikse: So far we have primarily been talking about the West accepting the ideas and teachings of the East. If this is to be a true spiritual integration of East and West, doesn't that also mean that the East must accept the appropriate ideas and teachings of the West?

Yogananda: Absolutely.

Leichtman: I think the East is far more advanced in absorbing Western practices than vice-versa, though. Would you agree?

Yogananda: I would agree.

Leichtman: But that is true. Integration must occur in both traditions, leading to a unified one.

Japikse: To put it in terms of your staircase analogy, true integration would seem to be a matter of the West learning from the East how to get up the stairs and the East learning from the West how to get down the stairs.

Yogananda: Precisely true.

Japikse: Now, in pursuing this integration, how much difficulty is created by the difference in language? It is my understanding that the Eastern languages are a good deal more figurative and symbolic in nature than our languages in the West, which tend to be literal and precise. Is that a problem? When you talk about devotion and love of God, does that mean something different to an Easterner than a Westerner?

Yogananda: Yes, the context is different, and it is worthwhile for people in the West to take that into account. Let me draw an example out of your own literature. There is a very fine American author, William Faulkner, whose works are generally set in the American South of the early twentieth century. To understand his writings, you have to know something of the customs and traditions of the locale in which they are set. If his novels were translated into Arabic and read in Lebanon or Syria, it would be very hard for the average reader there to penetrate what is going on, even though the translation might be a very good one. The culture and traditions are so different that it would be very hard to understand the context.

Now, if you can conceive of that as being a problem, then the difficulty of translating books on the Eastern spiritual tradition into the languages of the West, so that they can be understood in the context of the latter twentieth century, is immensely more complex. Devotion definitely does mean something different in the streets of Calcutta than in the streets of New York City, even to the masses. Among spiritual aspirants, the differences may be even more pronounced, because they have been schooled in their respective traditions. Of course, once a certain level of enlightenment has been achieved, the differences begin to fall away and the similarities emerge, because the individual is dealing more with the love and wisdom behind the tradition, and not the tradition itself. Those are universal realities.

In India, a love for God and devotion to God is a love for a transcendent God, the universal, benevolent force which is the source of all life, the one life we all share. Devotion is the outpouring of love and respect which puts you in touch with this underlying unity. As I am talking now about love and devotion, I am tuning into these qualities. From my perspective, the few words I am saying about them are simple and immensely crude, for they are inadequate to convey the fullness of devotion and love I am experiencing.

If you were my students, and for the purpose of this interview, let's say that the three of you are my students, I would not teach you about the nature of love and devotion by lecturing you about them at great length. I might say a few words, as

I have just done, but my major way of teaching you would be to create an atmosphere of intense devotion to God and flood your little group with it, drawing you into this atmosphere so that you experience a true level of devotion and love in my presence. And that's how I would tell you about devotion and love—not in words, but by sharing with you the presence of God. And that should tell you much more than I could ever say with words.

Leichtman: Oh, yes. Of course, I would hope that this is a method of teaching which the good teachers in the West use, too.

Yogananda: I think it is. But it's a *tradition* in the East, much more so than lecturing. And so the words we use to teach are more simple, in comparison, but the people in India expect that. They have had the personal experience of devotion many times, at the feet of their guru, and do not need a lengthy explanation of what it is. In the West, it is not quite that way. Here, it is possible for people to talk about the virtues of devotion to God on the one hand but turn around and claim on the other hand that everyone outside their own religious sect—the Jews, the Baptists, the Catholics, the Lutherans, or whoever—are evil, pagan, and worthy only of condemnation. They have no trouble, apparently, handling that paradox, but in the East it would be recognized as an absurdity. It would be unthinkable and incomprehensible to the average Indian mind, although some of this attitude does get expressed in the conflict between Hindus and Moslems.

I'm not sure I'm answering your question.

Japikse: Oh, you're doing a very good job.

Yogananda: The Western tradition is focused much more on the mental level and has a much stronger emphasis on the precise articulation and verbalization of ideas, spelling out the nuances and variations in subtle shades of meaning. I appreciated that focus during my career and I am perhaps appreciating it even more today, as I throw my darts through this highly developed Western mind. The Western intellectual tradition has carried this art to a very high degree. It is one of the great strengths of the West, allowing you to elaborate upon the details and finiteness of love or devotion or any other topic. But it also has its weaknesses, when used without wisdom. The Western mind can break things down into such finite elements that the central meaning is lost. You can take a rose, for example, and pull it apart, dissecting every element, analyzing the chemical structure of its perfume, and developing a whole array of theories—but you no longer have the rose you started with. What you have, scattered on the table, does not look like a flower or smell like a flower. All its perfume, grace, and beauty are gone. The thirst of the mind for knowledge has destroyed it.

This is not the tradition in the East. There, the idea is to pull things back into their basic oneness, into their essence, which is God. The Easterner would not dissect the flower but seek to identify with its essence, and within that essence he would discover the joy which is within the flower, the beauty which is within the flower, and by experiencing that joy and beauty, he would worship God. Now, it is a lot harder to describe that rather abstract joy and beauty in precise scientific terms, which are more suited for labeling the various parts of a rose. So the Easterner doesn't bother; he leaves behind words and concepts and tries to communicate the experience, the feeling, the knowing, and the awareness. Generally, that communication is not in words or writing.

Japikse: The reason I asked that question is that it seems to me that the integration of East and West is not accomplished just by reading some books about the East or even by following a guru from the East. Both traditions need to be understood in their fullness before they can be integrated, don't they? We're not just mixing the two traditions together and magically producing something better, are we?

Leichtman: Yes, there has to be a process of digesting both the differences and the similarities, before integration becomes possible.

Yogananda: Well, the work of integration is very poorly understood, and so I am quite delighted to have this opportunity to talk about it today. Let me try to sketch out for you what this digestion, as you call it, would involve. I'll put this in terms of integrating the East into the West, although the reverse process is just as necessary.

The first step is bringing the East to the West, a process I was happy to participate in. This is done in many ways, by writing books, by teachers of all kinds of Eastern practices coming to the West, and by translating sacred Eastern texts. But the Eastern traditions must first be brought over. And in some cases it is necessary for the teachers who come over to teach their material exactly as if they were back in India or Pakistan or Malaysia or China or wherever.

In a way, I suppose it would be something like taking the haute cuisine of the finest French restaurants to the Texas of one hundred years ago. You couldn't just send over a few cookbooks; you would have to bring over some of the chefs, to actually demonstrate how it is done. And at first, it would be interesting only to a few people, and not well understood or appreciated by most. Now, I could have picked any state in America, but I chose Texas, because I understand that it has its own culinary traditions which are substantially different from the French. And so, it would take quite a while before the French cooking came to be understood and appreciated, and during that time, it would have to be taught as it is taught in France. Eventually, however, it would be accepted, and then the ideas of French cooking would be adapted and incorporated into the cuisine of Texas, producing something new and probably better than both of the original kinds of cuisine. At some point of time, even the average cook in Texas would be using various French techniques—not the sauces which require six hours to prepare, but many of the basic practices.

I think this illustrates the steps which are being taken to integrate Eastern ideas into Western practices. The first phase is to bring the teachings of the East to the West and present them as they would be taught in the East. Gradually, as Westerners become exposed to them, they will begin to appreciate the inner value of these practices, what they consist of, and what they will achieve. As this occurs, the people of the West will begin to see how these techniques can be adapted and used by the Western individual. They will pick and choose, leaving out some things while embracing others, until they arrive at a workable synthesis of the Eastern tradition and their own.

In saying that, I do not mean to imply that there is anything bad about the Eastern traditions and practices. I am simply pointing out that the Westerner must be discerning and recognize that some of the Eastern philosophy and practices will be more appropriate than others.

Leichtman: What would be some of the elements of Eastern philosophy and practice which are inappropriate for the West, or must be very carefully adapted before they can be truly useful in the West?

Yogananda: I would encourage Westerners to realize that the Eastern traditions have been practiced now for thousands of years in the East, and the culture in general and even the individuals in particular have built up certain safety valves which protect them from misusing the techniques. The Western individual, not having been born in the East, does not innately have these safety valves, and must proceed with common sense and caution in experimenting with Eastern practices.

Let me explain this from the perspective of the Easterner first, and then transport the idea so that it applies to the Westerner. The Eastern tradition, as we have said, is very devotional by nature. You would say that it is a more emotional approach to God, carried out on the wavelength of love. But it is this very wavelength of love which protects the Eastern individual from any abuse of the techniques of his spiritual tradition. The upbringing of the Easterner is steeped in a climate of devotion to and trust in God. Any mantra, technique, or transfer of energy he might use would therefore be practiced in the context of this devotion and trust. And you must understand that this is a very rich climate of devotion, which has been built up in the culture for centuries and centuries. It tends to mute the potential for gross abnormalities.

The Westerner, on the other hand, who has not been brought up in this climate or inherited such a strong mystical tradition, would find himself in very dangerous waters trying to use certain techniques from the East. He is not likely to have the strong sense of devotion and trust in God which protects the Eastern individual using the same techniques. In fact, because the Westerner is physically oriented—and by that I mean adept at producing results on the physical plane—the Westerner would tend to view many of these techniques as ends in themselves. He would think of the *techniques* as being the pathway to God, which is not true. They are training maneuvers which, when used on a day-to-day basis, enhance a union with God which already has been established, and has existed since early age, *for the Easterner!*

I hope you are beginning to see the danger of transporting some of these techniques with only a superficial awareness of their purpose. The Westerner is quite apt to take a specific technique and view it as the beginning and end of spiritual growth, without any regard for the character of the individual using the technique, the condition of his subtle bodies, or the refinement of his consciousness. He is willing to believe that the mere repetition of a particular technique will automatically establish union with God. This is an illusion.

Leichtman: Yes, I've seen this happen when Buddhism is brought over to America. I know a number of angry and aggressive Americans who have embraced the spit and polish of Buddhism without understanding its basic truths, and they've just ended up being angry, aggressive Buddhists. That's an abortion of Buddhism.

Yogananda: In my teaching, I tried to present the ideas of the East in precisely the way I have just been discussing—that without an intense devotion and love of God, these techniques can be dangerous and should not be attempted. The first criterion of spiritual growth is to cultivate a profound attitude of love and devotion. Techniques should be seen as practices which supplement that love and devotion, *not replace them*. Even the best of techniques can be misused, after all. But when they are used with the right attitude, right living, and the right approach to God, the worst consequences of misusing them are muted.

Leichtman: I'm glad you are making such a strong point of this, for it is something that is very dear to my heart—that the *quality* of consciousness is the real key to spiritual growth, not chanting or hyperventilating or levitating.

Yogananda: That is true. And there are many ways you can measure the quality of consciousness, but to me it was the strength of one's devotion. If you love God with the whole of your heart, all the time, every day, then the techniques you practice will work as they are supposed to. In the final analysis, the techniques are secondary to the quality of consciousness.

Leichtman: In this vein, then, I would like to carry your analogy about introducing French cuisine into Texas a step or two further. If the people of Texas one hundred years ago did not know anything about French cooking, wouldn't it be hard for them to separate the imposters from the chefs with cordon bleu training? There must have been plenty of Frenchmen one hundred years ago who were lousy cooks and unable to make it in Paris who would be tempted to go to Texas and take the poor suckers there for a ride. And it would seem to me that the same can be said regarding the East. There are different levels of spiritual attainment among the people of India. Some of the ones who have come to America have been highly enlightened, such as yourself, and we would be missing a great opportunity if we did not welcome them. But others might simply be people who could not make it as a guru or swami in India, and so came over here—to take us poor suckers for a ride.

Yogananda: Well, that can be a problem, but it tends to be a self-correcting one. A phony in the East is not that much different from a phony in the West. Eastern phonies may dress a little differently and have a different accent, but most people in the West would know how to spot them. Their strangeness may throw you off the scent for awhile, but sooner or later they will have to pass the scrutiny of common sense, discerning thought, and careful observation.

I don't want to say anything which would tend to encourage the reader to become overly skeptical; because there are differences in the cultures of the East and the West, it is rather important that the West give the teachers from the East the benefit of the doubt for a while, and be willing to make allowances, until the Eastern tradition is better understood. But yes, there are imperfect people in all walks of life, including the spiritual teachers of the East, and it is important that the "buyer beware." Yet it's like anything else; if you were going to buy a new car, you would want to go to a reputable dealer, not a crook. If you are going to entrust your life and approach to God to a new teacher, you should be intelligently cautious and be sure you are making a good choice, before you "buy into" that particular guru or philosophy.

What is amazing is that so many people do not use their common sense in this way. If they would, they could protect themselves from being deceived.

Japikse: Well, let's put common sense to the test. Is it really a spiritual tradition in India to spend five thousand dollars to learn to levitate? *[Laughter.]*

Yogananda: Of course not. That's unthinkable.

Japikse: In fact, are techniques for learning to levitate a valid part of the Eastern tradition?

Yogananda: Why, sure. But not if they cost five thousand dollars. And not if they obscure the central theme of learning to love God.

Japikse: Would you care to demonstrate your expertise?

Leichtman: There he goes. He didn't take Paul's body with him, though. *[Laughter.]*

Japikse: That doesn't count, then.

Yogananda: You mean I have to lift the body up, too? *[Guffawing.]*

Leichtman: We'll let you practice on the cookies.

Yogananda: The phenomena of spiritual growth are the natural results of having taken certain spiritual pathways. When any phenomenon, including levitation, is approached as an end or a goal in itself, rather than a byproduct of spiritual transformation, then you are setting the stage for great self-deception. Unfortunately, some people do view the *phenomena* of the spiritual life as the goal. That is an error.

Leichtman: Is there any way in which knowing how to levitate would improve your ability to love God or know God? Does transcendence of gravity imply even a smidgen of transcendence over one's immaturity?

Yogananda: A smidgen?

Leichtman: Yes, a smidgen.

Japikse: A Sanskrit term. *[Laughter.]*

Leichtman: It means an itty-bitty little bit.

Yogananda: Well, that's a difficult question.

Leichtman: Aha. That's enough of an answer. *[Laughter.]*

Yogananda: I'm glad you recognized it.

Leichtman: Well, let me continue to pursue your analogy of the enrichment of Texan cuisine through the introduction of French cordon bleu cooking.

Yogananda: Actually, some of us would consider it more of an enrichment if it had been brown rice instead. *[Laughter.]*

Leichtman: Of course.

Yogananda: I'm sorry. Do go on.

Leichtman: Well, I wanted to make sure that it is clear that you are not suggesting that the Texans should totally abandon their cuisine, but rather that they build upon it, by introducing new elements. Many people who become interested in the East seem to think that they must renounce any Western approach. I know this is not what you meant, but would you care to comment briefly on which traditions of the West are valuable and can be built upon?

Yogananda: Well, let me make a prefatory statement first. The Western individual loves to make broad, sweeping generalizations. He says, "Let's find out what is best for everyone and then make sure that everyone does it." That's the Western style, and it's an outgrowth of the rich mental tradition you have followed in the West, with its emphasis on discerning the principles and formulas which are inherent in the cosmos and the plan of evolution for the whole of humanity. And, of course, these principles can be discovered—that's what the ancient wisdom is all about. It has been articulated through the holy scriptures of many major religions and the writings of esoteric teachers for tens of thousands of years. But when it comes to the finite question of what to do with this one individual or group of individuals, there are no simple answers or generalizations which can be followed without variance. Some people in the West *are* going to have to have the experience, at least briefly, of living the spiritual life exactly as the Hindus live it or the Buddhists live it. And to do that, they may have to reject the traditions they grew up with, at least for a while. Once they understand the Eastern traditions thoroughly, then perhaps they will see where they are able to adapt them and incorporate them into Western life.

I like the cooking analogy because the food we eat physically can be a lovely symbol for the spiritual food we are meant to consume. I noticed you had a yummy dessert for lunch today.

Leichtman: Oh, the Kahlua pie. Yes, it *was* marvelous.

Japikse: An ancient Hindu specialty. *[Laughter.]*

Yogananda: Well, suppose someone gave you the recipe for that Kahlua pie. The first time you made it yourself, you would probably want to follow the recipe exactly as it was written down, so that you could see how it went together—and how it was supposed to come out. But after you had made it a time or two exactly as it was written, you would probably start to vary it somewhat, and adapt its taste and the technique of making it to your own preferences. Gradually, it would become your own version of Kahlua pie.

The same principle applies to the process of investigating the Eastern spiritual tradition. It is marvelous to be able to go down to the local metaphysical bookstore and be able to buy books on the Eastern tradition, or a copy of the *Bhagavad-Gita*, or the sutras of Patanjali. But if your investigation of the Eastern tradition consists of reading such books casually for an hour or so now and then, you will be more of a dilettante than a devotee. I don't want to discourage anyone from reading in this fashion; it is commendable to read widely. But I would hope that anyone reading on that level would appreciate that these investigations can also be pursued at a much greater depth.

Now that I've said that, I will answer your question. It may startle some people, but the Western individual who starts out to explore the Eastern traditions ought to begin by becoming familiar with his own spiritual traditions—the spiritual traditions of the West. He ought to be enough of a student of Western civilization to know where its strengths lie. Notice that I haven't said anything about the problems of Western civilization. I have emphasized the strengths and values of Western civilization and the Western spiritual tradition. With that kind of preparation, and a sufficiently open mind, he should be able to make sense of the East and comprehend the unique value of the Eastern traditions. He will be able to see how the light of the East can complement his own spiritual needs and the traditions of his own civilization.

Of course, by understanding the Western tradition I am not suggesting that people need to spend eight years researching the subject or earn a Ph.D. in it. But there should be some familiarity with the rich mental tradition of the West and the basic themes of Western civilization.

Japikse: How would you define those basic themes?

Yogananda: I'd put the traditions of brotherhood and service at the top of the list. You put a great deal of emphasis on spiritualizing civilization, on being the thoughtful steward of the resources of earth, and on developing the enlightened, discerning mind. The whole work of bringing the richness and beauty and inspiration of heaven to earth is very well promoted in the West. And that is not a spectacular insight; it should be a matter of common sense to the average intelligent Westerner.

Leichtman: Let me ask this. What would the integration of the East and the West result in?

Yogananda: The proper balance between the realization of the God transcendent and the realization of the God immanent, as well as the full development of techniques and practices for interacting with both of these aspects of God. I could say more, but everything else would be derived from these basic ideas.

Japikse: So that would be a healthier way of defining the work of integration than, let's say, the balancing of the mental approach of the West with the more emotional approach of the East.

Yogananda: That would be involved, too, as a means of working toward the overall goal. Westerners tend to know more about an enlightened and active use of the mind. Easterners tend to know more about an enlightened use of the emotions. And they have a great deal to learn from one another. Easterners tend to know more about how to find God and contact God. Westerners know more about how to use divine inspiration and divine force once they have contacted it. Easterners know more about how to face the light and hold themselves steady in that light. Westerners know more about how to radiate that light into their personality and self-expression to produce practical results. But these activities are complementary, and need to be integrated, at some point, by the enlightened individual. Collectively, the activities of East and West are also complementary and need to be integrated to achieve the same result in the entity which is the human race.

Japikse: Would you talk a bit more about the quality of devotional love? You referred to it earlier as a pillar of love, which I thought was an apt way to put it. In English, the word "love" is used in so many different ways that it tends to become confusing. I certainly almost never hear it used in any sense close to your idea of a pillar of love. In fact, it is usually just the opposite, and tends to have whatever meaning the person using it wants it to have.

Leichtman: Yes, how about the people who claim they love an abstract God but don't demonstrate very much love for any of God's creations?

Yogananda: Well, as I indicated before, I'm not sure I would try to explain the "concept" of love. Instead, I would try to create an atmosphere in which my students could experience devotion and love for themselves. Then they would know what it is. But if I had to explain it, I would define it as "deep respect"—a deep respect and awe for God. I am certainly not talking about selfish, emotional "love" and the possessiveness of the lower emotions. I am speaking of a deeper love—a deep respect for life and creation, and the proper devotion to that.

Leichtman: Of course, there are certain gurus making the rounds here who say much the same thing, but what they *solicit* is adoration of themselves, as representatives of God's love.

Yogananda: That is a perversion of love. The good teacher will always be the first to decry any personal representation of God. To make the claim that one has a license from God is the grossest form of misrepresentation and should be met with a skeptical eye.

Japikse: So, the love of God can properly include a healthy measure of skepticism? If someone comes along and says, "You ought to love me in order to love God," would it be consistent with the ideal of loving God to reject the attempt of this person to confuse you?

Yogananda: In principle, yes. True love and respect for God is something which must come out of each person individually. It is not possible to love God through someone else. So if someone comes along and tries to teach people that the only way to love God is through *him,* why that would be nonsense. And I believe an outright rejection of such nonsense is the appropriate reaction.

Japikse: I brought that up because many people would claim that *any* form of rejection is the antithesis of love.

Yogananda: Well, I'm not talking about rejecting this nonsense by yelling and stomping and screaming at the person. It would be a silent, inward rejection, a quiet affirmation that this is not the path to enlightenment, and so it is not for me. This person may have something to offer, but it is not my road to God. That would be an appropriate form of rejection. It doesn't have to involve discrediting the other person, which doesn't do anyone any good anyway. That would not be appropriate.

Leichtman: One of the things which has always troubled me about the East has to do with this issue of love. You defined love as "deep respect for God," which I think is very good. In the East, this deep respect is almost entirely focused on the God transcendent—the universal, omnipresent, benevolent, creative life force. We would call it the "God up there." But there is also a "God down here," a God immanent, dwelling in each one of us and expressed, to one degree or another, through our acts. The East seems to often neglect making contact with this God within us. And yet, isn't it a necessary part of "deep respect" to extend that respect to the God within all people and all life forms? I'm referring to the concept of reverence for life as demonstrated by Albert Schweitzer. I just don't see this kind of reverence for life as a dominant theme in the Eastern tradition.

Yogananda: Well, it's not. In fact, in many ways the Eastern tradition is "anti-life." It encourages the individual to divorce himself from mundane life and achieve union with the God transcendent; there's no question about that. And this is one of the reasons why the integration of the East and the West is important, so the Easterner will begin to learn that the individual is an expression of God, and in fact a reflection of God in the physical plane.

Leichtman: The reason I brought that up is that I know a number of people here in the United States who assume they are on a very spiritual path, but they are really rather self-centered and indifferent to the needs of their fellow spiritual aspirants, to say nothing of humanity as a whole.

Yogananda: Well, I always found that most of the people who loudly claim to be spiritual, aren't.

Leichtman: Oh, yes.

Yogananda: Self-delusion is a very common illusion in the spiritual life. The person who takes it upon himself to estimate his evolutionary stature, for the purpose of letting everyone else know what it is, generally overestimates by a substantial degree. *[Laughter.]* This indicates a deep problem in personal integrity.

The good teacher or leader is one who goes about his business in the quiet realization that he is a humble servant of a most magnificent enterprise, and that it is a distinct honor to be able to live and experience a tiny bit of this magnificence and glory. He serves with a sense of joy that he is able to contribute to this important work in some small way.

If you keep that model in mind, it will be easy to determine who is speaking with authority and who is simply speaking from self-delusion. I would even go so far as to say the degree of authority is inversely proportional to the vigor with which a person announces it, or brags about it, or insists upon it.

Leichtman: Yes.

Yogananda: The more an individual claims to be in direct contact with God, the more it is probable that he is not. The legitimate teacher or leader offers his help or presents his ideas without claims of being Jesus incarnate or the representative of something otherworldly. He simply says, "This is what I'm here to tell you. You can take it and use it or ignore it as you see fit. If you can use it, then I am glad."

This is getting a little easier now. I'm a bit more comfortable.

Leichtman: Good.

You have commented that the Western tradition has emphasized a more mental approach to God, while the Eastern has stressed the more emotional. In adapting Eastern meditative practices, is it important to modify them somewhat so that the mind is used more actively?

Yogananda: That would depend on the individual. The

value of a teacher, of course, is that he is able to tailor the teaching to the needs of his students.

Leichtman: You mean not everyone should be assigned a one-syllable Sanskrit mantra as his or her exclusive spiritual practice?

Yogananda: Of course not.

Japikse: What on earth are you referring to?

[Laughter.]

Yogananda: One of the phenomena of bringing the East to the West which is fascinating is the attempt here to teach spiritual practices *en masse.* I suppose this is an outcropping of the glamorous and showy aspects of Western society, but treading the spiritual path is an intensely personal thing. It requires individual instruction, and while there are certain general rules and techniques which can be given in books and lectures, there is no one technique which is universal and no one dogma which fits every individual.

Leichtman: But that is not to say that anything goes, is it?

Yogananda: Anything goes? Of course not. But the true teacher tailors the techniques to the individual. Through his spiritual perception, the teacher is able to understand where along the road of development any given individual is, and based on that, writes the prescription which is right for that person. This could be anything from holding your breath or standing on your head all the way to intense devotional or intellectual meditation. He might be able to find a small group of people with similar needs, and teach them together, but the attempt to teach five thousand people a single technique in two hours or even a day is probably not going to produce worthwhile results.

Japikse: Is this description of the true teacher an ideal, or are there thousands or even hundreds of teachers to be found who can operate in that fashion? I've run into very few who would fit the bill, I'm afraid.

Yogananda: No, there aren't that many who do live up to the ideal. I think I'd better amend the statement I just made a bit. There are certain introductory techniques which can be taught to anyone, but once these introductory techniques have been learned, and the student has a glimpse of what the spiritual path entails, he must tread the path in his own individual way. And the only kind of teacher who will really be able to help him is one who is willing to provide individual instruction. There are very few who are.

Japikse: Didn't you teach your kriya yoga technique to thousands of people?

Yogananda: Yes. That was an introductory technique.

Leichtman: You also taught raja yoga, didn't you?

Yogananda: I taught a number of different things. There were certain principles and practices I thought everybody could hear, but there was a lot of other instruction I gave only on a one-to-one basis. For me, the true teaching was being able to work with an individual one-to-one, and tailor a program just for that person. That is the true teaching. You don't make much money at it, but it's the real way to help an individual.

Of course, if I found that a group of three to five people were ready to hear the same thing, I would teach them together. But it is still essentially an individual approach.

Leichtman: What is your opinion of the usefulness of kundalini yoga and hatha yoga in the West? Some doubt their validity for the Western individual.

Yogananda: Let me say this. There are many different kinds of yoga, all with the goal of helping the individual become more aware of his union with God. The different yogas are the individual lessons and techniques the spiritual aspirant must master on the spiritual path. Each one is valid at some specific stage in growth and can be helpful for those people who are at that stage. The enlightened instructor will be aware of the benefits of all the yogas, and use them as appropriate to help the students who come to him. I don't think any of the yogas is destructive to the Western individual, as long as it is prescribed to the right people and in the right circumstances.

Let me once more reiterate that any technique should be

seen only as a stepping stone. We make a mistake if we hang our hat on the technique and forget to cultivate the love of God.

Leichtman: I've noticed that some people develop a very materialistic and earthbound consciousness as a result of practicing hatha yoga.

Yogananda: That can happen, yes.

Leichtman: And they are worse off than before.

Yogananda: It sounds as if these people are failing to cultivate the devotion and love which is the first and foremost requirement of any yoga. When I taught kriya yoga, for example, I always stressed the need to develop the attitude of devotion and love.

Leichtman: That sounds like bhakti yoga.

Yogananda: It was a combination of the two, I guess. But you need a goodly amount of the love and devotion of bhakti yoga in combination with any other yoga technique to be safe. I remember being disappointed when any of my students would lose sight of that.

Leichtman: What you are talking about, then, is the need for practicing the presence of God in whatever endeavor you happen to be engaged in.

Yogananda: Yes.

Leichtman: And that the most important time to practice the presence of God is when you are doing spiritual exercises, whether it is standing on your head or running your kundalini up your chakras or just saying a prayer. To run through a technique in a mechanical, rote way may have significantly less value, or even be harmful.

Yogananda: Absolutely.

Japikse: So the spiritual aspirant should look not for a teacher who has a good technique but for a teacher who has contact with spirit.

Yogananda: That's right. The true teaching occurs in the transference and molding of consciousness, as the teacher interacts with the student. The techniques which may be given out are secondary to the realizations of the student.

Japikse: Well, let me play the role of advocate here. Some of our readers may be scratching their heads. On the one hand you say that if a teacher claims that he has contact with his spirit, it is probably an indication that he doesn't, and on the other hand you say that finding a teacher with contact with his spirit is more important than finding one with a good technique. I know what you mean, but how does the average aspirant sort that out?

Yogananda: I don't think it matters, and I will explain why.

Leichtman: Yes, I want to see how you get yourself out of this.

Yogananda: There are a number of people up here waiting to see it, too. *[Laughter.]* Where I draw the line is between the early student and the advanced student. For the person who has tread the spiritual path for some time, it is a simple matter to discern the level of contact a teacher has. He will intuitively grasp it; he will know by knowing.

Now, if a person isn't able to discern the level of contact of a teacher intuitively, it's not important that he know. He will learn something about distinguishing truths from untruths, in any event.

Leichtman: This is the idea that even a bad teacher can teach us something worthwhile, I take it.

Yogananda: Yes.

Leichtman: Well, that's a profound idea and I hope the readers will take the time to think it through. It's very worthwhile.

Yogananda: Why, thank you. While we're still on the subject of spiritual techniques, let me add a comment which may help clarify a question you asked a while back. Some of the techniques which work extremely well in the East and are simple enough to do can be a problem for some Westerners, because there is a difference in your subtle bodies. They would produce an emotional sensitivity which would be unacceptable in the West, because it would interfere with the basic Western lifestyle of living an active life and working in public offices and factories. In India, a person can easily meditate for hours every day without any significant interference with his lifestyle. But in the West this would be unacceptable for most people. Yet it's difficult to get this point across.

Also remember that when these techniques are taught in the East, they are presented in a context of gentleness and patience, with the realization that they are going to help the student love God better and find God more quickly. Over here, people get all wrapped up in opening up their chakras or running the kundalini up their spine. They approach the techniques mechanistically, and often with a very intense effort. And that makes some of these techniques dangerous to the Western individual.

The intensely ambitious approach to life is so impregnated in Westerners at an unconscious level that just warning them about the danger of it in spiritual practices does not really stop them from plunging ahead anyway.

Leichtman: Can you give an example of how that might distort the intent of an Eastern exercise?

Yogananda: Well, in the East, when we tell someone to quiet down the mind, relax, and go within, the Easterner knows how to do that without becoming totally withdrawn from life, and without "blanking" the mind. In the West, however, the eager student tends to practice overkill, rejecting the body, rejecting the physical plane, and rejecting the mind. I know that some people believe that to be a big problem in the East, but it's not quite the problem there that it is thought to be, because the culture is different. Relaxation is not approached with the same militancy which is found in the West. It is a quiet letting go—the body and mind are still there, but the attention is being absorbed in the love of God. It's more a state of dispassion, rather than rejection, although it sometimes does get overdone.

In the West, however, the ambitious, eager, "let's take heaven by storm" mentality tends to get into some serious problems, by not understanding the subtle distinction between letting go and rejecting.

Leichtman: I appreciate what you are saying, but it does seem to me that the East has been somewhat culpable in spreading propaganda against the mind. I've heard many Easterners speak of the mind as the destroyer or slayer of spirituality, and put a strong negative connotation on the misuse of the mind. A lot of them talk on and on about all the problems a stupid mind can create, but give very little emphasis to the potential of the human mind to be enlightened and creative, or play a constructive role in spiritual practices.

Yogananda: Well, the Eastern tradition is based primarily on the emotional and devotional approach to God, and the mind *doesn't* have much of a constructive role in that method of approach. It mostly does get in the way. But it is a gross error to assume that there are not other ways of approaching God, in which the mind does play an important and constructive role. God certainly can be approached through the mind; it just happens to be a different mode of operation, which can either be used instead of or in conjunction with the devotional mode.

Leichtman: They should be compatible. But I find the Eastern tradition has done relatively little to explore the full scope of the uses of the mind. It has tended to present the mind primarily in terms of concentration and observation, but the power of the mind certainly extends far beyond that. There's very little said, for example, about the abstract nature of thinking and the fifth-dimensional use of the mind.

Yogananda: You have a very valid point here, and I believe the development of the mind as a spiritual vehicle is the next step in human growth. I would be so bold as to say, however, that the perfection of the emotional path to God was necessary before humanity moved on to learning the mental path to God, and learning to use abstract mental faculties.

Leichtman: I would agree. My problem is with people who teach that the mind is an obstruction or impediment to spirituality.

Yogananda: Well, it can be—but so can nasty, angry emotions. But you're right—it's usually the mind which gets the blame for obstructing the spiritual life, not the emotions. Which is wrong. But it is easier for people who are approaching God through the devotional nature and the love of God just to set the mind aside for the time being.

I would remind them, however, that setting the mind aside means that they are not integrating the whole of their being with God. It may be a necessary step at a certain stage, but eventually the mind must be developed.

Leichtman: So the person who would love God must also ultimately learn to comprehend God?

Yogananda: Exactly. We all must learn to perceive and understand God's presence, and see and comprehend His workings in everything. And learning this is an important stage in spiritual development. But not everyone is ready for this stage, and a teacher might be quite justified in teaching certain people to set their minds aside temporarily so they can explore the emotional and devotional approach to God more easily.

Let me add this thought, which may startle a number of people. The act of loving God is not just limited to an activity of the emotions. When it is, it often just becomes an indulgence in sentimentality. But the love of God is meant to be much more encompassing. As the Christ put it—and as you know, I have a great respect for the Christ and His teachings—there are two commandments, to love God with all your heart and mind and soul and might, and to love one another. In other words, loving God is not just an activity of the heart, not just an emotional experience; you must also love God with your mind and soul and might.

There are very few people, either in the East or the West, who know what that means—and even fewer who are doing it. Most people, whether they are Christian, Hindu, Buddhist, or something else, love God with their heart, but they don't know what it means to love God with their mind or soul or might. It seems to be a mystery even among the priests and ministers! *[Laughter.]*

Now, I am not in any way downplaying the importance of learning to love God with the emotions. As I have already said, this is something the West needs to learn from the East. There are many very accomplished and brilliant people here in the West who have sadly neglected the development of goodwill, faith, and devotion, and they are in dire need of adding some of these emotional qualities to their self-expression. They need to balance their lives.

I know you frequently discuss the danger of spiritual practices which simply emphasize loving God, loving God, loving God, as if that is all you need, but it is important for the spiritual aspirant to start there, and learn to love God. If he doesn't, then he's running a terrible risk of not knowing how to use, wisely and sensibly, the knowledge he develops. It's very easy to become destructive with the mind, unless an underlying foundation of goodwill has already been established in the aspirant's character and life expression.

Japikse: Yes, I've seen that in a number of people. The mind is very sharp but the emotions are not properly attuned to the life of spirit. As a result, they go through great crises of doubt and self-destruction, because they have not learned to turn and face the light of God as a source of comfort and strength.

Yogananda: Yes.

Japikse: Could you comment out of your own experiences about the depth of the power of loving God, and the nature of the union with God which results from the proper expression of devotion and love?

Yogananda: If you love God persistently, you become aware of God's love for you, as a direct experience of divine love flowing in you and through you.

Japikse: There seem to be a lot of people who believe that God's love is flowing through them, but give little evidence of it in their lives. How can one be sure he's been touched by God's love and not just an emotional goose?

Yogananda: If it is divine love, it will lead to a transformation of your thinking, your philosophy, the way you act in life, the way you react to others, your morality, and your values. These changes are the result of invoking God's love for you through your own love of God.

That's an important statement.

More esoterically, it could be said that the genuine act of loving God leads to a downpouring of divine love through the personality, moving you beyond the realms of form into the life of spirit, in the key areas of your character and activities. You become more motivated by spiritual matters, and how the spirit builds, than by the expectations and desires of the personality.

It should be remembered that the human personality is primarily concerned with the forms of life—the perceptions of the physical senses and the daily experiences and duties of life. It is designed to interact with forms, manipulate forms, build and destroy forms, understand forms, and nourish forms. But as the aspirant begins to invoke the love of God by loving God himself, this very quickly reorients the personality to the perspective of spirit.

Leichtman: How quickly is "very quickly"?

Yogananda: Well, it might take a whole lifetime, but that's very quick from my perspective. *[Laughter.]*

Leichtman: Yes, it is.

Yogananda: Now, spirit is not concerned with form at all; it functions in terms of consciousness and builds through the focused use of divine love, which is magnetic. The soul has a qualitatively different approach to life than the personality of the average person. But as a person begins to work with love, that helps him change his perspective relatively quickly, so that he begins working with the life of spirit.

That's easiest to do if the aspirant starts with the emotions. The mind can learn to work with the perspective of the soul, but it's not as easy. It's better to gain the experience first on the level of the emotions, and then add to it the creative potential of the mind. The third phase, once that had been developed, would then be to invoke divine will and learn how divine will functions.

I don't want anyone to get the impression that this is like stacking up a three-layer cake, and you can't put the second layer on until the first layer is there. Anyone working with devotion to God will also be using something of the mind and something of the will. The stages do proceed simultaneously, to some degree. It's a matter of focus.

Leichtman: Where does the use of mantras fit into all of this? That is a practice from the East which has been given a lot of attention here lately. Is the sounding of a mantra a complete technique for meditation?

Yogananda: The use of mantras is an introduction to the meditative state. To enter a meditative or contemplative state, the proper attitude must be attained. The physical, emotional, and mental vehicles must be held in the right posture, and a mantra can be useful in achieving the correct attitude. It is a device for recollecting one's heritage in consciousness and for preparing to receive new understanding and enlightenment. It quiets the personality vehicles so they are more responsive to the soul than to external stimulation.

Unfortunately, many people confuse the use of a mantra for the actual act of meditation, which it is not. It's a good preparation for meditation. Of course, for the beginner, the act of quieting the mind, the emotions, and the physical body through the use of a mantra may be quite a profound experience, when compared to anything else he's experienced before. It's unusual, and if it happens to be accompanied by a glimpse of the inner realities of consciousness, it may even be deemed a most extraordinary experience. If that happens, the beginner is quite ready to believe that the mere repetition of this mantra is all that is needed for enlightenment.

Of course, that just isn't true. Repeating a mantra throughout a whole meditation is like stopping after you've read only the introduction to a book and saying, "Boy, this is a tremendous book." But instead of going on and reading the actual story, you go back and reread the introduction, over and over again. *[Laughter.]*

The purpose of a mantra is to adjust the vehicles of the personality to the proper attitude. Once that has been achieved, the mantra should be left behind and other techniques employed. Students who do nothing but repeat a mantra for a whole meditation will sooner or later find that it is not fulfilling and will go on to something that is.

But you will also find certain individuals who are perfectly happy to spend their lives in rereading the introduction, firmly believing that they are loving God and understanding God and that God is loving them in return. Actually, God is saying, "Why don't you go on to chapter one and start reading the book?" *[Laughter.]*

Leichtman: It has been my observation that the people who continue using the mantra in this way, while they may be happy, are also unaware of the fact that their lives are quietly falling apart—they are less active, less productive, less competent, and more spaced out. They are not only less spiritual, but they are less human as well.

Yogananda: This would be the net effect of pursuing any activity which was basically useless. Now, mantras are not useless, by any means, but they have their place. They are a very good way to set the tone for meditating and getting into a meditative state. But they are not the meditation itself.

Leichtman: Should the mantra be a word or phrase you understand, or can it be a nonsense word?

Yogananda: It would be helpful if you understood the mantra and had a reason for using it, but that isn't necessary. Some mantras are better than others, however.

Leichtman: I was thinking—

Yogananda [interrupting]: There's someone here chanting, "Noo-noo, na-na." *[Laughter.]*

Leichtman: Yes, that's one I used to use. It's *very* esoteric. *[Laughter.]* Roy Davis [one of Yogananda's students and the author of *This is Reality*] suggests that you could use the phrase

"Prince Albert tobacco can" and it would work as a mantra, at least in terms of quieting yourself down. However, it might be better to repeat something like, "Be still and know that I am God."

Yogananda: Or a short prayer is fine, too. The Lord's Prayer is an excellent mantra to begin a meditation with.

Leichtman: Some people have the illusion that a mantra can be only one or two syllables long, but I've always thought a whole prayer is superior, because it does more than just quiet down the vehicles. It enriches one's consciousness, too.

Yogananda: No, a mantra doesn't have to be limited to just one or two syllables. But when you start talking about using a prayer to enrich consciousness, you're using it for something other than a pure mantra.

Leichtman: Yes.

Yogananda: A mantra is a quieting mechanism. It can be any word or phrase or symbol that works. There are other ways in which those same words or phrases or symbols could be used meditatively, but then you are moving beyond the classic definition of mantra.

Japikse: Let me get this straight: the term "mantra" applies only to the introductory, quieting step? It can't be used to describe the sequence of quieting, attuning, and then intoning?

Yogananda: I would limit the idea of a mantra to quieting and attuning.

Leichtman: Then the words of power a person might use to summon an order of angels or connect himself to an inner plane ashram are not what you are calling mantras?

Yogananda: No.

Japikse: What would you call them?

Yogananda: What would I call them?

Japikse: Yes. I want to hear the Sanskrit. *[Laughter.]*

Yogananda: Noo⁄noo, na⁄na. *[More laughter.]*

Leichtman: Darn, I thought it would be na⁄na, noo⁄noo.

[Giggling.]

Japikse: From heaven to earth, from earth to heaven.

Leichtman: Shhh—you're not supposed to say that. It's one of the big secrets. I'm not sure it's ready to be given out yet. *[Laughter.]*

Yogananda: There are some authorities who would expand the use of mantras to include invoking, banishing, or stimulating certain forces. But the term "mantra" is probably best restricted to quieting the mind and emotions.

Of course, there are words or sounds other than mantras which can be intoned on the subtle planes, "spoken" with the mind or the emotions, that have the value of energizing specific forces or vibrations within your consciousness. They can be used to summon certain forces and intelligences—or to banish them. The use of these words or sounds is well developed in the occult traditions of both the East and the West. But I wouldn't call them mantras.

Japikse: Since we've talked a great deal about devotion and love, could you give an example of a set of words which would be useful in summoning the divine quality of devotional love?

Yogananda: Well, there are many. I'll try to use something that would be appropriate to the West—"divine love permeates the whole universe." Now, just dwell on that thought and mentally sound it with the mind, and the emotions, and your soul. "Divine love permeates the whole universe. "You can sound it on the buddhic plane, too, if you have conscious use of the buddhic vehicle. I'm sounding this phrase very mildly now and am experiencing quite a build up of divine love.

Are you experiencing it?

Leichtman: Oh, yes—it's very powerful.

Japikse: Yes, you may not get me back to ask any more questions. *[Laughter.]*

Yogananda: It's still building up. Once it starts, it begins to snowball.

It's very easy for me to do that. Of course, it may not be so easy for everyone reading the book to do it. It's important to keep in mind that the more refined a person's experience of love becomes, the more refined his devotion becomes. The experience becomes richer and richer. It grows with practice, until it become extremely powerful and can be invoked rapidly.

Japikse: Let me ask—

Yogananda: Let me say this first. This is the way we teach in the East. A student asks a question, and the guru says, "If you want to know, sit next to me, and I will show you. Be quiet and I will be quiet and I will demonstrate the answer to you, so that you can experience a fraction of what I am experiencing. I will create the experience for you in my presence, so that you can subconsciously and unconsciously observe how I do it and learn, eventually, to do it on your own." Then there would be a long pause in which nothing would be said, until the guru sensed that the student had gotten the lesson. In the West, a lot of stock is put on long lectures and lengthy discussions, as though that conveys the whole teaching. It is helpful, especially for the Western mentality, but it isn't the whole teaching.

I'm sorry. Do go on.

Japikse: I recall from reading your autobiography that even when you were here in America, you maintained a strong rapport with your guru. Apparently, you had a strong rapport with many people in that way. I was wondering, as you were demonstrating the way of contacting devotional love, if you would comment on the wider range of spiritual contacts which can be developed.

Yogananda [laughing]: We have to be careful here—I could go on for hours and might end up invoking more power than any of us wants to bring into this experience today. I'm not even sure it's a good idea to list the wider range of possible contacts, *unless* the reader absolutely understands that no meditative contact is worth pursuing until a continuous capacity to experience divine love has been established. I'm not going to make absolute statements or issue rules for spiritual aspirants, but I do hope the reader will appreciate the immense value and protection that a rich and full experience of divine love adds to the rest of one's spiritual development in life. I cannot overstate that. I suppose I can be charged with being somewhat prejudiced about this, seeing as how I spent my whole life, not to mention many previous lives, championing this idea. Once you are able to experience the love of God on a continuous basis, you see, then any other power or force that you contact and express in the world will be conditioned by your goodwill and love. And that's very important.

If you contact the divine will or certain other divine elements before the love nature is properly developed, the force of the power you contact might turn you into a megalomaniac or destructive bully or a sensualist.

Having said that, I can answer your question. Yes, there's a whole world of archetypal forces that can be contacted, as well as the different orders of angels, various centers of force, and the many qualities of life on the inner planes. Even as a little child, I was very much aware of the line of gurus that I belonged to. And that tradition is a kind of hierarchical link into higher realms of divine force and power and love. To me, this is my family, that I am one in an unbroken line of spiritual teachers. In the East, this is one of the ways we establish lines of force from heaven to earth and from earth to heaven. Spiritual teachers are meant to keep reestablishing this link, so that students can plug into the connection as they are drawn to the teachers.

There are parallels in the West, of course, whether it is devotion to a Catholic saint or devotion to Mary, Mother of Jesus. In those cases, the lines of force are established by entities who remain in spirit and project the energies and qualities to their devotees on earth.

It's even possible to contact other planets—not exactly people on other planets but the divine force coming through a planet. For example, right now I am quietly contacting the force of God's love and devotion coming through Mars.

Leichtman: There's love and devotion on Mars?

Yogananda: There's love and devotion on all the planets.

Leichtman: Of course. There's one thing I would like you

to clarify before you go any further. When you talk about quietly contacting the force of God's love, what does that mean? Is it a feeling or an emotion or something else?

Yogananda: A feeling of love would be the personality's response to divine love. The feeling is not love itself. The difference is enormous—like the difference between tasting a sip of water and all the water in the Pacific Ocean. When I contact the force of God's love, there is an emotional response—but my contact involves much, much more than just the emotions. That is just a tiny part of it.

The difference here is a point of confusion for many spiritual aspirants. Obviously, it is through the emotions and our emotional responses that we first develop an awareness of devotion and love. As a result, our first experiences of God's love are sensations, good feelings about God. We have moments of ecstasy and rapture, which are, of course, feelings. But these sensations and feelings are just the response to divine love. At a certain point, you move beyond that response and begin to identify with the pure force of divine love.

There are many shades to these experiences; you can have a realization of divine love and then spend the next fifty years or fifty lifetimes deepening the quality and intensity of that realization. The experience of contacting divine love is not just something that happens and then it is over. It becomes part of your life, because it is much more than a feeling or a sensation. It's an experience of oneness, of infinite benevolence, of consciousness itself. I'm using words which may mean nothing to many readers, but if they don't make sense, I would hope they would ponder very carefully on what I have said, because there is a richness of insight there which is worth pursuing.

Leichtman: Well, for the record, I can say that the comments you just made communicated something quite real to me, and it's not coming across as mush or vagueness at all.

Japikse: Perhaps we could say that there is a language of love—or any divine quality—that the student must learn.

Yogananda: Yes, but it is a language which the student

learns on his own, as he attunes himself to love. I would encourage students not to be afraid to pursue this on their own—and not to be too eager to compare notes with other travelers on the spiritual path. It's your own intimate and rich experience, and it varies from individual to individual, not because God is different for any of us, but because we are different, with different perceptions and needs and past experiences.

Leichtman: One of the questions Carl and I wanted to pursue with you is the whole subject of passiveness in meditation. We've often noted that many people are far too passive in their meditative style, and that tends to hold them down in emotional reactiveness. They don't strike out on their own and pursue the kind of realizations you've been advocating—and they aren't much encouraged to, either. The reason why we thought we'd ask you about this is that many of the techniques which have come out of the East seem to promote passiveness.

Yogananda: In the East, meditation is passive, because the student is striving to develop a receptive awareness of the transcendent God. That is not the goal in the West, however, as we've already discussed. In the West, the goal is to bring the life of spirit into fruition on earth. So a different type of meditation is required. You are absolutely correct—too much passiveness is not helpful to Western meditation.

Here again we run into the problems of merging two spiritual traditions. You are taking passive meditative techniques and trying to adapt them to an active spiritual context. In the initial stages, some of the people will miss the mark.

Japikse: Has passiveness had a long-term benefit in the East?

Yogananda: I think it has. You have to remember that life is but an opportunity to develop along certain lines. If an individual soul is going to take a series of incarnations in the East for the purpose of spiritual growth, it can be presumed that the traditions and practices popular at those times in the East are probably what the individual soul needs. Certainly there is a time and a place in any soul's growth for not focusing in the physical plane and for learning an essentially passive form of meditation. So meditating in a passive format would not be harmful to such an individual; it would be part of his development.

But the West is not the place for a passive meditative format. In fact, if an individual soul incarnates into the West in order to utilize the experiences and opportunities available in that tradition, it would be missing something valuable to leap into a passive meditative practice. It would constitute a lost opportunity.

Leichtman: Are you saying that if someone is born into the West, in a Western family, it is probably not his destiny to take up Zen Buddhism?

Yogananda: That's what I'm saying, yes.

Leichtman: And if he did, it would be inappropriate for that particular lifetime?

Yogananda: Yes. Whether it would be detrimental or not would depend on what the person did with the Zen Buddhism in the context of the Western culture. It is possible to undergo the rigors of Zen Buddhism and still remain active in Western culture.

Leichtman: Yes.

Yogananda: But I'm assuming you're talking about the people who get caught up in the passiveness of Eastern meditation and disregard where they are and what they are supposed to be doing. This is primarily a problem of being in the early stages of the integration of East and West.

Leichtman: Some people just don't seem to be able to make the switch. They get so far into a passive meditative system that they become victims of it. They are unable to function in their careers, and even if they stop meditating, they don't seem to be able to recover from the damage that has been done.

Yogananda: If you study the Eastern cultures, you will see that they have adapted to this problem. The passive person has a place in the culture—the culture recognizes the validity of that stage in spiritual development. That is not the case in the West.

Leichtman: Yes. It has been my observation that one of the valid reasons for a passive orientation in meditative technique is to pursue the astral-buddhic line of development. That does require some passiveness, but is it necessary to go to the extreme that is often found in the East?

Yogananda: Of course not.

Leichtman: It would be possible, then, to pursue a mystical line of development, leading to awareness on the buddhic plane, while living in harmony with the active lifestyle and tradition of the West.

Yogananda: Sure. It is the intent of the spiritual life that it be a complement to the normal activities of being a productive member of society. In this particular era, it is not necessary to cease all worldly activities in order to pursue spiritual endeavors. In fact, it is quite possible for an enlightened individual to enjoy a full spiritual life as well as a full life in society, working hard, enjoying pleasant personal relationships, and making an enlightened contribution.

Leichtman: Won't that require substantial modification of some of today's commonly accepted spiritual and meditative techniques—perhaps even elimination? A friend of mine, for example, went to a Buddhist priest of very high rank for a two-week session, and all that he was instructed to do for the whole two weeks was sit quietly and visualize himself being surrounded by green light, with the awareness that this green light and the qualities associated with it would heal him. When the two weeks were over, he went home to his regular routine, only to find that he was very irritable, uncomfortable, restless, and fatigued. The whole experience was basically a big bust. I thought that meditative technique was highly impractical for him.

Yogananda: The effect of meditative work should be to transform a person's attitudes toward life, so they become more spiritual, rather than create major disruptions or changes in that person's daily activities and duties. Regardless of a person's work or activity, meditative exercises should enhance his productivity and increase the joy of making a worthwhile contribution to life, not interfere with it. While a certain measure of passiveness in meditation may serve to help relax and focus the vehicles, anything more than the small amount required for this purpose could in fact be destructive.

Leichtman: Certainly destructive to the mind. A healthy, normal mind has an active associative mechanism which is never meant to be stopped. Controlled, modulated, and refined, yes, but never stopped until the death of the mental vehicle.

Yogananda: Yes.

Japikse: Perhaps we should ask what your definition of meditation is? I'm getting the impression that meditation may mean something different in the East than in the West.

Yogananda: I would define meditation as the art of recollecting one's true nature so as to express the soul and personality in harmony.

Leichtman: Just what do you mean by "recollecting"?

Yogananda: Recollecting the personality into a state where it reflects the soul.

Leichtman: Ah, the right remembrance of one's *true* nature, then—not just remembering a memory?

Yogananda: That's right.

Leichtman: That definition would seem to imply a very active and intensely disciplined process.

Yogananda: In the West, yes. It might not in the East, but we'll just pretend we're not talking about the East.

Japikse: The What? *[Laughter.]*

Yogananda: The purpose of meditation, then, would be to enable the personality to live the life of the soul.

Japikse: That isn't what is always stated as the purpose of meditation, though. Some of the systems which use the word "meditation" claim that their purpose is to help people cope with stress.

Yogananda: Then those systems aren't teaching meditation. It sounds as though they are teaching relaxation. That's a prelude to meditation, not meditation itself.

Leichtman: Some systems even go so far as to claim that

there is no purpose at all to meditation—if you have a purpose for doing this, it's not meditation.

Yogananda: I see no purpose in bothering with such a claim. *[Laughter.]* Sometimes the personality might not understand the purpose of certain legitimate meditative techniques, but there is always a purpose served from the perspective of the soul.

Leichtman: So meditation is a means of spiritualizing the personality and the lifestyle, a means of honoring the life of the soul in all that we are and do. Is this correct?

Yogananda: Yes, meditation is a way of doing that—but it's not the only way, as you know. A person can attain very close harmony between the soul and the personality without meditating a single day.

Leichtman: An example of that would be karma yoga, wouldn't it, where the spiritual practice lies in carrying out one's duties in daily life as lovingly and as responsibly as possible?

Yogananda: Yes.

Leichtman: Well, your definition of meditation makes good sense. It stresses the need of the individual to achieve union with the divine forces which created him. But I have run into many teachers of Eastern philosophy who had such different ideas about meditation that I question not only their wisdom but even their integrity. In effect, they deny the value of individuality, saying there is no soul, just God, and that individuality is not important, just union with God. The implication is that once a person is totally absorbed in the Godhead, he, as an ongoing individual entity, has no usefulness, no purpose, nothing. To me, it's just nihilism.

Yogananda: I don't think this is a problem of the integrity of these teachers, but rather their inability to translate what they have been taught, in the Eastern context, into something that is meaningful for a person with a different karma and dharma. I'm not going to defend these teachers, but I will say that consideration should be made for the tradition they have come out of. There are bound to be mistakes and misrepresentations of these ideas in translating the tradition of the East into something meaningful in the West.

In point of fact, it is not inappropriate for an Easterner to state that the soul does not exist, that once we have achieved oneness with God any realization of self disappears. In the full context of Eastern philosophy, it is ultimately true—but it is a misleading statement and in fact untrue in the context of the Western tradition.

Leichtman: I understand what you're saying. What I am objecting to primarily is that I do not think it is ever spiritually appropriate to regard the physical plane collectively, or our physical identity individually, as something to escape from.

Yogananda: Oh, absolutely not.

Leichtman: It can be transcended and *should* be transcended—but it is not something to escape from. After all, it is part of God's creation. And even after the physical plane has been transcended—indeed, even after a person has taken those initiations which take him beyond the level of the soul—he is still concerned about participating in the work of God. He is still concerned with the redemption of the physical plane in some way.

Yogananda: This is true.

Leichtman: Even the masters, who have long since transcended the physical plane, are still indirectly concerned with and involved in the overall evolution of all the planes of matter and form. But some people take it as an absolute article of faith that the physical plane is something to be thrown off as early as possible. They want to escape to heaven and just keep on going. *[Laughter.]*

Yogananda: That indicates that they are not yet ready to cast off the physical plane, doesn't it? When one has reached the point where he is, in fact, able to cast off the physical plane and not be bound by it, that is precisely the time when he discovers the real creative potential of the physical plane. He will return to the physical plane not because it is necessary for his further growth, but because it is part of the work he is doing on the Father's behalf. His love of God is what brings him back, not his love of physical existence. He doesn't even think in terms of coming back or not coming back; it's not an issue for him.

Leichtman: You talked a bit earlier about what the integration of the East and West would represent, in spiritual terms. What will be the more practical results of this integration?

Yogananda: I'm not sure this will answer your question, but one thing that is going to have to happen is that there must be a distinct transformation in world conditions permitting more legitimate teachers to appear. Even though we are less barbaric than we were two thousand years ago, it is very difficult for enlightened beings to incarnate in the world today. It is quite a risk for them to incarnate.

The system that will evolve over the next two or three hundred years will include all the various yogas and meditative systems, presenting them almost like a menu for the aspirant to pick from, as appropriate to him. Each of these meditative systems will have its place, and they will all be looked upon as tools to enhance an individual's communion with God—tools to help transform the personality into an expression of divine love and wisdom.

Leichtman: That sounds as if it will be just a new mixture of what we already have today. Are you saying that there won't actually be anything new, or a weeding out of ancient practices which are no longer applicable?

Yogananda: I don't think it will be a totally new system, no. It will be an amalgamation of techniques and ideas already available, *but they will be presented in a new perspective.* I do not mean that the current systems will simply be classified and put in their appropriate categories. But the proper use of each technique will be better understood, and certain paths which are already in use on the planet will become more widely known and used.

As you well know, it is hard enough to get people to use anything good.

Leichtman: I thought there might be a movement *away* from some of the techniques which I refer to as "esoteric materialism," which concern themselves more with the subtle *form* of consciousness than with consciousness itself. I'm referring to the heavy emphasis some people put on hatha yoga, the chakras, and kundalini yoga.

Yogananda: Of course. Still, it is necessary to preserve these techniques in some form, because they are useful at certain stages of development. But the basic understanding of meditation will evolve as humanity itself evolves, and the focus will be more on developing and training the mental apparatus. Meditations will become more mentally focused and less emotionally and physically focused.

Leichtman: I was just thinking that perhaps we ought to ask you to define spiritual living. We may have implied at times that an individual's spiritual life is measured in terms of his spiritual practices, such as meditating, and that would be misleading, wouldn't it?

Yogananda: Terribly misleading. As I said, a person can lead a very spiritual life without having meditated a single minute.

Leichtman: Well, what are the qualities that make a spiritual life spiritual?

Yogananda: There are a number of measures and ingredients to the spiritual life. It involves treating other individuals with compassion, love, wisdom, and harmlessness, and acting with responsibility in handling the duties of daily life. The basic indicator of a spiritual life is that spirit is honored in everything the person does and thinks and feels. He reveals God. We could have had the whole interview on just this subject.

Leichtman: Yes, I know, and I think it is important to stress that. Incidentally, I know that Eastern philosophy makes a big deal about *harmlessness,* but is that really the divine virtue—or is it *helpfulness?* After all, a rock can be harmless but no damn good.

Yogananda: Well, there are degrees. Harmlessness is the minimum requirement. Helpfulness is much better.

Leichtman: Some people seem to be very smug about the practice of harmlessness, but all they are doing is doing absolutely nothing.

Yogananda: That's a good distinction to make.

Leichtman: I consider that attitude to be sanctimonious and hypocritical.

Yogananda: Of course, you must realize that for some people just practicing harmlessness *is* a tremendous virtue. *[Laughter.]*

Leichtman: Yes, I guess it is better than throwing bombs. I'm talking about the people who smugly believe that they are helping God mightily by their total lack of effort. *[Laughter.]*

Yogananda: Oh, them. *[More laughter.]*

Japikse: In line with what we've been discussing, let me ask this. How important is it for a student in this era to search out a physical plane teacher, as opposed to learning to rely upon his own inner teacher—the soul?

Yogananda: In the East, of course, the tradition has been to find a teacher and study with him. In the West, this is not nearly as necessary, and in some cases would not be the right thing to do. Let me again say that there are no hard rules which must be followed by everyone. Some people can definitely benefit from being in the company of a teacher for a period of time. It might be an afternoon's conversation, a weekend workshop, or several years of work. It might even involve entering an ashram or monastery or convent, for several years or perhaps a lifetime. But in the West it is right and proper for the majority of people to take the time required to get to know their own spirit and to learn how to invoke its guidance and wisdom. This would be their inner teacher, and learning to listen to this inner teacher is part of the Western occult and mystical tradition. It's part of the Eastern tradition, too, but it is not emphasized as much. Eventually, everyone must learn to contact this inner teacher, but there is still immense value for many people, at different stages on the spiritual path, to be a part of a group and take instruction from a teacher, assuming that they find a good teacher. The teacher can help them make sense of their lives, point out the blind spots, and advise them on adapting techniques to their own needs. A teacher can also be very helpful in warning them about what to do and what not to do, where to limit activities and where to put the major emphasis.

The role of the teacher is to help the spiritual child grow into the spiritual adult. But just as the physical child can only rely so much on his physical parents, and then must do some growing on his own, the same is true for the spiritual aspirant. Eventually, he must realize that he must exercise responsibility on his own. He must learn to meditate on his own, read on his own, and practice his own devotion.

There are a lot of people in the West who can move pretty quickly through the phase of needing a teacher and then be able to develop mostly on their own. You are at a point in civilization where you have the tremendous advantage of many marvelous books containing a great deal of spiritual and esoteric wisdom. So it is possible to do much by yourself, and it is acceptable to develop the spiritual intuition so that you truly do find the inner teacher, or even an inner planes teacher who comes to you.

Japikse: How does that contact develop—through a proper meditative program, the development of psychic abilities, or what?

Yogananda: It need not involve that at all. It doesn't even require meditation. Someone who is taking his responsibilities in life seriously and compassionately, who is trying to be the right person and do the best he can, tends to invoke this inner teaching. He may never go to a church or temple, he may never meditate, he might not even read much, but the singleminded focus of pursuing the responsibilities of life with care and love and thoughtfulness does tend to invoke guidance. It comes as a variety of inner knowing, not as a traditional psychic experience.

Japikse: So we don't need a clairvoyant impression of someone dressed in robes and surrounded by candles, with angels chanting in the background, in order to receive instructions from an inner teacher. *[Laughter.]*

Yogananda: Not only is it unnecessary, it's highly unlikely that a real teacher would show up in that way. For some it might. But that sort of thing is more commonly a dream experience than legitimate spiritual instruction.

Leichtman: Many aspirants seem to have the problem of confusing a high level of their emotions for the actual life of spirit. Many people following Eastern methods, for example, will believe that they have achieved a high level of samadhi, yet all they have really achieved is a high level of feeling good about themselves.

Yogananda: That is a very common problem, yes. Of course, for many people it is an experience that they have to go through, in order to learn discernment. In most cases, it is a stage which cannot be avoided. I would just hope that the people who repeatedly have these intense devotional experiences, where they feel overwhelmed by the love pouring through them and break into tears and get very emotional, would appreciate that there is something beyond that sentimental, emotional experience—something much more substantial. I would encourage them to hang in there with the understanding that there is something more beyond that experience, for if they do, they will be able to grow toward it.

These people really do become filled with love. They take it to be a divine rapture and are moved to tears. This is an emotional reaction to what they are experiencing at a higher level, and handling it is very difficult, because the reaction tends to keep them from reaching the higher level consciously. I will simply say that the genuine spiritual ecstasy and rapture produces almost no external reaction. To achieve that level of ecstasy, the emotions and mind must be totally subdued—not stopped, but subdued. So you are not dealing with any of the reactiveness of the emotions or personality.

True samadhi is experienced completely in consciousness, not in sensation.

For the people who repeatedly have an intense emotional experience in meditation, sometimes the next step for them is to contain some of that intense devotion and move up to the level of the mind, trying to experience some of that quality of love on the mental plane. They must ponder on what it means to love God with the mind. This is a part of the spiritual life which is not all that well understood in the East but needs to be considered. It is a part of the Western dharma.

People who want to learn to love God with their mind might begin by bringing the focus of their attention up to the throat or the top of the head and then adding—to what they call the love of God—a trust in God, a dedication to God, and the attempt to comprehend God and the wisdom of God through study, an understanding of the events of daily life, and meditation.

Now, that is not the way it would be traditionally approached in the East, and I want to emphasize that. But it is a way which would be appropriate for Westerners, and I presume I am speaking largely for a Western audience in this interview.

Of course, I don't mean to imply that this is the next step for every Western aspirant. That would not be true.

Leichtman: Let me ask you about ashrams, which are a common tradition in the East. Is retiring to an ashram or a monastery going to become a significant part of the Western tradition?

Yogananda: I think it will be less necessary. Ashrams are designed to be retreats which take the individual out of his or her day-to-day activities for periods of recollectiveness. Such periods are quite necessary, but we are moving into an era when the activities of the world will have to be combined with the spiritual life, not retreated from. It will not be the standard to disavow worldly activities and move into an ashram. But they won't totally disappear, because there will be individuals who will incarnate specifically for the purpose of living a number of years in an ashram.

Leichtman: I presume certain spiritual practices do require a steady climate of love and compassion and reverence for life, and for the person interested in pursuing those practices, an ashram is necessary.

Yogananda: Yes.

Leichtman: What about the new age concept of an ashram without a physical structure—meaning an ashram on the inner planes?

Yogananda: These do exist. Many people who do not belong to a physical plane ashram do indeed belong to an inner planes ashram and are in continuous contact with a group in that way.

Leichtman: I've had a hunch for a long time that many people who need an ashramic contact are going to have to find it telepathically, with their inner planes ashram, because the right ashram for them just doesn't exist physically. If they need solace and tranquillity or certain spiritual energies, they are going to have to learn to link themselves in periods of meditation with what might be called the "home office."

Yogananda: The home office? I don't believe that's what we called it in India. *[Laughter.]* The problem you pose may be less of a problem in the future, as more and more members of these inner planes ashrams incarnate.

Leichtman: So there will be more and more physical ashrams to go to?

Yogananda: Yes.

Leichtman: How would an individual know if he had a legitimate telepathic connection with an inner planes ashram?

Yogananda: I don't think it is necessary to know. If he didn't know, he probably doesn't have the connection.

Leichtman: That's a good answer. Those who are members of an ashram will eventually come to suspect it, for various good reasons.

Japikse: A question I would like to ask is: what scriptures and other writings from the East would you recommend to people here in the West? I'm thinking of the kind of person who wants some good references for learning about the spiritual traditions of the East, without following one particular teacher. Of course, your autobiography and the other books you wrote would be a good place to start.

Yogananda: I'm glad you think so. The autobiography was meant to be a quick overview of the philosophy and spiritual practices of India. I think it's fairly easy to read, and a good place to start.

Japikse: Oh, it's delightful to read.

Leichtman: Yes, I don't think there's anything else quite like it in print, in that it recounts such a broad panorama of the phenomena of Eastern spiritual practices. Of course, its charm is that it is a personal account.

Yogananda: Yes, it's not encyclopedic. It's meant to be an intriguing invitation to the East. I'm glad to see it is still popular.

Well, among the scriptures, I think the most important texts to read would be the *Bhagavad-Gita,* which consists of the dialogues of Arjuna and Krishna, and the sutras of Patanjali. There are many translations and commentaries on both of these books; the difficulty is finding a good translation. I believe there is a good translation of the *Bhagavad-Gita* by Saraydarian. A.P. Sinnett's *Esoteric Buddhism* also has much of value in it.

There are many good books on the life and traditions of India. Paul Brunton's *A Search in Secret India* is just one example.

Japikse: What should a Westerner look for in reading these books?

Yogananda: Any of these books, even my own autobiography, can be read as a kind of adventure book, with the attitude of, "Let's see what these strange foreign people are doing." Or, in some cases, "Let's see what the heathens are doing." I would hope that people would not even bother looking into life in India and its rich spiritual traditions unless they were motivated by a love of truth and a respect for what they are reading about. This is not an unreasonable request; it's based on the awareness that there is one God and this one God created all people. God is the force behind the different civilizations of the world and the different religious practices, and they should be respected as expressions of the divine. If the readers can pursue these writings with this attitude in mind, then virtually anything they pick up and read will be found to have something of value in it.

More specifically, I would encourage people to try to see, through these writings, what the Easterner is looking for in his spiritual practices and what he is indeed finding. How have these practices enriched life in the East—and would these practices be able to similarly enrich life in the West? Now, in all fairness, the full answer to those questions cannot be gotten from reading books. That's just a start. The person who wanted the full answer would have to go to the East and spend time in the different countries, soaking up the culture of the peoples, and getting direct experience in the practices and techniques. It's one thing to watch a slide show of someone's summer vacation in Finland and quite another thing to spend two years living in Finland. The same idea applies to learning about the spiritual traditions of the East. But since it's not practical for most people to live in the East for two years, reading is a very good way to explore some of these themes, as long as it is approached with a healthy sense of appreciation.

Leichtman: Let me ask this question about the years you spent teaching here in the West. Were you satisfied with the reception given to your ideas?

Yogananda: Oh, absolutely. I loved what I was doing and it gave me great pleasure to work with the people I was associated with. I think I was able to teach them something about God and I know I learned a great deal from them. I did what I was supposed to do.

Japikse: Did you find the West more bogged down in materialism than you thought you would?

Yogananda: I really didn't pass judgment on that. I knew

I was supposed to come to the West to teach, and I found that the people I dealt with had the same qualities of humanity that the people of India have. The people in the West were pursuing different activities, but humanity is humanity, and I found the same love and compassion in the West as in the East.

Leichtman: I guess we ought to ask, "What are you doing now?"

Japikse: Other than throwing darts. *[Laughter.]*

Yogananda: I am rather intensely involved in bringing a stream of certain aspects of God's love into the earth realm. These are energies which come from beyond the planet, and I am involved in qualifying them and helping to transmit them so that they are more suitable for expression on earth. This consumes a great deal of my attention and effort, and is a project which is very close to my heart. I'm doing this now, as I'm talking about it. Are you experiencing it, too?

Leichtman: Oh, yes. There's a very strong sense of sixth ray devotional love.

Yogananda: I'm still present occasionally in the earth realm and can be depended on to pass these energies along. As some of my students know, I can be reached.

Leichtman: So, in some ways, even though you have transcended earth, you are still concerned with earth.

Yogananda: Oh, yes. I am deeply involved in the evolution of earth and am concerned about the development of the people that I worked with in particular and humanity as a whole. My efforts are dedicated to helping the being who is the planet evolve.

Leichtman: From what you've just said, then, it sounds as if union with God is not the final objective of spiritual growth and living. Once this union itself is achieved, there follows vast possibilities for working in harmony with God and divine energies.

Yogananda: That is true. The goal of spiritual growth is union with God, but then comes the responsibility for using that attainment in an enlightened manner, to help the evolution of life on this planet. Other planets, too, but primarily this one.

Leichtman: And whatever pathway you follow to achieve this union, even the passive pathway, eventually there comes a time of rather intense activity.

Yogananda: Yes, we all end up at the same place working for the same goal.

Japikse: Well, that doesn't sound like the usual description of nirvana, where you lose yourself like a drop in an ocean. What you're describing doesn't sound like that at all.

Yogananda: Nirvana is not a goal; it is just a means for achieving other ends. It is the activity of returning to the source to become renewed, so that you can begin your outer activities again.

Leichtman: In occult terms, you might say that you face the light for a certain period and then become a transmitter of the light—but you never get lost in the light. Is that right?

Yogananda: That's right. You don't disappear into nothingness.

Leichtman: Oh, thank God! *[Laughter.]* Of course, I could stand to lose a few pounds. *[More laughter.]*

Yogananda: Yes, couldn't we all.

Leichtman: Do you have other questions to ask?

Japikse: I think we've covered the territory pretty well.

Yogananda: Then let me make a few concluding remarks. I would hope that the intelligent Westerner, the person who has a love for truth and a dedication to doing good work, would appreciate that Eastern traditions can make a valuable contribution to the West and even to his own life. But this can only happen if he investigates the Eastern traditions with thoughtfulness and, most of all, love. It's easy to condemn practices you don't understand and reject them as heathen, but I invite all good people to look beyond that level and delve into the rich and valuable and profound traditions of the East, which have been a blessing to this planet for thousands of years. These traditions are well worth studying, pursuing, developing, and preserving. That is not to say that they should be used without adaptation, but there is much of value to be found there.

In some ways, the East is ahead of the West. In other ways, the West is ahead of the East. But to the genuine spiritual aspirant, the notion of who is ahead of whom is not even a legitimate question. The East is not competing with the West and I would hope the West is not competing with the East. The East and the West are twin elements of the spiritual path to divine life. There is much of value in both traditions.

I will leave it at that, hoping that the men and women of goodwill who will read these words will understand that they are said with love and with the hope that the integration of East and West will be approached with enlightenment and wisdom and a good deal of love.

And if I may, I would like to add a personal comment to those I worked with and to those who have read and studied my material. I would like to say that I am still present. The people I have known and the people who have studied with me, not only in the physical plane but also on the inner planes, are dear to my heart and I am still here. I will be with them as long as they need my help and love and guidance.

But I would also ask them not to rest on my teachings alone, but to begin to add to them and to look beyond them, because there is more wisdom and love in this world than can be expressed through one individual. While I am with them always, I would hope they would take what I have taught and listen to what others teach and continue to grow, moving always toward their own union with God.

Leichtman: Very good.

Yogananda: Thank you. I send my love.

CARNEGIE RETURNS

"Poor and restricted are our opportunities in this life; narrow our horizon; our best work most imperfect; but rich men should be thankful for one inestimable boon. They have it in their power during their lives to busy themselves in organizing benefactions from which the masses of their fellows will derive lasting advantage, and thus dignify their own lives. The highest life is probably to be reached, not by such imitation of the life of Christ as Count Tolstoy gives us but, while animated by Christ's spirit, by recognizing the changed conditions of this age and adopting modes of expressing this spirit suitable to the changed conditions under which we live; still laboring for the good of our fellows, which was the essence of His life and teaching, but laboring in a different manner.

"This, then, is held to be the duty of the man of wealth: first, to set an example of modest, unostentatious living, shunning display or extravagance; to provide moderately for the legitimate wants of those dependent upon him; and after doing so to consider all surplus revenues which come to him simply as trust funds which he is called upon to administer, and strictly bound as a matter of duty to administer in the manner which, in his judgment, is best calculated to produce the most beneficial results for the community."

In these few sentences, the heart of a larger article on "Wealth" which appeared in *North American Review* in 1889,

Andrew Carnegie set forth the basic principles of his "gospel of wealth"—a philosophy which became the keystone of modern American philanthropy, as well as the basis for Carnegie's own public service.

At the time this article was written, Carnegie was already one of the wealthiest men in America—and one of the most powerful figures in the growing steel industry in this country. He also had the reputation of being able to earn money and increase capital faster than anyone else then alive—and this during the time of the most rapid expansion of business and free enterprise in the history of America. Nevertheless, in a world where materialism was king, Carnegie's ideas were bold and challenging—and undoubtedly threatening to many. It is a testimony to their value that they became the inspiration for many of our modern philanthropic and charitable organizations—the Rockefeller and Ford Foundations, as well as many others.

Andrew Carnegie was not born wealthy; he created the vast fortune he eventually distributed through public projects by his own hard work, brilliance, and organizational talent. Born in Scotland, he emigrated to the United States with his family at the age of 13, settling in the Pittsburgh area. Because the family was poor, he started working as a young teenager, first in a cotton factory and then as a messenger boy for a telegraph office. This led to employment with the Pennsylvania Railroad, where he was responsible for introducing the first Pullman sleeping cars. In his twelve years with the railroad, he rose to become superintendent of the Pittsburgh division, leaving in 1865 to start his own company at the age of 30.

Carnegie recognized the growing importance of iron and steel to an industrialized economy, and concentrated his efforts in its manufacture. The Carnegie Steel Company eventually became the giant in the industry, and when he sold his interests in it to J.P. Morgan in 1901, it became the core of U.S. Steel.

From that point on, Carnegie devoted himself to putting his philosophy of wealth to work, distributing his wealth for the good of his community and nation and working tirelessly for the cause of world peace. By the time he died in 1919, he had given away 350 million dollars—a sum which would be worth many times that figure in today's dollars.

One of Carnegie's major tenets, however, was that money should not just be given away, but *invested* in activities and causes which promote the good of humanity in general. As he put it in his article on "Wealth":

"In bestowing charity, the main consideration should be to help those who will help themselves; to provide part of the means by which those who desire to improve may do so; to give those who desire to rise the aids by which they may rise; to assist, but rarely or never to do all. Neither the individual nor the race is improved by almsgiving."

True to his philosophy, Carnegie chose the projects he funded carefully, favoring those which would inspire people to educate themselves—and inspire communities to engage in their own charitable works. He provided, for example, the funds to build and equip a great number of public libraries in the United States, Great Britain, and other English-speaking countries—but always on the condition that the local community supply the site and maintenance. Millions of people have in this way benefited from the charitable spirit of Andrew Carnegie—most without even knowing it.

Carnegie also funded formal educational projects. He founded the Carnegie Institute of Technology of Carnegie-Mellon University in Pittsburgh, the Carnegie Foundation for the Advancement of Teaching, and the Carnegie Institution of Washington. He was a generous benefactor of the Tuskegee Institute, founded by Booker T. Washington, and many other colleges and universities, both in this country and his native Scotland.

His other great interests included the development of the principle of individuality and world peace, and these, too, figured prominently in his charitable work. He set up a fund for the recognition of heroic deeds and founded the Carnegie

Endowment for International Peace. He financed construction of a Temple of Peace in the Netherlands and a Pan-American Palace in Washington.

But Andrew Carnegie was not just a wealthy man who decided to give away his millions. Throughout his life, he was deeply interested in the arts, philosophy, and literature. He wrote extensively, contributing articles on all of these subjects to many leading periodicals. He was devoted to the concept of free enterprise and individual success, and was one of the first and strongest voices to speak out against Communism, which was then just an untried theory. He freely shared his "secrets" of success with others, and helped many associates launch hugely successful careers. His ideas, for example, became the central core of the philosophy of Napoleon Hill, who became world famous through his numerous books on success, such as *Think and Grow Rich*.

To me, Andrew Carnegie is therefore an outstanding example of a true priest of enterprise and wealth—a man who not only became successful in his own right but shared that success with his fellow man—both literally and figuratively. The fact that he made his fortune and then devoted it to the good of mankind during an epoch in American history which is most commonly remembered as the time of the "robber baron" makes his example even more dramatic.

In the interview that follows, Carnegie clearly relishes the opportunity to enunciate once again, and for a new generation, many of the principles which motivated him while he was living on the physical plane. It was also clear to me, as the interview progressed, that Carnegie was enjoying the chance to restate these principles from his current perspective on the inner planes of life. Far from changing his belief that the free enterprise system is the best mankind has yet evolved for the functioning of a healthy economy, Carnegie now believes more firmly than ever in the need for an unrestricted system which is able to operate in harmony with what he calls "the natural laws of energy."

When most people talk about money, they are usually concerned with how to get it—or make more. The focus is on acquisition. Carnegie makes it clear that anyone who wants to understand the nature of money must see that it has two sides—the earning side and the spending side. Only the person who can work with both of these aspects of money in an enlightened way will become truly successful.

Each of these two aspects, he then explains, is governed by natural laws which any intelligent person can observe and comprehend. Money is earned by taking initiative and becoming productive. Capital is expanded by operating efficiently and providing a useful service or product which benefits mankind. But like a lake which will grow stagnant unless there is as much outflow as there is inflow, the acquisition of wealth must be balanced by an enlightened, intelligent use of money. It must be reinvested or spent in ways which foster the good of humanity.

Carnegie describes money as a form of energy—the energy of productivity and the finite resources of the planet. He states that the laws which govern the transfer of money are very similar to the laws which govern any transfer of energy. If used wisely, money can be a tremendous force for good. But like any energy, it can be squandered or misused. He speaks especially eloquently about the need to be in harmony with the natural flow of this energy through the economy. As the interview unfolded, I was deeply impressed that I was speaking to a man who not only is inspired by the archetypal forces of money, wealth, and productivity, but is an active agent of them!

Carnegie's ideas will be helpful to anyone striving to look at money and wealth from a spiritual perspective. But they also have direct and immediate importance to all thoughtful and intelligent people who are interested in economic issues and the political decisions which are made about the economy. In particular, he observes that the government has become the largest single factor in the economy today—a situation which is much different than when he was alive in a physical body.

Moreover, the government is spending money in ways that compromise the productivity of present and future generations. So much is being diverted from the productive members of society to the unproductive members that the economy is becoming dangerously imbalanced. Eventually, the natural laws of money will move to restore a proper balance. This correction, he states, will come with the same force and certainty of an earthquake occurring after decades of unrelieved tension along a fault line. We cannot be sure *when* it will occur, but we can be certain it *will* occur.

The subject of governmental interference in the natural flow of money is explored in great depth by Carnegie. There will undoubtedly be people who will disagree with what he says, but as Carnegie himself explains, they are likely to be part of the ranks of the nonproductive themselves. To those who are productive, and dedicated to making a contribution to humanity, his comments and explanations should be a breath of fresh air and common sense—an invigorating tonic after decades of platitudes and fiscal foolishness at the federal level.

In my opinion, however, the heart of our discussion was Carnegie's comments on his philosophy of charity and the use of wealth for the betterment of humanity. He explains that since all wealth is drawn from the vast resources of abundance which it is humanity's right to share, it is the responsibility and duty of those entrusted with wealth to reinvest it in the good of civilization. Yet he makes it very clear that it is not the right nor the role of government to step in and abrogate this duty of the wealthy, even if the wealthy fail to fulfill it. When government does step in, as it has, then the natural laws of money are upset.

He also warns that a serious disease is spreading throughout society—a disease which has corrupted the American Dream and left it in ruins. This is the disease of envy—envy of the wealthy, the productive, and the talented. According to Carnegie, this is a new disease in America, one which did not exist in his time, when the wealthy and the industrious were respected and used as role models. All this has changed, however, and the common person now resents wealth and productivity. The common person therefore thinks it is a good idea for the government to redistribute wealth—and may even think it justified to try to destroy large corporations or wealthy individuals. Yet envy is never a constructive force. It is a poison, a disease, and it kills the person who harbors it, not the rich and productive. It kills the American Dream.

The more I reflect on the life of Andrew Carnegie, and the ideas he presents in this interview, the more I am convinced that his life stands as a powerful symbol not only for the power of success, but also for the right use of spiritual opportunity. Money is a symbol of productivity. It could be the productivity of the assembly line worker, the housewife who toils in domestic work, the artist, the attorney, the office manager, or the one who serves the spiritual life. If we are involved in work which benefits mankind, we will draw our just compensation. If we happen to draw a large compensation, we have a second opportunity to help humanity, through the way in which we spend what we do not need for our own support. In this way, we can double our productivity—or perhaps increase it by an even larger factor.

The right management of money therefore gives us each a spiritual opportunity, both to earn it and to spend it wisely. This spiritual opportunity is richly demonstrated in the life and works of Andrew Carnegie—and the interview that follows. He was truly a "rich man"—because his use of the treasures of earth revealed the treasures of spirit. He was *twice rich*—rich by virtue of what he earned, and rich by virtue of how he spent it. It should be the goal of every spiritual aspirant to become rich in this way.

The medium for this interview was Paul Winters. I am joined in asking questions by my friend and colleague, Carl Japikse. The interview was conducted in early 1982.

Carnegie: I don't have a prepared statement. There is

much we can talk about, but I think I will let you propose the direction and set the tone of the interview. That way we will all be spared long lectures from me. *[Laughter.]*

Leichtman: Why don't we start with the enlightened use of wealth? You were not only wealthy, but also a premier example of American philanthropy. I guess we can call you American, can't we? You don't seem to speak with a Scottish accent, at any rate. *[Laughter.]* What is the correct use of money?

Carnegie: I would like to answer that question by outlining my basic philosophy of money. I am going to make some fundamental statements here that we can then explore for the rest of the interview. But it may make the most sense to spit them all out at once, so you see how they fit together.

Leichtman: All right.

Carnegie: To me, money is a form of energy. It is the energy which taps and distributes the material resources of the earth. The correct use of money, therefore, is the transmission of the energy of the earth's resources in an enlightened way. I always thought of myself as an energy transmitter, you see.

Now, there are two sides to the transmission of money. There is the act of earning money, and there is the act of spending money. And there is an enlightened philosophy both for earning and for spending money.

The only justification for the accumulation of money is so that it can be used to meet a specific need. Unfortunately, many people view the accumulation of wealth as an end in itself. Their goal in life is to accumulate as much of this energy as they can, without regard for the need it will serve. But this is not the way the energy we call money is meant to be used. The enlightened use of accumulated wealth is critically important. The opportunity to use wealth to meet specific needs is in fact the main reason why vast resources are sometimes bestowed on certain individuals. But whether they use these resources to meet these needs, or merely divert them to their own use, depends upon how the individual responds to the opportunity. Those who are entrusted with the wealth of this planet take on a great responsibility, for in effect, they become the channels for the transfer of one of the natural energies of society. If you think of the planet as a whole, it is quite clear that there are finite material resources here for the use of humanity. Money is the medium for the distribution and use of these resources. In order for humanity to operate efficiently on this planet, it is therefore important that the people who are entrusted with the earth's limited resources, by virtue of having wealth, live up to that trust. It is important that they use the money they control wisely.

Leichtman: That would certainly be ideal. But it is hardly how it is working out in this day and age. We have a situation where large amounts of money are being accumulated by rock and roll stars, baseball players, the Mafia, and others who are not known for their enlightened philosophies of money. Certainly these people are not responding to the legitimate needs of society, are they?

Carnegie: Some are and some aren't. I don't want to muddy what I am talking about with the side issue of accumulating money through illegal or unworthy activities; it is somewhat pointless to talk about the responsible use of money in the context of someone who gains it illegitimately. But in the case of people who do accumulate a sizeable amount of money in legitimate ways, there is a distinct responsibility to use it and put it to work in an enlightened manner. Some do and some don't. And I will not hesitate to add that those who don't use their wealth in an enlightened way are creating real problems, not only for themselves but also for society in general.

Leichtman: That principle is certainly recognizable today—and historically as well.

Carnegie: Now, I want to make myself clear. There is absolutely nothing wrong with a musician or athlete or businessman or anyone else using his or her particular talents to accumulate a great deal of money. If the talent is great, then the reward should be, too. It is in the way the wealthy person *spends* his or her money that the responsibility lies. It is in the outflow of this energy that the real potential for an intelligent and creative transfer of the resources of the planet lies. This is a major responsibility, and one which must be borne with intelligence and compassion.

In some cases, it is handled well. In some cases, it obviously is not. It depends on the individual.

Japikse: You are implying, then, that the person who accumulates a great deal of wealth has a certain obligation to use it in ways which enrich humanity and civilization.

Carnegie: Yes. Probably the biggest mistake that anyone can make is merely to consume it for his or her own selfish needs.

Japikse: Why is that a mistake?

Carnegie: It is a mistake because it leads to a stagnation of those resources.

Now, I want it to be understood that I am talking about the use of substantial sums of money. The person with modest means must divert almost all of his income into supporting himself and his family, and that certainly is not selfishness. It is self-sufficiency. Even the person with substantial sums of money has an obligation to use a portion of that money to support himself and his family, and these obligations should not be ignored or stinted. One of the rewards of being productive is the opportunity to live well and comfortably—and the person who is truly at ease with money will be able to use it to support a comfortable lifestyle.

That would certainly be an ingredient in an enlightened use of money. But there must be a healthy balance between the amount diverted for personal use and the amount put back into constructive work in society. If an unduly large amount of accumulated wealth is used merely for selfish purposes, to consume the resources of society, then something is definitely amiss. This is not an intelligent use of money.

It is not too much to say that one of the principles of the right use of money is that the more a person invests in the productive work of society, the more he will accumulate.

Money which is spent in productive work has a regenerative capacity—it has the tendency to reproduce itself. Money which is spent for selfish pleasures, on the other hand, is basically money down the drain.

If this principle were understood, it would be seen that it is possible for a person of wealth to use only a small percentage of that wealth to support his own needs. The rest could be put into constructive activities for the benefit of society.

Let me add this observation. There is a certain idea promoted in some "spiritual" circles that the wealthy individual is a person who has earned the right to be wealthy in earlier incarnations, by virtue of work which went unrewarded or because he suffered through many impoverished lives. And therefore, these true believers maintain, the wealthy person has earned the right to accumulate his wealth and spend, spend, spend.

Nothing could be further from the truth. The wealthy person has been entrusted with part of the planet's resources. He has a responsibility to use those resources wisely, no matter how poor he may have once been. Money should not really be seen as a personal reward.

Leichtman: You make this sound as though the enlightened use of money is not just a lovely idea which is praised by saints and martyrs and angels, but is somehow a matter of natural law.

Carnegie: Exactly. Money is a type of natural energy. Like all energies, there are certain principles or laws which govern its natural flow. Those principles and laws must be honored if money is to be used in an enlightened way.

There are any number of stories of people who have gone from rags to riches, acquiring a substantial amount of wealth, but never acquiring an understanding of how that wealth operates. They become so overwhelmed by the personal, selfish elements of money and wealth that they never assume the responsibility for disbursing their wealth intelligently.

Leichtman: And they are ruined by it.

Carnegie: Sure. They spend their money in very irresponsible ways and end up back where they started, penniless. Bankrupt. There are stories of this nature in the papers all the time. And it has nothing to do with economic conditions. It is a personal failure to understand the workings of the natural laws of money. These people are not using the resources they accumulate in a reasonable manner.

And mind you, reasonable is all that is required. It is not necessary to have a great purpose and lofty spiritual goals in order to use money in accord with natural law. It is only necessary to handle this flow of energy in a reasonable way—in a way that is beneficial to society.

Leichtman: I take it, then, that if someone were to use his money with this philosophy and intention it would somehow attract to him more resources, new opportunities, expanded power, and greater talent.

Carnegie: Sure—that's part of the working of the law. Spending money in an enlightened way is like priming the pump. It creates the beginning of the flow of the material resources of life and sets the pattern for the building of momentum. This is the whole basis for philanthropy, which is the enlightened use of money for the benefit of humanity in general.

Leichtman: Well, let's talk about philanthropy for a bit. In this day and age, with the growing concept of a welfare society, there is grave concern as to what is the best way to help people who are unable to support themselves—and to help groups and organizations, too. It is recognized, at least by some, that just throwing money at a problem may actually make it worse. I know that this was an issue of concern for you as well, and it shaped the way in which you went about giving away the bulk of your fortune.

Carnegie: The big problem is that the government has jumped into the middle of the whole issue and changed everything. Over a period of time, it has taken more and more of both the power and the responsibility of philanthropy away from the people who have earned the right to wield them.

Leichtman: They have taken the money away, too.

Carnegie: Right. Instead of a situation where the wealthy person has the opportunity to use 10 or 20 or 30 percent of his wealth—or whatever he deems appropriate—to fund activities which benefit humanity, we now have a situation where the government taxes up to 50 percent of his wealth and then decides how and where that money is to be spent.

Now, if you have been following the implications of the comments I just made on the natural laws of energy and money, you will be able to appreciate the problems attending philanthropy today. Over the years, the people with tremendous resources of wealth and earning power abdicated their responsibility to use that energy in an enlightened and constructive way. And so the government has stepped in and taken much of the responsibility for philanthropy away from them—and much of the money, too. Their wealth has been diverted into the coffers of government, not for the purpose of running government, but for the purpose of supporting the welfare of the people.

This has created a serious problem. The people who are spending this money—the government—have in no way earned the right to spend it! They have not earned it—they have merely siphoned it off from the productive members of society. They are therefore assuming responsibility for distributing and spending money which they have not earned, and this creates a fundamental disturbance in the natural flow of the energy we call money. It sets the stage for enormous waste.

It is very clear to me that a person is much more careful in distributing and spending resources he has earned through his own effort than he is in investing or spending money earned by others. It is the person who has earned the money who has the greatest opportunity to use it in an enlightened way. A government employee who has never had to earn the huge sums of money and resources he distributes is not *capable* of making an enlightened choice as to how to spend the money.

Leichtman: Would you say that a committee of very well educated sociologists, psychologists, and humanitarians would be able to make those decisions wisely?

Carnegie: Oh, absolutely not! *[Laughter.]*

Leichtman: That answer will come as a surprise to a lot of people, I can assure you. *[More laughter.]*

Carnegie: Now, I am not saying that committees such as you are describing should not have some input into how the funds available can best be spent for the betterment of society. They have a valuable role in making recommendations. But the ultimate decision and responsibility for the spending of resources lies totally with the one who has earned them. And that is not the situation today.

Japikse: Do these comments extend to publicly supported charities? The decisions of how to disburse the resources of public charities are generally made by the executive or operating committee of the charity, not the people making the contributions. Take a college, for example. Colleges are very dependent on the support of their alumni, but it would hardly be feasible for the alumni to sit in on every decision as to how the money was spent.

Carnegie: That's very true. But you must keep in mind that the case of a public charity or educational institution is very much different than the case of government. When an individual donates money to a charity or a college, it is very clear how that money will ultimately be spent. The institution is governed by a charter which expressly states the purposes for raising and spending the money. And so the individual giving the donation is able to decide, for himself, whether or not this is a good place to spend his money, before he gives it. The responsibility is still in the hands of the one who earned the money.

What I have been talking about is the case where the money is blindly thrown into a common pot and then some faceless bureaucrat makes an arbitrary decision as to where the money is going to go.

In the case of the public foundation or university, the person giving the money is able to see his individual intention carry through to the actual spending of the money. In the case of government, this is not true. The natural energy which this money represents is diverted from its rightful course. The cycle is not completed.

I want you to understand that I am not speaking figuratively when I describe money as energy. Money carries with it a specific charge of energy. The enlightened use of money requires that this charge be harnessed in an intelligent way, for the benefit of humanity. The person who has earned the money has the responsibility to direct that charge into meaningful activities and enterprises. This cannot be done effectively under the current appropriation of wealth by the government.

Leichtman: I understand the theory of what you are saying, but isn't it a bit unrealistic? It sounds as though you are suggesting we should just do away with taxes and depend entirely upon the beneficence and philanthropy of the wealthy members of society. And yet you said that this whole current problem developed in part because these people abdicated their responsibility. Are these ideas workable?

Carnegie: The ideas are workable, sure. The question is whether or not we are willing to make them work. If you look at history, you will find that the times when the greatest progress and the greatest leaps forward have occurred are precisely the times when the government is not draining the wealth of its citizenry and the wealthy members respond to their basic obligation to use their money in an enlightened, philanthropic way.

Leichtman: But those were also times, quite often, of crushing poverty for large numbers of people—times when the school systems were inadequate, and environmental health problems were neglected, and other services we deem necessary today were ignored.

Carnegie: What you say is true, and the pendulum does swing from one extreme to the other. That is a basic fact of life in society. I am not in any way suggesting that welfare and education are not functions of government. I am primarily suggesting that the funding of governmental programs should be set up in accord with the natural laws of money—not in opposition to them—and that we should be careful not to let government usurp the responsibilities which naturally fall to the wealthy members of society.

Japikse: How could the funding of governmental programs be set up in accord with the laws of money?

Carnegie: The money which is taken in by the government through taxes should not be thrown into a common pot, but should be earmarked for specific programs. The programs and the amounts to be spent on them would be voted on by the citizens, and the tax rate would be determined as a result of those votes—not by a bureaucrat.

Let me add this. There will always be people of wealth who abuse their responsibilities. But we are talking primarily about what constitutes an enlightened use of money. And I don't think any enlightened person of wealth would ever hesitate to spend a portion of his or her accumulated wealth for the education of the masses.

The problem today is not whether or not the people of wealth will live up to their responsibilities. The problem is that the pendulum has swung so far to the opposite extreme that these people do not have a real opportunity to exercise their responsibility. They have virtually no input into how the money which is taken by the government to fund its programs is spent. And this is not the way it should be.

Japikse: No. With our current system of taxing up to half of the income of highly productive people, it has occurred to me that we still have a system of slavery in this country—but the slaves are the highly productive. After a certain level of productivity has been reached, they are essentially working for nothing. They are slaves to the government.

Carnegie: And there are very few voices crying for their emancipation.

Leichtman: No. In fact, the loudest voices are those who want to take even more of this responsibility and power away from the wealthy and the productive. The voices we hear are from the labor organizations, the welfare organizations, and the various minority groups, all of whom are crying out for greater governmental control of the distribution and spending of wealth. And these groups seem to have the numbers needed to dominate a democratic system.

Carnegie: And this illustrates the point I have been making all along. These groups are asking for money they have not earned. They are not just asking to be given the money, but more importantly, to be given *control* of the money. And that is where philanthropy ends and governmental abuse begins.

Leichtman: Of course, they assume it is their divine right to have this money.

Carnegie: Well, it isn't!

Leichtman: And those who don't believe in God assume it is their legal right. *[Laughter.]*

Carnegie: Yes, I know. But these assumptions are not in harmony with the natural laws of money. The only person who has the right to control the way money is spent is the person who has earned it.

Now, I don't want anyone to misunderstand me. The person with money has a responsibility to be compassionate toward those who do not have enough money to buy food to eat or clothes to wear or shelter to protect themselves from the elements. It is a shameful state when real poverty exists in a wealthy and productive society. But giving people money—or giving them control of money they have not earned—is not an antidote for poverty. I always tried to use the resources I had to help people learn how to set up their own energy chain— to learn how to earn money of their own and spend it wisely, so that they would begin to accumulate the fruits of their labors for themselves.

This approach, of course, is *not* being taken today.

Leichtman: Well, there are some programs in government which give job training to the poor and guarantee loans to small businesses, so that individuals can become more productive members of society.

Carnegie: That's very true, and these programs should be viewed as models of the ideal involvement of government in helping the poor and needy. But these programs represent only a tiny portion of the transfer of wealth by the government from the productive members of society to the nonproductive. The major programs simply give money. Yet the goal of any *compassionate* program for helping the downtrodden and the poor should be to help them earn money on their own, not just give them funds.

Leichtman: If I understand you correctly, you are suggesting that genuine assistance to the poor consists of promoting self-sufficiency, providing opportunities for education, and programs of that nature. Yet this would often require a radical change of individual attitude, self-image, and philosophy on the part of the people being helped.

Japikse: They might even fail to take advantage of the opportunities you would give them, and then society would feel as though it was not doing an adequate job of helping them.

Carnegie: This is true. But let me add this: I am not excluding the need to help the destitute obtain the bare essentials for living. It is the duty and requirement of society to make sure that no one is suffering unduly from the lack of the necessities of living. It is ridiculous to have starving families in a wealthy and productive society.

Leichtman: Well, given the current conditions in our society, what can you recommend as practical ways to genuinely help poor people?

Carnegie: I would start by advocating a change in governmental philosophy. I would take a long, hard look at all the blatant "take from the productive and give to the non-productive" programs and see how they could be modified, so that the money could be invested in educational and job opportunities, rather than outright grants of money. Of course, the current state of the democratic process in America does not lend itself to this kind of review, and it probably won't happen. The people who demand something for nothing are a very substantial voting bloc now, and they would never stand by and let the programs that benefit them be jeopardized.

But that's where I would start.

Leichtman: It sounds as though something must be done in society to promote the value of personal responsibility and personal achievement more fully. We hear stories all the time, for example, about workers in industry who are discouraged from working too hard or productively because it embarrasses their co-workers who are not as ambitious or as competent as they. The ambition, competence, and industry of the worker often go unrewarded, and society does not seem concerned. I wonder if the basic attitudes of society need revising before it would be possible to really push the kind of philosophy you are advocating.

Carnegie: Yes. And let me carry that idea a step further. As the unions have gotten stronger, and have demanded and won strict wage guidelines, the productivity of the American worker has suffered enormously.

In my day, an unemployed worker could walk in off the street and say to an employer, "I will do the same job as that fellow over there, but I will do it faster and take less pay." And the employer would say, "Fine—give it a go." And if he could do the job better and faster, and was willing to work for less, he would get the job.

This kind of bidding had a great impact on productivity, because the people who were the most competent and the hardest workers were rewarded. It was a great boon to industry in general. But today, because of collective bargaining and fixed wages, a person who is out of work does not have the opportunity to walk into a shop and bid for a job. There is virtually no competition among the labor force, and the direct result of that is a loss of productivity. It also makes it very hard for unemployed people to reenter the labor market.

Leichtman: Do you think there is even the slightest ghost of a chance that a bidding system could be restored to the labor market?

Carnegie: Of course not.

Leichtman: Well, what can be done to restore the virtue of productivity?

Carnegie: In part, it is a question of learning to recognize how the pendulum swings back and forth in these issues. I would be the first to admit, for example, that the working conditions in my day, when we had the bidding system, were not the best. Employees were not treated by their employers with the respect they deserved. Management created many, many problems for labor. The labor movement arose in order to remedy the excesses of management, and this was justified. I don't think anyone could effectively argue that the labor movement was not justified.

But in our desire to remedy these excesses, we have in effect created new excesses. The pendulum has swung to the opposite extreme, and it is now labor which is guilty of excesses and not treating management with the respect it deserves. This is certainly true in the whole area of productivity and rewarding competence. Some of the current attitudes of labor and society actually hinder growth and progress—and must not be ignored.

Leichtman: Of course, these trends have gone even further in Europe than in this country. We hear stories about how factories in Italy are not allowed to shut down, even though they are losing money, because it would put the workers out of work! The government subsidizes a losing proposition to keep it alive.

Carnegie: The ultimate end of that, of course, is bankruptcy. But let me say this. In the end, the people who will survive such bankruptcies, and the major economic upheavals which will go with them, will be those who are productive. They may not have currency to trade with and use as energy, but they will have their own individual energies and talents, and that will give them the capacity to survive. This is what really separates the productive from the nonproductive—the capacity to survive in a time of major economic upheaval. That alone should be sufficient incentive to propel anyone who is nonproductive into becoming productive.

Leichtman: That's fine, but is that where these trends are leading us? Do we have to push ourselves to the point of a massive depression again before people will appreciate the value of a decent job and productivity? Is that where it all ends?

Carnegie: That's precisely where it all ends. It ends with the changing of the order and the reversal of the pendulum, so that it swings in the other direction for a while.

Leichtman: Is this where we are actually heading, or are you making a theoretical prediction in order to explain your point?

Carnegie: I'm making a theoretical prediction, not a literal one. There are too many variables involved to even try to make a literal prediction as to what will happen. Suffice it to say, however, that the natural laws which govern the flow of money are being violated. Unless these problems are corrected, it is only a matter of time before the remedial power of these natural laws will assert itself, in order to get the flow of money running smoothly again.

Leichtman: From what you've been saying, it sounds as though these laws operate best in a free enterprise system—not necessarily in our free enterprise system, but an ideal one. Are these laws able to operate in a totally different economic system, such as in a communist state, where the state is the landlord and the owner of all industry? Those systems do thrive, at least to a limited degree. Are they based on the natural laws of energy you are citing?

Carnegie: To a degree, yes. An energy transfer does take place, in that the resources are funneled through the central government. The productive worker does reap benefits from his productive work, even though indirectly. So the energy flow is there, and it does work. But it doesn't work very efficiently.

Let me give you an analogy. You can operate an electric motor at ten percent of its capacity, and it will work. It just isn't working effectively. You can operate it with rusty bearings and worn out belts, and it will still drive a machine—but it is not an ideal way of using that motor. By the same token, the natural laws of money do operate in communistic and collective societies—but they don't operate at anywhere their peak efficiency. They are running at 10 or 20 percent of capacity.

Leichtman: It's a well-known fact that after the farms were collectivized in Russia, productivity fell dramatically. When the cane fields in Cuba were nationalized, the same thing happened. And we have seen it now more recently, when the factories and oil fields in Iran were nationalized. Productivity fell way off. And it's odd that in some of these countries, especially the communist societies, they are now starting to introduce capitalistic methods for promoting individual incentive. But no one seems to be getting the message about the basic superiority of a free enterprise system—and the value of productivity to society. It makes me very pessimistic about the capacity of society to observe the obvious.

Carnegie: Yes.

Leichtman: It's as though the "laws" of greed and stupidity are a good deal more powerful than the laws of productivity and money.

Japikse: I would call it the law of sinking into dullness. *[Laughter.]* I think it is excellent that you are talking about money as a form of energy, and I hope our readers will appreciate the full implications of this idea. I was wondering if you would care to pursue it from a slightly different angle. When Bob and I are teaching people to harness their personal energies, we talk about the need to cultivate patience, detachment, and other skills of enlightened living. Are those kinds of skills useful to the person who wants to learn to work with money as a form of energy? Or how would you define the talents and skills a person ought to have in order to handle money wisely?

Carnegie: To talk about the skills of handling money wisely, it is important once again to distinguish between the two sides of money—earning it and spending it. There are separate sets of skills which must be developed for each of these activities. The mere capacity to earn money does not guarantee the capacity to spend it wisely.

Most of the people who are able to use money wisely and productively bring a unique set of character traits and inner skills with them into their incarnation. It is just as much a talent or skill as an artistic or musical talent would be.

Leichtman: Is it possible to refine and develop those talents and skills during the incarnation?

Carnegie: Absolutely, absolutely. Now, in talking about specific skills in handling money, let me say that the most important skill would be the talent to understand the natural laws which govern energy and be guided by them. It is the capacity of an individual to tap into these laws and use money in accordance with them that most insures success in working with money. Of course, this ability to work in harmony with the natural laws governing money is usually an unconscious one—the person has no idea he is doing it. This is why I make the point that the talents and skills of working with money are often brought with the person into incarnation.

Japikse: The person is able to work in harmony with the archetypal forces governing money.

Carnegie: Yes. And this would usually be a talent the person has developed in many previous lives, just as an artist or a musician would spend many lives developing and perfecting his creative talents. Many of the people who are born into wealth, or into conditions which give them the opportunity to become wealthy, have in fact earned the right to deal with this wealth because they have spent a lot of time in earlier lives learning the skills of handling wealth. And depending upon the skills they have, they would specialize either in earning wealth or in putting their wealth to work. It depends on the lessons in living and the focus of work set by the higher self for that particular lifetime.

Leichtman: Yes.

Carnegie: And now that I've said all that, I think I can answer your question. The specific skills which are developed as a person learns to work wisely with money, lifetime after lifetime, would be very similar to the skills the two of you teach in your classes, because they are skills in using energy effectively.

I suppose the very first skill to be mastered is detachment

or dispassion in the handling of money. Most people are very personal in their use of money and very much attached to the money they accumulate. This makes it extremely difficult to handle money wisely. Keep in mind that money is strictly a kind of energy, nothing more, nothing less. And therefore it is an energy for living—for doing good work. It is a constructive force. It can be used in harmful ways, of course, but we are specifically talking about the enlightened uses of money, so we will stick to the assumption that the person wants to learn the skills of using money in a constructive way.

Leichtman: Yes.

Carnegie: The person who is greedy and possessive of money, and the goods that money can buy, is unable to be attuned to the natural laws and rhythms of money. He is controlled only by his own greed and possessiveness. So he will not be able to use money in an enlightened, constructive way—not until he learns detachment. By learning detachment, he discovers that money is not an end in itself or a goal of living. It is an energy which makes it possible to transfer one's talents into services, one's potential into opportunities, one's industry into goods, and one's wealth into an enriched life, individually and in society.

The second skill would involve learning to work with the law of increase. This is the idea that the energy of money seeks to increase itself, to expand its influence. The businessman learns about the law of increase by making investments which return a profit. Gradually, as skills in handling the law of increase are developed, the motive for investment moves away from personal profit and more and more into enlightened contributions to life.

Now, as I said before, there are certain basic priorities in the use of money which must take preference over all others—providing food, shelter, clothing and the other essentials of living for yourself and your family. But as you begin earning more than you need to pay for these essentials, an interesting challenge arises. You must determine how the excess is going to be spent.

Will it be spent on self-gratification and luxuries, or will it be invested in a new business opportunity, thereby setting the stage for the law of increase to work? Or perhaps it will be invested in educating yourself further or given to a charitable foundation to further its capacity to contribute to society. These would be other examples of cooperating with the law of increase.

Not very many people have thought about the relationship between the law of increase and the use of money, but to me it is an important key to the right use of resources.

Japikse: Yes, it is something I stress quite heavily in my management seminar, as one of the most important skills of business—to make sure that every action taken contributes to the increase of the business and the community in which the business operates. It strikes me that you are indirectly encouraging people to recognize that they are making a statement about what they value and the ideals they serve by the way in which they dispose of the excess income or wealth that they have.

Carnegie: It reveals their basic motivation, yes. As soon as some people come into a little extra cash, they gather it all together and drive to Las Vegas and blow it playing craps. Or they spend it all on luxury items because they have an enormous appetite for possessiveness that they must satisfy. But other individuals are motivated to donate their extra funds to charitable organizations which are promoting causes or ideas they consider worthwhile, or use this money to help the disadvantaged. Or they invest it in artistic endeavors and cultural events which enrich the quality of civilization. So you are right, the way they spend their excess money becomes a part of their self-expression.

Motivation also applies to the way a person earns money, by the way. I want to draw an important distinction, and this is that an intense desire to *earn* money is not the same as an intense desire to *have* money. I am describing here the basic difference between responsibility and greed. Some people think that any desire to acquire money is a sign of greed, but this is not true at all. It all depends upon the motivation. If a person is motivated to earn great sums of money in order to start a worthwhile business enterprise, or to do charitable work in society, or to support the arts and education, then this is a sign of maturity and responsibility. But if a person desires money only because of the prestige or self-importance or possessions it can buy, then this is a sign of greed.

There are many stories of individuals who have come into great wealth, only to have it destroy their lives, because they did not know how to wisely invest or spend any money in excess of what they needed to live. In part this was because they had not earned the money in the first place, but it is also partly an indication that they lacked skill in using the principle of increase.

Now, a person who has learned to work with detachment and the law of increase will also discover, sooner or later, a third principle in the use of money: that the less a person uses his wealth for himself, the greater the increase will be.

This is a complex idea, so I want to make it very clear. This principle does not apply to money which would be spent on self-sufficiency—on providing basic necessities such as food, clothing, shelter, an automobile, and so on. It applies only to the way we choose to use monies over and above our personal needs and responsibilities. The more we funnel this money into selfish and egocentric pleasures, the less value we receive on the dollar. And conversely, the more we dedicate this money to productive and constructive uses in society, the more the energy it represents will increase. This productive and constructive use can cover a very broad spectrum, running all the way from using these funds to prepare for the education and well-being of our own family on the one hand to becoming a patron of the arts and charity on the other. And there's a lot in between, but I think I've already mentioned most of it.

The point I am making is that the more the energies of our personal wealth are used to help others and benefit civilization, the more active the law of increase will become in our life. But the more selfish we are and the more we indulge in conspicuous consumption of the resources of society, the more the law of increase will become a negative factor in our life. It will go into reverse, if I may put it in that way. This does not mean that the earning capacity of the individual would diminish—keep in mind that I have separated the earning capacity from the skills of spending. But selfishness does have a negative effect on the person. It can become a very destructive force, mentally and emotionally.

I guess you would say that it leads to an impoverishment of consciousness.

Leichtman: Yes. Let me ask a clarifying question about this last point. There are books which have been published on how to become wealthy that promote the idea that if you contribute your money to a worthwhile cause, God will reward you by making you wealthy. And so people will give money to charities with the ulterior motive in mind that this will make them wealthy. Is this an abuse of what you have been talking about?

Carnegie: Of course. It's also very naïve, because these people are blurring the distinction between the earning and the spending functions of money. If anyone who reads this interview is ever confused about this issue, the solution is very simple. Just remember that there are two separate and distinct categories in the right use of money. One is earning and one is spending. They are totally separate and must be kept separate.

It is not possible to "prime the pump" by giving money. That is not the way the law works. It never has and it never will. The best way to prime the pump is to develop the skills and talents which are required to earn money.

Japikse: But that seems like a contradiction to what you said earlier about priming the pump.

Carnegie: It's not a contradiction. It's an issue of whether you are priming the pump for your personal benefit or for the good of humanity.

Leichtman: Yes. And I think what you said earlier about selfishness is very appropriate here. These people aren't really giving their money—their true motivation is selfishness, not charity. So they get the reward of selfishness, not charity.

Carnegie: Of course. To me, it's just a form of spending money, not giving it.

Leichtman: You mentioned a little while ago about people building up the talents and skills needed to handle money over a number of lifetimes. Can you give us any hints as to how you developed the skills you used so masterfully in your life as Andrew Carnegie?

Carnegie: Well, the Andrew Carnegie incarnation was the culmination of many lifetimes in which I was involved in commerce and industry. It was a sequence of lives devoted to learning the skills of money and industry. As one progresses through a sequence of lessons of this nature, one becomes more and more responsible and attracts greater and greater opportunities. My lifetime as Carnegie was the culmination of that particular sequence. I've had it with money now—I'm going to move on to other challenges.

[Laughter.]

Leichtman: Well, very good. Let me ask this, while we are on the subject of your life as Andrew Carnegie. In your autobiography, you described how you were called to Washington at the outbreak of the Civil War to work for the War Department. And you mentioned that President Lincoln would come down every now and then and wait in the office for telegrams to arrive or messages to be sent, and you got to know him.

Carnegie: He was a very powerful being. It was quite a pleasurable and awe-inspiring event for me to be in such close contact with the President of the United States. Of course, President Lincoln was not as revered at that time as he is now. He was chastized and criticized as most Presidents are, while they are in office. He had his problems; he had his enemies. But he was a very determined man who knew what he had to do. I'm not sure he knew why he was pursuing the particular course he followed—the larger perspective of it, I mean—but he certainly had the conviction and the strength to carry it forward.

In general, he was a no-nonsense individual. He was very kind and friendly, but didn't have much time for levity, as the weight of the times was upon him. It was a very serious time.

Leichtman: Of course.

Carnegie: His way of lightening up the situation was to reminisce about his younger days. His ideal of relaxation or recreation was to get out of the city and back into nature, and he often talked fondly about his life on the frontier.

Leichtman: Very good. Well, when we interview Lincoln we'll give him equal time to tell his side of the story. *[Laughter.]*

Carnegie: I was happy to have the opportunity to serve the country in that small way. Of course, we didn't have as many people in those days, and so if you were in any way competent, you were usually called upon to rally during times of emergency.

Leichtman: When I was reading your autobiography, I noted that you did not have a high opinion of the officials in the government, and especially in the army, at that time. You thought they were grossly incompetent.

Carnegie: Of course—the people who were competent would not take a public job in those days. It was the period of personal initiative. Anyone who had any talent at all would try to make it on his own and would not rely on "taking a job," so to speak. So there was just as much incompetency in the government then as there is now, perhaps even more so, since the rewards of private enterprise and making it on your own were so much greater then than now.

Leichtman: Yes, it is often the case today that the government will pay better than private industry. It is not uncommon to find street sweepers earning $20,000 a year, which is a liveable wage, I do believe. *[Laughter.]*

Carnegie: Well, in my day, when you made a dollar you kept a dollar, and it was easy to compound your income and snowball it into something very meaningful very quickly—if you had the talent. It is much more difficult today, because the tax collector is not only taking half of any business income you might be making but is in fact taking substantially more than

I ever thought possible in my day. It would have been considered highway robbery to make the suggestion that the government should take half of what any business makes.

Leichtman: Well, what can be done to restore incentive to the private sector?

Carnegie: Lower taxes! I said this earlier, and I will say it again—the person who earns the money has the right to determine how that money is to be spent. But this right is being abused. The money which is being earned by business and by individuals is being taken by the government and spent wherever and however the government wants.

If you think back to the birth of this country, it was the expressed intention of the Founding Fathers that money be made available for defense and for running the government—but that was virtually it. There was no intent at that time to tax the productivity of the nation—none at all. There was no intention to have the government branch out and become a huge machine which transfers money from the productive to the nonproductive. But this is what has happened.

And it is not in accord with the natural flow of energy.

Leichtman: I suppose we ought to remind our readers that at the time of the founding of the United States, only people who owned property had the right to vote. And so the direction of goverment was controlled at that time by the productive members of society—not the nonproductive members, as it is now.

Carnegie: Yes, and as long as there are more rewards to being nonproductive than to being productive, there is no effective way to restore incentive to the private sector. The incentive is the opportunity to reap the rewards of one's hard work, and not have them diluted by someone else's so-called right to dip into the public till.

You mentioned, Carl, that the highly productive members of society are the twentieth century equivalent of slaves. I will go a step further, and state that it is a parasitic society that takes away such a substantial portion of the money an individual or business has worked so hard to earn. In my day, we had virtually twice as good a chance to become successful and do something meaningful as you do today.

Leichtman: Could you do it all over again, if you were alive physically today and just graduating from college? Could you make a fortune again in some industry or business?

Carnegie: It obviously can be done, but it would be significantly more difficult.

Leichtman: Without becoming a rock and roll star?

[Laughter.]

Carnegie: I wouldn't be able to do it in steel, that's for sure. And I don't think it is possible to do it on your own. It is virtually impossible for one person to begin an enterprise today and have it grow into a substantial size without taking in massive amounts of outside funding to keep the operation going.

Leichtman: Why is that?

Carnegie: Look at the figures: half of what you make is taken by the government, and so that half is not available for reinvestment and for financing the growth of the business. But there are certain stages in the growth of an enterprise where it is necessary to put as much of your profits as you can back into the operations, in order to keep it growing. If the money isn't there, because the government has taken it, then you have to go to the bank and to outside investors to find more capital that can be put into the business.

In my day, you might have gone to a wealthy investor to get the initial money needed to start a company, but it was quite unusual to have to keep finding additional investors to fuel the growth of a business. The money you made could be pumped back into the company. And since you got a dollar for a dollar, it was much easier to grow. You had twice as much money. And so it was possible for a single individual to build a large company. That can't be done today. You have to continually find more and more investors. And so an individual cannot become as wealthy, individually, as he could in my day.

This does not mean that you cannot become wealthy today

or that you cannot make a significant contribution to society. It is still quite possible. But the laws have changed the circumstances and conditions for making money. They have significantly redistributed the resources available for new enterprises.

Leichtman: Some people, of course, consider those changes to be very good. They talk with great glee about the fact that the robber barons could never make it in our modern society.

Carnegie: But who are these people? They are precisely the people who have never tried to create wealth. They are the takers, not the givers. It is to their benefit to encourage society to redistribute wealth, because it makes it easier for them to acquire money they have not earned.

Leichtman: This is not to say, however, that there are no ills in business, is it? It is certainly commonplace in this day and age to pick up a newspaper and read about business paying millions of dollars in bribes overseas to obtain contracts. These problems cannot be glossed over, can they?

Carnegie: Of course not. The greater the freedom, the greater the opportunity for greedy individuals to abuse the freedom. But I would pose the following question. Which is worse—a stagnant and declining economy in which there is no incentive to create wealth, or a free and vigorous economy which is open to abuse but also to enormous growth? I know I would much rather deal with a few charlatans and cheats but have the freedom to conduct business as I saw fit, than be stuck in a stagnant and dying economy.

Leichtman: Yes. Well, let me pick up on some of our earlier comments about labor. It seems that organized labor today almost always takes an adversary position against business and management, as though their interests were isolated from and antagonistic toward the interests of business. This hardly seems intelligent to me. Do you have any comments about enlightened labor relations?

Carnegie: I would merely say that the success of a company is directly related to the success of the individual employees. Employees at all levels partake of and contribute to the basic success of the company. Unfortunately, this basic reality is sometimes forgotten by both management and labor.

In my day, it was often the other way around. Businesses practically mowed down their workers. The workers were generally treated as second-class citizens. There were exceptions, of course, but all too often factory workers were treated poorly—in some ways like slaves. They were thought of as a necessary evil. The business could not be run without them, but they were not respected.

This was a wrong attitude, and the labor backlash of the late nineteenth century was a direct result of it. Today, however, the pendulum has moved to the opposite extreme, and labor seems to think of itself almost as a separate entity which has no interrelationship with the fortunes of the enterprise which provides these jobs. This can create real problems in labor-management relations, particularly when the success of the company depends on the efficiency and cost effectiveness of labor. There are many examples from recent history where the increasing demands of labor have virtually bankrupted a company and driven it out of business. And this is not good, either.

Leichtman: No. It is said that the labor movement has become even more capitalistic than industry itself, because it has managed to create a legal monopoly. Labor has amassed a tremendous amount of power and is protected by the government. And yet in many ways the unions oppress the average worker.

Carnegie: Well, they certainly are oppressing the industries which employ their members, and that is not good. But neither were the conditions that gave rise to the unions 100 years ago. So you could make a case that the conditions of today are the result of the inevitable backlash against the conditions of 100 years ago.

Leichtman: Do you see the pendulum swinging back?

Carnegie: My scouts up here are telling me that labor is slowly becoming more aware of the negative impact it is having on industry, as a result of its enormous greed, and of the subsequent impact this has on its own prosperity.

It is slowly learning that greed does not a viable company make.

Leichtman: Well, the unions often give the impression that their wage demands have absolutely nothing to do with the health of the company they work for—and in fact, they seem to have the attitude that if the company can't pay for these enormous increases, it's certainly not the fault of labor. It's as though they think the only function of management is to make enough money so that labor can get its huge wage increases.

Carnegie: Well, I think we are heading toward a time when both management and labor will realize that the success of the company depends on the cooperation of both. Both management and labor have a job to do, and indeed, the first job of both parties is to insure the continuation of the enterprise.

This is already the case today in many smaller companies, where there is a much closer interaction between the management team and the workers.

Leichtman: Are you suggesting, then, that perhaps organized labor should have a direct or indirect role in management decisions? Would something like that, or a profit sharing plan, help the labor force appreciate more fully that its welfare is bound up in the health and productivity of the whole company?

Carnegie: Those programs can work, but you can't force them on management. You can't guarantee labor a very high wage and then on top of that give away a percentage of the profits—not without seriously jeopardizing your ability to reinvest in the business and keep it prospering.

Leichtman: You are not in favor, then, of cooperatives?

Carnegie: Oh, I'm very much in favor of them, but the very nature of a cooperative entails a change in the usual way employees are paid. The virtue of a cooperative is that it gives the employees an incentive to increase productivity. Unfortunately, this incentive is usually missing today—particularly in unionized shops.

Leichtman: Well, what is needed to restore this incentive in the work force?

Carnegie: One step would be to educate the workers and their representatives about the factors which are necessary for healthy businesses to stay healthy. We have been lax in educating people about the workings of the economy, the overall dynamics of free enterprise, and the kinds of pressures which can undermine the health of a company. If the individual were taught to look at the company and the industry it is part of *as a whole,* rather than just his or her individual job, that would be a major step in the right direction.

Japikse: Just teaching management to think in those ways would be a major step in the right direction.

Carnegie: Well, that's a whole different problem. *[Laughter.]* The second step would be to increase communication between the labor force and the managers of the company, not at the level of bargaining for wages, but at the level of decision making, so that the workers have a part in some of the decisions which are made affecting the direction and operation of the company.

We are heading in this direction in many companies, and that is good.

Leichtman: Isn't there a tremendous problem to overcome, however? A lot of workers seem to think that they deserve everything they can get and that the only thing management is interested in is exploiting the workers. Some even believe that it is evil to make a profit. In some cases, these terribly distorted points of view seem to have been carefully fed by union leaders. Is it really possible to overcome them with education?

Carnegie: I don't know if these beliefs can be overcome, but I would hope that the attempt would be made. If these beliefs can't be changed by education, then I guess the only way they can be changed is by way of another shake-up.

Leichtman: You're talking about an upheaval again?

Carnegie: Yes, another one of my theoretical upheavals. *[Laughter.]*

Leichtman: One nice thing about theoretical upheavals is that they can be solved by theoretical solutions.

[More laughter.]
Carnegie: Isn't that wonderful?
Leichtman: It's ingenious.
Carnegie: I think there's a good chance the steps I recommended would be successful if attempted. I will go on record as predicting that we are coming into an era when more and more cooperation between labor and management will be possible. As more and more businesses become less and less solvent because of the excessive demands of the employees, it will become apparent that labor will have to curb its demands, lest all of its members lose their jobs. I think this reality of the work place will result in more and more decisions being made by labor which favor the health of the enterprise.

Leichtman: Yes, that exact scenario has already occurred in some major industries which are teetering on bankruptcy. Labor has had to take cuts in its benefits and wages and in many cases is going along with it. Of course, it is usually a choice between that or nothing at all.

Japikse: I have a question along this line. Should government be stepping in and bailing out ailing companies?

Carnegie: Absolutely not.

Leichtman: Even if it is a huge corporation employing hundreds of thousands of people or more?

Carnegie: It is not and should not be the responsibility or function of government to bail out a company which is going broke, no matter how large or small. But having made that statement of policy, let me add this. The government, unfortunately, has already assumed far too much responsibility for setting policies which control the economy and directly affect the fortunes of business. And one of the major reasons why businesses are failing at this time is because of the regulations government has imposed on business and the constraints it has placed on trade. So when a business does fail in this day and age, the government is responsible for that failure in a very real way. And so there are strong pressures to bail out the company and keep it going. But that is not the solution to the problem.

The solution is to get government out of business entirely. The problem cannot be solved by increasing government's role in business, *because that is the problem!*

Leichtman [whispering]: Did you follow that?

Japikse: I followed it, but I'm not sure where it took us. *[Laughter.]*

Carnegie [chuckling]: Well, this is where it took us—there is no answer to your question, because the government is part of the problem. Until the government realizes that and decides to stop trying to run the businesses of this country, there can be no solution.

If the present trend is allowed to continue, the government will soon end up running all industry.

Japikse: That's just what I was going to say. Short of your theoretical upheaval, it sounds as though everything will be run by the government in a decade or two, because the government certainly doesn't show any real signs of slowing down its involvement in business.

Carnegie: I will go on record and state that you are absolutely correct in that assessment—and this would not be a healthy turn of events.

Leichtman: It certainly has not worked in England.

Carnegie: Isn't it fascinating that there are examples all over the world that government interference in business just does not work, and yet the United States shows no signs of heeding these warning signals.

Leichtman: This is certainly something which continually amazes me. When the Founding Fathers established the government here in the United States, they very carefully studied the governmental systems of other nations and evaluated what worked and what didn't work, and then tried to take the best elements of those systems and put them together in ours. But even though our whole system of government was founded on the idea of learning the lessons which history would teach us, we seem to have abandoned this fine and sensible approach to government, in favor of greed and stupidity and expediency.

Carnegie: I couldn't have said it better myself.

Leichtman: Well, let me pick up our discussion about labor again—I have a few more questions, and then we can move on to something else. Do you think the labor movement ought to be subject to our anti-monopoly laws? So far they have been immune to them, but in many ways they are bigger monopolies than any business ever was.

Carnegie: I don't think any laws are necessary to correct the imbalances in the labor movement. This will all balance itself out as a result of economic realities. We don't need any more government interference in these areas.

Leichtman: Let me ask you this, then: are you in favor of the minimum wage laws?

Carnegie: Absolutely not. I'm not in favor of minimum wage laws at all—they prohibit the natural process of bidding for jobs. In my view, these laws actually reduce the number of jobs available. A company that is unable to hire people at the minimum wage simply will not hire—period. And that means that someone who would be willing to take a job at the bottom of the ladder and work his way up to a better paying job is prohibited from doing so. A whole section of the economy has been eliminated due to the minimum wage.

Leichtman: Yes, and it is often the very poorest people who bear the brunt of the problem.

What about the laws which now require companies to hire a certain percentage of people with green skin and a certain percentage of people with purple skin, and so on? Should the government be in the business of insisting on quota systems for minorities?

Carnegie: When those laws were first passed, I think they were necessary. You had a situation where racial discrimination and prejudice were inbred into the thinking of society and individuals. People were not being given job opportunities strictly because of their racial heritage or social standing. It's a historical fact that this was going on.

Leichtman: Yes.

Carnegie: So, the question was really a social question, not a business question. And what opportunities does a society have for promoting racial equality? Well, the only real way to do it was to establish strict quotas for equal opportunity in business, education, and the other major areas of individual opportunity. And I think the laws which set those quotas were definitely appropriate for the time in which they were passed. They forced narrowminded and prejudiced individuals to strain themselves and hire minorities and people from all races—something they would not do on their own.

At this point in time, we now have a whole new generation of business people who are accustomed to working with all of these minorities in the work force, and it has become a natural part of doing business. To a large measure, the prejudices have been overcome—because the laws enforced a quota system for hiring and educating. And I think it is fair to say that the changes these laws were designed to produce have come to pass, and the laws are not necessary now. In fact, in some cases, the laws work against their intended purpose, because they sometimes force business people to hire people for positions they are not prepared to handle. And because they then perform in substandard ways, the old prejudices tend to be revived. So at this point in time, perhaps the quotas should be phased out, over a number of years—provided, of course, that the old racial biases do not reappear.

Leichtman: So ultimately it should be a person's talent, productivity, and competence which determine how well he or she fares in society—not the color of that person's skin, or racial heritage, or sex.

Carnegie: Of course. The laws have done their job. The quotas were good, but if we keep them too long, they will become restrictive.

Leichtman: Okay, let me move on to a different topic and ask you about a statement made by Admiral [Hyman George] Rickover just after he retired. Admiral Rickover was the man who devoted his career to building our fleet of atomic submarines. He said that this country is spending a ridiculous amount of money on the military, and it is like throwing money into a hole in the ground. It doesn't really benefit anyone. Most of this money, he said, is being used to stockpile armaments which aren't really needed. Other than making a few select companies wealthy, this enormous expenditure of money is not helping the country and not even helping the economy.

So here's my question: is this a wrong use of money? Does spending money in this way violate the natural laws of energy you were describing earlier?

Carnegie: Obviously, any money which is thrown down the hole of excess spending is a violation of the natural laws of money. This is not to say, however, that spending money on defense is in and of itself a violation of the natural laws of money. Financing the legitimate defense of the people is a valid way of spending money. The only question here is the highly debatable issue of how much defense is enough defense.

I'm not in the position to comment on that—and I won't.

Leichtman: All right.

Carnegie: It is part of enlightened government in this world to provide for reasonable defenses against the forces of evil. But it is also a duty of enlightened government to know what is necessary and what is excessive, and not waste money. That obviously is an ideal which is not always achieved.

Leichtman: Well, let me broaden the scope of my question a little. It is apparent that government bureaucracies have very little incentive to conserve their funds or even disburse them efficiently. Their primary incentive, in fact, is to keep growing—to increase the size of their agencies as though public funding was a bottomless pit. What can be done to change this—to make the heads of these agencies more accountable and more concerned about conserving money and limiting their budgets?

In private industry, the need to make a profit becomes a strong incentive to conserve and operate efficiently. But that is not the case in government. How would you handle this problem?

Carnegie: By shifting the government into a profit making mode. You give the heads of these agencies reasonable budgets and then cut them in on anything they manage to save. The money they are able to save, by operating efficiently, would be the "profit" of government.

Leichtman: Ah, so there would be no incentive then to buy two electric typewriters for every employee.

Carnegie: Right. Let's say the head of an agency had a budget of five million dollars. If he is able to save one million dollars, you would give him a bonus based on a certain percentage of what he has saved—say, five percent.

Leichtman: That would be $50,000!

Carnegie: Right.

Leichtman: Well, that certainly would be an incentive. You could eliminate kickbacks and graft all in one fell swoop. *[Laughter.]*

Carnegie: Absolutely. The problem with this idea, of course, is that the public would have to understand the sound principles it was based on. The very good managers would end up making a lot of money, and some people would not understand that they had earned it. Let's say the head of the agency I was just talking about had a base salary of $50,000 and then made an extra $50,000 by running a tight operation. That makes a total of $100,000, and that would seem like an extravagance to a lot of people. They would throw a tirade and say it was unfair for this person to be making $100,000 running a government agency. But it actually is quite fair, because he has saved the Treasury one million dollars, and it only cost the public $50,000.

Managers in private industry are given these kinds of incentives all the time. Their effectiveness is well proven.

Leichtman: Of course some people would complain that such incentives would motivate the manager to cut back on the services the agency provides, just to save money and make a bigger bonus for himself, and that they would therefore not be in the public's interest.

Carnegie: It is assumed that these incentives would not cover the actual money put into the programs the agency was administering. These bonuses would be determined by how much the manager saved in administrative costs, not program costs. The point is to cut down on governmental waste, where two typewriters are being ordered for every employee, whether they can type or not—not to cut down on the money actually being spent on programs and services.

You would not give anyone a bonus for taking away some poor person's welfare check.

Leichtman: Well, let me ask you this question. In recent years socialistic ideas and philosophies have been gaining steadily in terms of acceptance by the public—especially the concept of large-scale government spending. And during this same period of time, the capitalist or free enterprise system has suffered great abuse. There has been an enormous amount of propaganda antagonistic to the free enterprise system. It is getting to the point where the average person now views capitalism as synonymous with exploitation and oppression.

If you were to head up an educational program to promote the values of personal endeavor and free enterprise, how would you go about correcting these misconceptions? How would you go about delivering your message to the public?

Carnegie: That is not an easy question to answer, since there are several brilliant individuals who are writing books and articles designed to do exactly what you are talking about, and yet they are not being given due attention by the public media. There are a number of us on this side who are working with these individuals, helping them formulate their ideas, but unfortunately the public press is not giving them the publicity they deserve. Of course, that's not surprising—the press in general has a very low regard for anyone who is speaking the truth.

The problem boils down to one of envy. This is a poisonous attitude which has crept into public opinion during the last fifty years and has increased far more rapidly than any of us would have expected.

I am talking here about the envy of big business, the envy of wealth, the envy of productivity, and the envy of talent. It is a disease which has crept into the American society, and it is extremely distressing to those of us on this side, because America used to have a noble dream. And this American Dream was that any talented, productive, aggressive, hard-charging individual could make himself a millionaire or billionaire through hard work, hard effort, productivity, talent, and a little luck.

In my day, the people who fulfilled this American Dream were respected, they were looked up to. The heads of large corporations, the artists and musicians who became the leaders in their fields, and anyone who demonstrated productivity and competence were given the highest stature in society. They were role models the rest of the public emulated. Wealth was not seen as something negative or exploitative; it was something to achieve.

In this century, however, the American Dream has been turned around, in part because of the interjection of socialistic and Marxist ideas into the thinking of the public. Those who have great wealth and are productive are viewed with disgust and envy. It is generally believed that these people could not possibly have earned their wealth as a result of their own talent and energy, because that puts the nonproductive members of society in a bad light by comparison, and so it is assumed that the wealthy have become wealthy only because they have exploited the masses. Of course, nothing could be further from the truth, but it is the way the masses often think nowadays. It is just envy.

This is a very sad condition. The greed and the envy of these people have torn down the American Dream.

Leichtman: Yes.

Carnegie: The discerning individual needs to understand that there is a fine line between respecting a role model and wanting to emulate him on the one hand and envying and resenting him on the other. Respect can turn to envy quickly, if it is discovered that it is going to be difficult to emulate and become like the object you respect.

Respect for achievement was always a strong part of the American Dream. A person just starting out would meet a productive, wealthy individual and say to himself, "Boy, I would really like to be like that individual, and I am going to work harder so I can achieve what he has achieved." That's respect, and it's healthy.

The envious person, however, sees a wealthy person, and instead of respecting his achievements, he resents the trappings of his wealth—the limousine, the mansion, the private jet, and the glamorous lifestyle. Instead of being inspired to achieve what the wealthy person has achieved, he says to himself, "If I can't have what he has, then he has no right to have it either." And so he does all he can to destroy that individual.

It is the growth of envy which has set the stage for the terrorist activities of recent years. Terrorism is envy taken to a violent degree. The terrorist operates on the notion that if he can't have as much wealth as the wealthy person, then the wealthy person has no right to exist. And so the terrorist tries to kill those who have wealth and power, or blow up their factories.

Now, as I see it, this envy is in large part an outcropping of the massive growth in government in the last fifty years and the creeping notion that "if I can't make it as a productive member of society, I don't have to worry because the government will protect me and give me an income." Actually, there is another aspect to this as well, because even if a person is productive, the government will take so much of his income that he doesn't have the incentive to work that a person did one hundred years ago. So the American Dream has been squeezed from both directions. The government has imposed so many restrictions upon an individual's ability to accumulate wealth that it is virtually impossible to achieve the American Dream without a substantial amount of good luck. And at the same time, it has made it possible for people to survive very comfortably without having to work or be productive. In these people, the Dream simply dies, and is turned into envy of those who are productive and wealthy.

This is a very sad state.

Leichtman: I agree. But what would you do to promote the enlightened ethic of productivity and wealth?

Carnegie: Well, as I pointed out, there are good people who are trying to promote it, but they are not getting very far. I'm not sure I can make any other suggestions. The envy is a major obstacle which makes it very difficult to promote an enlightened ethic without being misunderstood. The moment you propose reducing the size of the government and lightening the tax burden on individuals and businesses, those who are dependent on the government and envious of wealth will immediately raise their voices in protest.

The recent tax changes pushed through Congress by President Reagan are a good example. They were a step in the right direction, but absolutely minor in comparison to what needs to be done. And yet even these minor changes brought furious protests.

Leichtman: Yes, President Reagan was accused of stealing from the poor to give to the rich.

Carnegie: Absolutely—the program was seen by many as a gift for the rich. That's nonsense, of course, but it is an indication of how widespread and insidious this disease of envy has become.

Leichtman: Well, that rationale is based on the rather wild assumption that somehow the government really has a right to all of the income the citizens of the country produce, and when it does not tax a part of that income, it is somehow a gift.

Japikse: The slavery of the highly productive.

Carnegie: Absolutely.

Leichtman: Well, I find that line of reasoning hard to follow.

Carnegie: Yes, it's a perverted sense of reality. When this country was founded, it was assumed that the fruits of an individual's labors belonged entirely to him. If the government needed to raise money through taxes, it taxed property or imports or something of that nature, but it left the fruits of its citizens' labors to them. But in the last seventy-five years, since the introduction of the income tax, this whole philosophy has been perverted, and now we have reached the point where it is assumed that the government has a right to 100 percent of the fruits of an individual's labors, and can take as much of his income as it pleases.

As I have been saying throughout this entire interview, this attitude is totally at odds with the laws of money. And if we do not correct the situation ourselves, the natural laws of money will eventually correct it for us.

As a general rule, the worse the condition becomes, the more painful the correction will be.

Leichtman: And what would that correction be?

Carnegie: A return to a natural pattern of accumulating and distributing wealth and the energy of money. Let me draw an analogy to what happens in earthquakes. If you have a fault line where the two surfaces are moving a hundredth of an inch a day in relationship to each other, but then get stuck and cannot move as they are supposed to, the energy of the natural movement will begin to build up. And it may build up for two decades, but eventually the pressure will become so great that it will start those two surfaces moving again. But when that happens, the surfaces will not move just a hundredth of an inch. They will move a distance equivalent to two decades times a hundredth of an inch a day.

Leichtman: A big shake-up! *[Laughter.]*

Carnegie: Yes. Now, the same principle applies to the natural flow of money. The longer the flow of money and wealth is thwarted by governmental policies, the economic system, or the envy of the masses, the more this energy will build up. When it is finally released, it will be a big shake-up.

Leichtman: Not just a theoretical shake-up, but a big shake-up! *[Laughter.]*

Carnegie: You got it. *[More laughter.]* Sooner or later the natural laws of money build up to the point where they dramatically move to restore a proper balance to the flow of money. This is true not just in this country, by the way, but throughout the world. The Soviet Union, for example, has been violating these laws since 1917, but the natural laws of money will not allow that situation to continue indefinitely. It is just a matter of time.

Leichtman: I'm glad to hear that. Well, let me ask you this. Suppose you were put in charge of a foundation that had a net worth of 25 billion dollars. How would you spend that today in this country?

Carnegie: I would spend it in two distinct ways. The first thing I would do would be to go right to President Reagan and say, "I have a billion dollars to spend each year for the next 25 years. Why don't you give me a billion dollars worth of your social programs to take care of and cut your budget by that much?" And we'd sit down and I would pick the programs I thought we could administer. The reason for doing this would be to get the government out of the business of administering those social programs—which I think is absolutely necessary.

The other way I would spend the money would be to use it to promote educational programs which teach society to understand and respect the natural laws of increase. This would not be a mystical or esoteric education, either. It would be a basic instruction in economic history, which I think is totally lacking in our current educational system.

Leichtman: Using the mistakes being made in other countries as examples of what not to do, I would hope.

Carnegie: Sure, and what has worked and what has not worked, historically. There would also be an examination of the various kinds of economic systems, demonstrating which systems best fulfill the natural laws of money and increase, and which do not do a very good job. And most important of all, these programs would take a serious look at the role of government in the economy and try to teach the basic premise that government has no business whatsoever meddling in the economy!

Leichtman: That sounds very good. I suppose the object of taking over a billion dollars worth of social programs would be to demonstrate that they can be administered more effectively by private charities than by the government—and in a way that would promote genuine self-sufficiency, not the classic pattern of governmental paternalism.

Carnegie: Absolutely. One of the interesting aspects about providing for the welfare of the needy by giving them direct payments is that it upsets the natural law of money as it is working through the destinies of those individuals. We have been talking in this interview about the natural laws of money as they work through society, and we have commented on how government interferes with and distorts the natural flow of money through society. But we can also apply these same laws and principles to the case of an individual, both as an earner and a spender of money. And when a person is living solely on direct welfare payments, then obviously he is not earning the money he is spending. The natural laws of earning are being distorted in that individual's life. And just as it is a matter of time before society has to deal with the consequence of distorting the natural laws of money, it is only a matter of time before the individual must deal with the consequences of depending on welfare payments. It may not be in this lifetime that the consequences become obvious, but they do come eventually and must be dealt with. A truly effective welfare program would take this factor into account, and try to meet the needs of these people without forcing them to become dependent upon welfare handouts.

The spending side of this issue is even more interesting. The purpose of welfare programs is to help people acquire the necessities. And many people who are dependent on these programs do spend the money they receive on necessities—food, clothing, and shelter. These people are handling the spending side of welfare intelligently, and are therefore able to put the law of increase to work in their lives. They are able to confront the learning situations of their life and grow, whether it is a mother trying to raise ten kids without a husband to support her or a person with a physical handicap who is unable to work. There may be circumstances which keep these individuals from being self-sufficient, and yet they use the law of increase intelligently by spending the money they receive wisely and prudently.

But not everyone who receives welfare payments spends this money intelligently. Some are quite able to take care of the basic necessities on their own, but draw welfare payments so they can maintain a fancy lifestyle. They spend the money they receive not on necessities but on a bigger house or a bigger car, expensive clothes, a television set, or whatever. They take the attitude that this government largess is theirs to consume, and so they take everything they can get.

This, of course, is a perversion of the natural laws of spending. And so again, a good welfare program should take this factor into consideration and try to educate the people it serves as to the right way to spend money. It should teach them that if they spend the money foolishly or wastefully, they will eventually reap the benefits of their foolishness and wastefulness. And they will not enjoy it when it all comes back to haunt them.

Leichtman: Sometimes I think it takes a bit too long for their foolishness and wastefulness to come back to them. Most of these people aren't intelligent enough to get the message if it isn't immediate.

Well, how would you promote your educational system? Would these be programs you would try to introduce into the public school system?

Carnegie: The public school system is run by the government, and the government is not going to endorse an educational program which would advocate that the government stop interfering in business and the economy.

There are many ways to do it. Television would be one

avenue, and a whole new opportunity for disseminating information and ideas through computers is now developing.

Leichtman: But even if the money were available, would this program work?

Carnegie: It *could* work, yes. Whether it would or not is an interesting question.

I want you to understand something about this discussion. Education is not the solution. The real problem is not the ignorance of the people but the restrictions that government has put on free enterprise and the economy. The question is therefore not how to educate the people but rather how to remove all these restrictions.

Now, once you realize that the goal is to remove all of these restrictions and get government to stop interfering with the natural flow of money, then we ask ourselves, "How can this be done?" And one possible way of doing it is by educating the people. The idea would be to educate a generation of individuals who would grow up realizing that the previous generations had mortgaged the future of the economic system for their own short-term gains, and that the only way to restore vitality to the economy is to get rid of all the restrictions. That would be the goal of the educational programs.

Now that we have defined the issues in this way, we are still left with two questions. Question number one is: can we achieve this goal by countering the propaganda of those who want to perpetuate the system as it is—the propaganda of the nonproductive? And question number two is: wouldn't it be a lot easier just to remove the restrictions?

Leichtman: Yes. *[Laughter.]*

Carnegie: Can it be done without educating the masses? I don't know the answer to that question.

Leichtman: Well, it is certainly obvious that the most recent generation has mortgaged the future of the upcoming generations.

Japikse: Just look at the state of Social Security.

Carnegie: And the fact that a substantial portion of the

federal budget today is merely the *interest* on money the government has borrowed in the past. Not only has the government taxed the citizens of this country to the limit, limiting their productivity in a drastic and unhealthy way, but on top of that, it has also borrowed in excess of what it has earned, in order to spend even more.

Some people, of course, claim that the national debt is not unhealthy, but I don't subscribe to that philosophy. I was not a proponent of debt during my career, and I am still not a proponent of debt.

Leichtman: Yes, it is not part of the Scottish tradition, is it? *[Laughter.]*

Well, let me shift the direction of our discussion again. It is obvious that you had an enormous grasp of what it takes to achieve success in business, and in fact spent much of your later years passing this understanding on to others, so that they could learn what it really takes to be successful, too. And there was one man in particular who you taught these principles to, and he wrote them down in several books, such as *Think and Grow Rich*. Would you comment, not so much about Napoleon Hill, but about the principles of personal success?

Carnegie: The books speak for themselves. They may have become a little overdone and perhaps a bit too doctrinaire, but every work is imperfect. They certainly still stand with my approval on them.

The important aspects of success center around setting goals and then investing the whole of your being in moving toward those goals. And from this simple premise you can then branch out in many directions, talking about creating the right mental attitude, visualizing the goal you have set in your mind, seeing it, feeling it, living it, moving toward it, and making sure that the road to your goal is a direct one.

Leichtman: I remember when I read those books I was really quite impressed by them. They are filled with down-to-earth and very practical suggestions for becoming successful, whether it is in business or in a profession or in any other aspect of life.

I wanted to mention them here because I think more people ought to pick up those books and read them. They are still applicable today.

Carnegie: Oh, I'm sure they are. I'm very happy with them, even though they certainly have their limitations.

Leichtman: Some people, it seems to me, have the notion that being successful means working very, very hard and having lots of ambition and dedication. What struck me about your philosophy, as it was set down in those books, is that it was much fuller and richer than that very narrow idea. You took into account the Creator, and the people one would be working with, and the practical steps that would have to be taken to earn success. You didn't just unleash the greed of people—you evoked their talent and their humanity.

Carnegie: Yes. The mere desire to be wealthy does not suffice to make anyone wealthy. It is important to understand that in any worthwhile endeavor, the monetary reward is forthcoming as a result of the contribution which is made, rather than the other way around. And this is a basic principle which is not widely appreciated.

I would venture to say that not many wealthy people are really all that concerned about the amount of money they are earning. They are wrapped up in achieving their goals and making sure that the operation runs smoothly. I think it would be fair to say, for example, that an artist would be painting no matter how much income he or she earned, unless there was absolutely none. And this is true of most people who become wealthy, too. Their first love is for the work they are doing and the contribution they are making—not for the money they are earning.

Any worthwhile endeavor which provides a benefit to humanity will provide a reasonable way to earn a living. The money follows the endeavor. However, if you look at projects which have failed, you will often find that they failed because the only goal these projects served was the generation of money.

Sometimes, of course, these projects do succeed, even though their only goal is to make money. But if you look at them over the long term, you will find they do not last. There may have been a momentary success and a brief flurry of wealth, but the success cannot be sustained. Only those products and services which benefit humanity can provide a basis for continuing success.

Leichtman: I suppose that principle applies not just to individuals but also to corporations.

Carnegie: Absolutely.

Leichtman: Well, let me ask you this. In this day and age, corporations are treated as an entity, as though they were an individual. Is this the case esoterically as well as legally? Does a corporation somehow acquire a life of its own?

Carnegie: Of course. The corporation becomes the sum total of all the individuals that are contributing to it.

Leichtman: Is there sometimes even more than just the group mind?

Carnegie: Sure. It has a life of its own. The group mind is the best way to explain it, but it is much more complex than that alone. A corporation can be sick or healthy, it can be growing or shrinking. But a successful corporation will have its own character, its own energy. The comings and goings of the individuals who work for the corporation will have a relatively minor effect on the health of the organization as a whole.

Leichtman: Can a corporation be imbued with or charged with the dedication and humanitarian purpose of its founders or leaders?

Carnegie: Absolutely. This is carried from generation to generation.

Leichtman: But if the management becomes sloppy or greedy at some point—

Carnegie: The vitality of the corporation can definitely be dissipated. The companies which are healthy and prosperous are the ones which had good ideals and good seed thoughts to begin with, and have translated those ideals into good policies and procedures which safeguard the success of the company. And these attitudes and policies and ideas have been transmitted throughout the organization, from the highest levels to the lowest, and from generation to generation.

It is also quite true that an individual tends to take on the attitudes and characteristics of a corporation he is working for.

Leichtman: That is also true in many government agencies and offices. I think it is most noticeable in going from one branch of the Post Office to another. In one you may be treated hospitably and warmly, and in the next one you are treated as an obnoxious enemy who is interfering with their coffee break. *[Laughter.]*

Carnegie: Yes.

Japikse: Is this corporate character you are describing found entirely at the form level, or is there also a spiritual element which is associated with corporations and companies?

Carnegie: The corporate mind is actually much more apparent at the subtle levels of life than it is at the physical level. It is a very real thing and does exist at these subtle levels. And the connection of each individual member of the corporation to this corporate mind is a mental connection, not a physical one.

It can have a very powerful influence on the individual, too. Quite often, a corporate style of dressing and speaking and even thinking will develop, even though no one is consciously setting forth rules and policies which dictate this style. This is particularly true in terms of thinking. Certain patterns of problem solving will develop which are unique to that company, or at least consistent from department to department throughout the company. And as people move throughout the company, the patterns are continually reinforced.

In some cases these patterns become detrimental to the health of the company, but in most cases they are the patterns upon which the company first became successful, and they contribute to the longevity of the corporation.

Leichtman: Yes. I've visited the Hershey complex in Hershey, Pennsylvania, a few times. It has a long record of philanthropic work in the community and the business seems to continue to thrive. And their labor relations apparently are quite good. It certainly has a healthy glow about it.

Japikse: A chocolate glow, I presume. *[Laughter.]*

Carnegie: There are many companies in this country that are living testimony to the fact that the principles we have been enunciating in this interview are not only valid but also practical. And if people read this book and recognize that they are working for one of these healthy, successful, and public-minded corporations, they should feel proud, because they are contributing to the achievement and success of that company.

Leichtman: Doesn't this imply, however, that the personality of a company might occasionally become sick or neurotic or greedy or depressed, just as the personality of an individual can fall sick?

Carnegie: Of course.

Leichtman: Which begs the question: should we have psychologists to give therapy to these companies?

Carnegie: Corporate shrinks, sure. *[Laughter.]* They do exist, but they aren't called corporate shrinks. They are called consultants.

Japikse: Do they make house calls? *[More laughter.]*

Carnegie: Just office calls.

Leichtman: Very good. You mentioned earlier that you are busy at least in part inspiring some of the people here in the physical plane who are writing about free enterprise and the virtue of productivity. Can you give us other hints about what occupies your time now?

Carnegie: Well, I have some very close friends who are in physical incarnation now, and I am working very closely with them, helping them with their business ventures. This is one of the reasons why I am so well versed in contemporary problems. And in fact I am very interested in the economic issues of the day. I'm convinced that unless the United States changes some of the political decisions which have been made, we are going to lose the system which gave this country its phenomenal economic success. I am working very diligently here on the inner side to try to gain the ear of those that might listen.

Leichtman: Does that actually include advising prominent governmental figures?

Carnegie: Let's put it way. There are some of us up here who are talking at them.

Leichtman: But is anyone in the physical plane listening?

Carnegie: Very few, very few. But we are making headway, albeit slowly.

Leichtman: I occasionally hear comments from people such as William Simon and Milton Friedman which are very good.

Carnegie: The problem that many of these people have is that they set forth the fantastic progress which was made during the time when personal and economic freedom still existed in this country as a model for what could be done again in the future. But the people who are listening to them confuse the message, and think that they are advocating that we return to the conditions of a hundred years ago, and everything that entailed. And so they charge these voices with wanting to go backwards. But that is not the point. It would not be possible or desirable to return to what we once had. The freedom of one hundred years ago did produce an economic success unheard of in the history of this planet. But it would be foolish to try to recreate the exact conditions under which that success flourished. What we must do instead is try to work with and understand the principles which produced that success, and apply them to our current conditions.

We must look around at this country and see what economic freedom accomplished. And we must never forget that it was industry and productivity which built this country, not welfare schemes. We are perilously close to losing what we have built. We have moved too far away from the freedom and industry which built the country.

Unless the voices of economic and personal freedom are heard, and refuse to give up until their message is heeded, we will lose our dream. They must persist, and keep on reminding the public that there are more important things than greed and tomorrow's dollar. Sooner or later, the public is going to wake up and realize that public handouts are not the way to economic freedom. It will realize that the ultimate freedom is the freedom to honor the best and noblest within yourself, plus the freedom to do what you know is best, without interference or constraints. And the public will insist that the government restore this freedom.

Leichtman: But that sounds elitist. *[Laughter.]*

Carnegie: It's the exact opposite of elitist!

Leichtman: Yes, I know, but that won't stop the self-professed populists from thinking it's elitist. Sometimes the only thing you can say to these people is, "If our system is such a failure, why has it been such a success?" *[More laughter.]*

Carnegie: That's true.

Leichtman: But even that doesn't seem to faze them. I'm not sure these people are completely rational.

Carnegie: No, because they will counter your statement with this one: "Well, if the economy is so strong, then it won't hurt to take a few billion dollars more out of it." Yet that is like preferring a slow death to a swift one.

Still, there are a number of brave and intelligent voices out there, and I am heartily behind them and working with them to the best of my ability.

Japikse: Is there anything else you are currently involved in?

Carnegie: My hands are full.

Japikse: Well, that brings up a question we really must ask. A number of people we have interviewed in this series have told us that they left behind manuscripts or other objects that they secreted in mysterious hiding places. Were you thoughtful enough to leave behind some of your money, and if so, would you kindly tell us where you hid it? *[Laughter.]*

Carnegie: Well, let me tell you where I hid it. I had working for me a very pleasant young man who was a real genius, and just before my untimely demise, he developed a matter transporter. And we shoveled all my gold doubloons into this machine and transported them to Jupiter. And they are buried in a cave just left of the southwest quadrant of the planet. *[Loud guffawing.]* When you get there, I am sure you will be able to find them.

Leichtman: Well, now that you've mentioned gold, do you have any comments on the spectacular rise and fall of the price of gold and silver which occurred recently, or on the idea of speculation on metals and commodities in general? Is such heavy speculation a good or a bad idea?

Carnegie: It's neither a good idea or a bad idea—it isn't really an idea at all. It's an index of the health of the economy.

One of the signs of economic disruption is that it becomes easier and more profitable to buy a commodity and sit on it than invest the same money in a productive and meaningful enterprise. It would have behooved anyone reading this book to have taken all of his money at the beginning of 1979 and converted it to gold, holding it for the duration of the year, instead of working. But that doesn't mean it would have been a good idea. It just means the system was sick. Because something is dramatically wrong when it is easier to make money through speculation than it is by working. The system needs help.

Leichtman: In your terminology, then, making money through speculation and buying up futures on commodities is really a form of draining off energy and putting it in suspense, instead of investing it in something productive and beneficial to mankind.

Carnegie: Yes. Society does not benefit from anyone making money while sitting on his rear.

Japikse: I'm not sure I appreciate that statement. *[Laughter.]* Some of us are productive while sitting on our rears.

Leichtman: Yes, I really wouldn't want to type for very long standing up. *[More laughter.]*

Carnegie: Well, I will amend it. Society does not benefit from anyone making money while sitting on his rear doing nothing.

Japikse: Thank you.

Leichtman: Well, what is the best way to handle the problem of speculation? Do we try to turn the economy around so it is not profitable to speculate, or do we impose curbs and limitations on the ability to speculate?

Carnegie: Oh, absolutely not. You should not want to curb the freedom of anyone to speculate on anything he likes. In fact, the shackles should be removed.

I don't want to get into an in-depth discussion of the commodities market or the stock market or anything else at this point, but I will say this. When there is a greater incentive to put your money into speculation than there is to reinvest it in a productive enterprise or human service—something that will benefit humanity in general—then there is something drastically wrong. The problem is not that the commodities are rising spectacularly—the problem is that there is an insufficient number of places to invest capital profitably other than commodities.

In my day you would much rather use your money to start a little business than to buy gold and sit on it. It was much more sensible—and challenging—to invent some new widget which would be useful to others and then build a factory to produce them. It was great fun and really got the adrenalin flowing. And it not only got the adrenalin flowing, but it also benefited humanity.

The attractiveness of speculating in commodities and other markets is only another sign of the basic problem we have been talking about all along—the interference of the government in business and the economy upsets the rhythm and balance of the natural laws of money.

Leichtman: Let me ask you perhaps the most imponderable question I have asked so far. Who is running the show? Is it the people down here on the physical plane grubbing for a buck? Is it enlightened people like you running around heaven telling us down here what to do? *[Laughter.]*

Carnegie: From my perspective, I don't believe that any of the problems we have today have been consciously perpetrated by any group of people. There are, of course, obvious indications of greed throughout the world, and greed is the one factor more than any other that upsets the natural laws of money.

There are certain pockets of greed in a number of places throughout the world which are especially strong, but I don't believe I will mention where. They should be obvious.

Leichtman: I can't imagine. *[Laughter.]*

Japikse: Actually, I didn't realize they had pockets in those get-ups that they wear. *[More laughter.]*

Carnegie: But it really isn't useful to single out a specific group or nation and say they are the cause of all of our economic problems. It's easy to do that, but not really productive. The world has been through far more severe crises than the economic crisis confronting us today. As always, the solution lies in seeing what actions would restore the flow of money to its natural state, and then taking those actions.

What has happened is that the natural and normal flows of the energy of money have been diverted into pockets of greed which are not able to handle the energy effectively. This has created imbalances in many areas, either because there is too much energy or too little energy. And until economics and productivity are viewed from the perspective of energy which is earned and owned and then spent or given away, this problem will continue. And the same can be said about the need to view the individual as an energy-transferring unit—whether it is an individual person or an individual company or an individual nation.

The groups which are causing the problems today have a genuine desire to provide a better lot for mankind, but their methods of going about it are totally wrong. They have the wrong attitudes and a very poor understanding of the actual workings of economics.

Leichtman: Okay.

Japikse: How much do the different cultural backgrounds throughout the world affect the handling of money?

Carnegie: They influence the solution to the problem, but

they do not change the basic workings of the natural laws.

Leichtman: It's like saying the law of gravity works equally for everyone around the world.

Carnegie: Yes. Another way to look at it would be to compare it to sickness in a human being. Let's say a person has a pain in his foot. The Chinese might try to treat it with acupuncture, whereas in the West we would treat it with medicine. The sickness is the same, but the treatment differs from culture to culture. The principles of healing are the same, but the way the healing is effected differs. Of course, in terms of what we have been talking about today, the favored treatment of our modern age seems to be that the person complains about the pain in his foot and the government reacts by pounding his hand with a hammer. *[Laughter.]* The pain in the foot is generally forgotten as the hammer continues to strike the hand.

Leichtman: How about that—creative injury!

[More laughter.]

I suppose I need not ask, but I presume you do not have much of anything favorable to say for the Marxist system.

Carnegie: No, I don't, although you must keep in mind that some elements of the collective society do anticipate the final, ideal economic order. This ideal economic order will be a nation of productive, industrious people working together for the mutual benefit of all. This is the destiny of mankind.

Leichtman: Yet that is not incongruous with capitalism.

Carnegie: Of course not. What must be done is this: the principles of individual creation, growth, and fulfillment must be brought into harmony with the goals of the collective society. You cannot put the goal of collective humanity before the goals of the healthy individual and reach the final, ideal economic order.

Once the principles of individuality are fully developed and blended with the principles of collective humanity, however, then the ultimate ideal can be attained. And the ultimate ideal is this: that in the end, all must benefit from the work of the individual.

The mistake of Marxism is that it tries to create an economic unit where the goals of the group are put before the goals and the health of the individual. This is not the way the final ideal is to be reached. It should be sought the other way around. The individual must be given adequate incentive to achieve his destiny and the education he needs in order to act in a reasonable manner. And as many individuals are able to act successfully in life, then all of the little individual successes they are generating will prove very effective in providing for the collective needs of the whole.

Is that clear?

Leichtman: Yes, very clear.

Carnegie: Well, let me end with the following observations. In the next twenty-five years, we are going to witness a tremendous shift in economic thinking and a tremendous upheaval in the world economically. In this country, the last two generations have taken a beautiful economic system that they inherited from their fathers and grandfathers and have mortgaged it to the hilt. They have lived off the system like a bunch of bratty children, but have basically not contributed anything to it. The question is: when will the generation which will have the strength and forethought to rebuild the system and make it even better arise? Is it this generation? Or will it be another generation or two before it arises?

I want you to understand that I am not criticizing. These are normal cycles in humanity. Particularly if you look at world history from this side, it is easy to see that we have always gone through cycles of opportunity and cycles of mistakes. We grow from both opportunities and mistakes, after all.

The cycle we are in now has distorted our economic system. The freedom of the free enterprise system has been compromised. But it is not just our system; the communist and socialist systems are not working, either. In fact, they are working far more poorly than the free enterprise system.

Out of this mess, there will have to come some enlightened individuals who will develop a new system—a system which will take the best of capitalism, the best of socialism, and the best of Marxism, if there is any, and try to put these elements together.

I'm sure there are some benefits in socialism and Marxism. I personally don't know what they are, but I suppose somebody will be able to find them. Keep in mind that I'm an old advocate of the free enterprise, capitalistic system.

In any event, a new order is going to come out of all this mess. And it will combine the compassion of socialism with adherence to the natural laws of capitalism. It will be a difficult transformation for the world and this country, but it will be worth it.

Leichtman: Well, very good.

Carnegie: I think I will leave it at that.

Leichtman: That's a very complete statement, I think.

Japikse: Yes, indeed.

Carnegie: This has been very pleasurable. Thank you.

Leichtman: Thank you.

CHURCHILL RETURNS

There is no Nobel Prize for War, only for Peace. But for Sir Winston Churchill, an exception should have been made, for Churchill was an exceptional man, who performed an extraordinary service for England and the entire world. Throughout the Thirties, he warned that Germany under Hitler was preparing for war; he was ignored. On his own, without government support, he began to prepare for the inexorable conflict, so that England would not be totally unable to meet the crisis. And it was not, for when World War II arrived, against everyone's wishes, Sir Winston Churchill was ready. He stepped into the offices of Prime Minister and Minister of Defense and rallied England from near defeat to victory. Had it not been for Churchill, the configuration of the world government today might be completely different.

As it was, Churchill was presented a Nobel Prize—for literature. But it is not for his writing skills, as brilliant as they were, that we remember him. Nor is it for the many other contributions he made to England during the sixty years of his political career—and they were many. At different times, he held leadership posts in the Admiralty, the Colonial Office, and as home secretary and chancellor of the exchequer. As such, he was instrumental in shaping many of England's domestic and foreign policies. But all of these pale in comparison to his labors as Prime Minister during the war.

Churchill was not just a "man of the hour." He was no mere opportunist who happened to achieve fame only because he was the leader of a great nation at a time of crisis. He was, in a very real sense, a man who created the hour in which he served—a man who saw clearly what England had to do and rallied his nation to the cause, when no one else seemed able. He stared fate in its face, and refused to cower when given a responsibility which would have caused most men to tremble. He wrapped himself in power and plunged into the conflict, determined to emerge only as the victor. Many have found themselves in similar positions of leadership, but few have ever harnessed it with such genius—or produced results which so profoundly benefited mankind.

What was it about this man that made him so extraordinary? Was it his tremendous talent for oratory? Was it his magnetic influence on others? Was it his almost prescient vision of the future course of events? Was it his mysterious ability to get people to listen to him and follow his lead? Was it his grasp of history and awareness of its patterns—its tendencies to repeat itself subtly? All of these attributes and talents played their part.

Winston Churchill was no accident, no fluke of fate. It is obvious that he was a man born to lead—to become a priest of leadership. While others have a talent to educate or heal, to discover or create, Churchill had a remarkable talent to gather power, to focus authority, and to bring people together so that they could accomplish collectively what none of them could do alone. He worked hard to refine his talents of leadership, applying himself to a thorough study of history and accepting a broad range of military and governmental posts. He brought a ferocious dynamism to everything that he did. He had the gift of authority.

Few leaders genuinely do have this gift. Many have a talent for ambition, for charming other people, for satisfying their personal greed, or for lusting after popularity; they ride the crest of fads or capitalize on public bigotry. But they are not true leaders—just opportunists and troublemakers. They do not have the gift of authority. They accumulate power, perhaps, but they do not know how to use it. They end up slaves of the power they long so much to attain.

But men such as Churchill become genuine priests of authority, because they nurture an innate capacity to find the threads of national destiny and weave them into a tapestry for others to behold. These leaders see where the subtle and hidden currents of human nature and society are flowing and recognize what must be done, what must be avoided, to steer the ship of state safely along its course. These are men of great vision, not in the clairvoyant sense, but in terms of the ability to sense currents of power, the values the people hold sacred, and the wounds of society which need healing.

The leader who is blessed with the gift of authority knows when there is complacency and apathy which no one can stir; he likewise knows how to rouse the noblest passions of the people, before they turn destructive and angry. He is in touch with the hearts and minds of the people he leads, and knows how to rally them, so that the ship he steers will not founder.

The priest of leadership also manifests a marvelous sense of timing. There truly are tides in the events of history and our collective reactions to them; these tides, if recognized, can either work to our advantage or thwart our efforts. There is a time for reform, a time for launching new schemes, a time for returning to old values, a time for scrapping old ways, and a time for resting, in order to consolidate our gains. The true leader has a masterful sense of what is possible and what is not, and for picking the most favorable moment in time to push some special theme.

This kind of leader becomes a nexus for significant power, meaning that he can gather power from a variety of sources, give it focus and interpretation, and then implement it successfully. This is not personal power, gathered through charm or intimidation; it is a much larger power, gathered from a movement or ideal. The source of power could be the growing discontent among certain groups about some aspect of society—or the evolutionary urge within people who cry out for innovative change. The wise leader is able to spot these sources of power and thrust himself into the midst of them, giving them voice. This is no mere opportunism! It is the magnetic call of the focused will inherent in some level of society, evoking a spokesman to give it representation.

In some cases, the power derives from an inner aspect of life, rather than the rage of outward protest or the need for some mundane change. This source of power is especially difficult to perceive, as it tends to have little outward expression until championed by an appropriate leader. It might be the pressure of an evolutionary force impelling society to transform itself— or the power of a tradition, trampled by public hysteria, seeking to reassert itself. But whatever the source of the power, be it from God or from man, it is there to be harnessed. And for that we need agents of power, such as Churchill.

A study of Churchill's life reveals much about power and its use. It is clear that he was able to channel and direct power in a way that few other people have: he had the temperament to be a leader and to use power. In addition, he had the spiritual depth to contact the deeper dimension of society and humanity which is the source of genuine power. And he had the occasion to use this great power: the crisis of the second world war. These three elements are essential to effective leadership—the temperament to lead, the situation which demands leadership, and the latent power of the deeper dimension of life. Without problems to be solved or an appropriate crisis, there is no invocation to do more than just maintain the status quo. Without the proper leadership temperament, the position of power is likely to become intoxicating and unbalancing. And without contact with the genuine sources of power nothing will arise except rhetoric and smoke.

It is because Churchill so aptly fits this portrait of leadership that I chose to interview him in this series, *From Heaven to Earth*. Naturally, the principal topic for our discussion was the nature of leadership and power. Churchill proved quite ready to tackle this rather heady subject, and insisted on giving very practical suggestions. But I did not want the interview to be just a scholarly dissertation on the uses of power, so I inquired freely of his views on current political conditions in the world. His answers are often most provocative. He is quite bold, for example, in stating that the cause the Western nations fought for in World War II has not been entirely won, and that the threat from communist countries parallels that which he confronted from Hitler.

Churchill points out that democratic nations frequently are too meek in dealing with these threats to freedom—an inherent part of the democratic character. In a time when the true language of diplomacy is becoming more and more ineffective, he advises, the true leader must not be hesitant to speak whatever language will be heard. Speaking this "language" would include using the economic and industrial strengths of the West, as well as sanctions and pressures of other kinds.

Over and over, Churchill makes the distinction between the *leader* and the *dictator*. Both may appear to be strong individuals, but the difference is enormous. The dictator seeks to impose his will on the people he governs, forcing them to act as he would have them act. The leader seeks to understand the deepest will of the people, and help them to mobilize it in every aspect of society.

In response to a question, Sir Winston describes his solution for the problem of national selfishness, which has become so dominant in international relations today. He implies that utopian governments are impractical, and then sets forth a basis for world cooperation which deserves careful consideration.

At one point, I ask him about his deep interest in the first Duke of Marlborough, which prompts a lengthy discussion of the values of heroes in any society. The first Duke of Marlborough was John Churchill, a direct ancestor of Sir Winston's and the hero of the wars against Louis XIV of

France in the early eighteenth century. He became a source of inspiration and the object of a book by Sir Winston, *Marlborough: His Life and Times*.

Churchill also talks at length about the nature of the national spirit, a term which may be familiar to esoteric students but not to others. Briefly, the spirit is the essence and the force of the ideals, the destiny, and the character of any nation. It can be contacted and known, both symbolically and intuitively, and has a direct impact on the government of a country. Churchill speaks of the spirit of Britain in terms of how it guided him as Prime Minister and his understanding of it now that he is a spirit himself.

Time and time again, Churchill makes points which have direct relevance to our lives. We need not be in a position of leadership to benefit from this example of a priest of leadership; all of us are citizens, of one country or another, and therefore need to know something about leadership. We need to learn about invoking, appreciating, supporting, and contributing to good leadership, and there is much to be gained in this regard from the comments transcribed on the following pages. In addition, each of us does have the potential to be a leader at least in small ways—a leader of family, a leader of a neighborhood cause, a leader of some project at work, or whatever might be appropriate. Life calls upon us to lead, at least by setting a good example, and we can only respond if we have some understanding of what the ideal of leadership is. I hope that each reader will be inspired by what Churchill has to say to become a more effective leader in his or her life, as the opportunity arises.

I would likewise hope some readers will be inspired to read more about the life of this fascinating individual, Sir Winston Churchill. There are a number of good biographies in print about him, and then, of course, there is the rich legacy of writings he left behind. The most famous of these writings are the four-volume *History of the English-Speaking Peoples* and the six-volume *The Second World War*.

One surprise in the interview occurred when I asked Churchill about his relationship with President Franklin Delano Roosevelt. Churchill announced that Roosevelt's spirit was actually on hand and had been listening to the entire interview! He then asked if I would be interested in chatting directly with Roosevelt himself. I said yes, and Churchill withdrew briefly from the body of the medium, allowing his long-time friend to appear. As the switch was made, there was also a substantial change in the psychic radiation around the medium. It was clearly a different person than had been there a moment before. Whereas Churchill commanded the medium with a serious, direct, and formal bearing, Roosevelt exhibited his well-known charm and exuberance. He even characteristically tossed his head—the medium's head, that is—as he spoke.

The medium for this interview is a very good friend of mine, Paul Winters. I am joined in asking questions by my colleague and friend, Carl Japikse. For the record, the interview was conducted in the summer of 1980. Several references to current events will make sense only if the date of the conversation is kept in mind.

Churchill was the first to speak.

Churchill: I heard you provided cigars in the original set of interviews. *[Laughter.]*

Leichtman: That's true. Unfortunately, Paul doesn't smoke, and I don't either anymore, so I can't accommodate you.

Churchill: Well, that's a real shame.

Leichtman: And I don't have any brandy to offer you, either.

Churchill: This doesn't sound as though it is going to be my "finest hour," does it? *[More laughter.]*

Leichtman: Well, we can hope for the best. What would you like to talk about?

Churchill: I don't have a prepared statement, as my contributions to the world have been well publicized. Most of what I did is very public and speaks for itself.

Leichtman: Well, I suppose most people would regard your leadership of Great Britain during World War II as your greatest contribution. Would you agree?

Churchill: Well, as you know, in the course of any one person's evolution, he experiences many different types of lives, over many, many centuries. In a sense, my lifetime as Winston Churchill was a very intense and work-oriented life, with many goals to be met. From my perspective now, I suppose the achievement I most want to be remembered for is that I was one of a group of people who contributed to the fight against the dark forces, who were attempting to take control of the planet. It was my privilege to have been a leader of the forces of good at that time.

This is how I view my role now. Of course, when one is in incarnation and doing the job you are supposed to be doing, you do not necessarily have the luxury of understanding the wider purpose for what you are doing. You are too caught up in the day-to-day routine of what has to be done.

Leichtman: Sure. You are so intensely involved in what you are doing that it is difficult to see the beginning or end or overall purpose.

There are many questions I want to ask, but let me begin here. You seemed quite prescient about the danger coming from Germany, both before World War I and as soon as Hitler came to power. In retrospect, I suppose anyone with modest intelligence should have been able to recognize the danger of Hitler, but you seem to have been one of the few politicians of the day to perceive this danger and articulate it well. Were you particularly impelled to warn of this danger? Were you guided from higher sources of intelligence, or was it just a matter of common sense?

Churchill: It was some of both. The deep philosophical beliefs that I held were being bombarded by the knowledge and fear of what was occurring in the world. The economic times were hard and quite disruptive politically; it was all too easy for people throughout the world to look for strong leadership and follow after chosen idols. Of course, if the people choose a worthy leader, then all is well and good. But Hitler was not a worthy leader.

I attempted to be a voice of conscience for humanity in general and the peoples of Western Europe in particular. I felt I had a duty to speak out as to what I believed to be the truth. I could see the danger very clearly. I don't want to leave the wrong impression; I didn't sit in my study contemplating the role of good and evil on the planet. I just did not like the way the leaders of the Western world were responding to the threats before them.

It is a trait of the Western nations that they practically have to be hit over the head by the full force of a problem before they will accept it as even existing. That was certainly the case in the Thirties. The aggression by Germany was being dismissed as a series of independent events with no common meaning, in the hope that they would simply go away. This was very distressing to me, but the leaders of the time found it very easy to rationalize. Each instance of aggression was seen as an independent military action against this or that country—an event which was not going to affect the rest of the world, so why worry? The leaders hoped Hitler would stop, but did nothing to meet the threat. I was deeply disturbed by these rationalizations—deeply disturbed that people were not more outraged by the abuse of power and the abuse of rights that was occurring. I felt that there had to be at least one strong voice standing up and saying, "We should not be permitting these military actions to occur; it is a violation of everything we know to be just to allow them to continue."

Leichtman: Do you think that humanity in general and Western civilization in particular have changed their ways about recognizing the destructiveness and exploitation of countries led by oligarchies and dictators?

Churchill: No, nothing has changed. I would like to make this comment. One of the major difficulties of being a free country or a democracy is the strong desire to leave other countries alone. This desire leads them to make the assumption that people throughout the world appreciate the value of democracy and will recognize that what is best for a democracy—freedom and self-government—is also best for everyone throughout the world. As a result, the tendency in the West is to let other people alone. Unless faced with an utter disaster or emergency, democracies are slow to move; that's inherent in the system. It is government by consensus, and the price one pays for having a democratic society is that the mechanism of decision-making moves very slowly. Consequently, there is a definite inability in Western civilization to recognize problems in their early stages and take effective corrective action. This is probably *the* major flaw in Western civilization—it is not able to act until a problem reaches a state of crisis.

Of course, this is nothing new—and it will probably continue to be the case ad infinitum.

Leichtman: We seem to fumble along reasonably well despite all the difficulties, however. I remember your classic statement that democracy is the worst possible form of government—except for all the others. That says a great deal.

Churchill: That's why I said it. *[Laughter.]*

Leichtman: After the danger which Hitler represented had been crushed, it became quite apparent to you, as I understand it, that the danger of Stalin and his successors was perhaps even more threatening and imposing. I am curious: do you think you could have altered events if you had not been voted out of office in July 1945? Would you have been able to mold the events of the immediate post war period a bit more carefully?

Churchill: From the perspective I have now, it is clear that it was not destined to be that way. The lessons to be learned by the world at that particular time were not fully learned. And, I might say, they are still not fully learned. Had I been permitted to stay in office, I would have continued to express my outrage at what was happening: that a government which was intrinsically similar to the one we had just defeated was being allowed to spread its influence. I knew the fight had not ended. Nonetheless, I was not in office. My mandate had ceased, and in a real sense, I was very tired of carrying the banner. I hoped someone would pick it up and carry on, but no one did. As the years progressed, it became clear that we had not won the war; we had only won a battle.

Leichtman: Yes. I sometimes tell my Marxist friends, much to their displeasure, that communism is just Nazism warmed over. The big lie is different, the propaganda is better, but everything else is just about the same.

Churchill: It is important to realize that communist governments have also become more sophisticated as the years have gone on. They learned from Hitler's mistakes, and their own mistakes, and have realized that there are more effective ways to carry out their schemes. The world has become more sophisticated since Hitler's demise.

Leichtman: I will want to return to this point in a while, but first I want to pursue what you said a moment ago about the difficulties democracies have in responding to danger from within and without. What can we do? What would you recommend to those of us here in the United States and to people in other democracies throughout the world? What can we do to preserve our freedoms and our integrity in the face of threats?

Churchill: It is a question of good leadership. Who is in power? Who is providing the information about the problems the society confronts, and who is providing the analysis of those problems and the solutions to those problems?

In a democracy, the populace has the responsibility to choose the leadership. Therefore, the public has the ability to project into power individuals who are decidedly incompetent in dealing with subtle issues as well as major problems. Indeed, one of the major fallacies in a democracy is the tradition that in order to become a leader, one has to promise many things to the populace which may not make sense—and, I might add, generally do not make sense in the greater scheme of things. In America, for example, there are major voting blocs which have a very great impact on choosing the leadership of the country.

As a result, your leadership tends to be noted for what it can do for these particular segments of the population, or even for the population as a whole. Individuals are not elected to office because of their administrative abilities or their quick intelligence or their ability to handle sophisticated national problems; they are elected because they seem most likely to give people what they want.

Leichtman: In fact, the public is often threatened by people who are very witty, sharp, and powerful. I think the American public is frightened we might have another imperial President.

Churchill: An imperial President is not so bad.

Leichtman: Yes, I know.

Churchill: If you have the right imperial President. *[Laughter.]*

Leichtman: Yes.

Churchill: And that is a major difficulty. The leaders of democratic countries are not picked because of their competence or qualities, but because of the promises they have made. This state of affairs leads to a decidedly lower quality of leadership—which, I might add, we are suffering from at this time in a majority of the Western world.

Leichtman: Do you see any hope for us?

Churchill: I suspect we will go through a period in which the populace becomes quite disenchanted with the people who are in power, and as a result, will change the criteria they use for electing leaders. Until these criteria change, however, the problems will get much worse, because the leadership of the Western world is not particularly suited for making the hard, critical decisions which are necessary.

Leichtman: Do you see any risk of calling forth a charismatic demagogue instead of a genuine leader?

Churchill: There's always that risk, isn't there?

Talking with you here is quite enjoyable. I haven't had a podium to speak from for quite a long time.

Leichtman: I could tell, from reading your biographies, that you enjoyed holding forth, whether it was in Parliament or at home. It fit you. You seemed to have quite a magnetic effect on others, glowering them into silence or overwhelming them with your aura of power, no matter whether they were colleagues, subordinates, or enemies. It was said in one of the biographies that you were a veritable lightning rod for conflict.

Churchill: That was part of my role, I suppose.

Leichtman: And perhaps stimulated some deep thinking, too?

Churchill: Of course. I loved to argue. I loved to discuss problems, handle difficulties, tackle crises, point out shortcomings, and come out victorious.

Leichtman: Since we're on this subject, could you comment on what it takes to make a real leader? You obviously had a great deal of what we would call nerve, push, and an eagerness to take charge of things, but you also had an enormous amount of talent.

Churchill: I would say that the major requisite of leadership is being able to speak the truth as the conscience of humanity. That's a rather sweeping statement, so let me dissect it for you.

Leadership entails striking a chord in every individual in the nation or group you are leading, so that each individual will think that the leader is speaking the truth, is correct, and is representing what he believes. But it's not just enough to know which chord to strike; the leader must have the qualities which will enable him to act. He has to be able to take the large picture of his philosophical insight and translate it, through management skills, into decisions, trade-offs, and actions. Both are necessary; leadership isn't just boldness or having the guts to make correct decisions. It's also a matter of being able to understand and be in harmony with the philosophical premises of the group that is being led. Where all of these factors are combined, you have a strong case for effective leadership.

Leichtman: That's a striking and succinct way of describing genuine leadership. It sounds like the more uncommon aspect of it is the ability to be in rapport with the guiding principles of the group. That is something you would almost have to be born with, isn't it?

Churchill: Yes—it's more an intuitive "knowing by knowing," rather than something anyone can learn. It's the ability to understand humanity as a collective entity—being able to understand the basic beliefs and desires of a group of people, and being able to express them lucidly as well as understand them personally. It also requires the ability to demonstrate this understanding to the people and then, once your leadership position is established, having the intellectual capabilities and wherewithal to rally the public.

A leader has to do much more than just take charge of functions and responsibilities, *ex oficio.* He must be an individual of vision who can recognize what ought to be happening, and identify what is possible and what can be achieved. To do that, he must be in harmony with the basic premises of the group. That does not mean that he sends out a bunch of pollsters to find out what the public feels or likes about this or that subject. I don't mean that at all. The leader transcends the level of simple self-interest and strikes to the heart of the matter. He taps the core of the public's values.

As you mentioned, this is not always easy to do, but the good leader is able to tap this inspiration—and it is an inspiration—and then speak out. He speaks for the people, championing what they believe to be right, fighting for what they would fight for, and opposing what they would oppose. He makes their enemies his enemies; their heroes, his heroes. He leads the people where they want to go, but knowing, in some mysterious way, that they are pushing him.

A leader of people is aware of these guiding principles and then acts forthrightly, with tremendous skill and daring and courage, knowing that he draws his power from the people he leads. He therefore has a tremendous obligation to handle himself correctly—not just to worry about his own personal feelings and how history will view him, but to be more concerned with what is really right for these people.

Now, I'm not saying that the leader literally sits down and thinks through these steps; it's an innate, automatic process of aligning yourself with these forces. It happens intuitively and somehow the inspired leader manages to do the right things. To be successful, however, you have to have this almost mystical rapport with the people you lead. You have to have nerve. You have to have courage. You have to take on the opposition and challenge them and bargain with them and fight with them and argue with them—whatever is necessary to honor the interest of the people you serve.

The leader himself is led by the people he appears to lead. He is the man who most successfully follows their innermost heartfelt values and convictions.

Japikse: It seems important to me to stress that the genuine leader is led by the *inner* ideals and goals of the people, not just their whims and prejudices.

Churchill: That's true, but I don't want anyone to get the idea that a dreamy-eyed visionary is going to be a good leader. He isn't.

Japikse: No.

Churchill: He may be nothing more than a powder puff in a hurricane. The real leader has the ability to articulate clearly what needs to be done and take appropriate action. He takes on the moral responsibility and the physical problems of seeing a cause through to its logical end. He must be an intensely practical person, a master psychologist who can read human nature accurately and deeply and then work realistically with it.

Leichtman: From what you've been saying, it also seems that the leader would have to know a great deal about civilization and where it is headed. You seem to be thinking in terms of the evolution of civilization itself.

Churchill: Yes—the evolution of civilization in the physical plane and life as it exists on the planet, rather than the more esoteric elements of civilization. Those would be more intuitive realizations.

Leichtman: You had a tremendous grasp of the traditions

of your own country and of history. This seems to be something which is sorely neglected here in America, but then we are still a young country. Would this be one of the ways one might prepare himself to perceive and absorb the philosophical perspective of a group of people, by studying the history of its traditions?

Churchill: Absolutely. A thorough study of history is almost mandatory in being able to understand the tides of civilization and the problems humanity has dealt with. Remember this: many of the problems humanity is dealing with today are merely subproblems of a greater problem. The subproblems have occurred throughout history and will continue to recur until the lessons involved are fully learned.

As you read history, even though you may not understand why all these patterns are occurring, you certainly begin to discern the patterns and problems that have been dealt with before. You also begin to see that they are recurring again—and are being managed now with only slightly more competence than before.

Leichtman: Yes. The nation which most frequently accuses other nations of imperialism is probably the most imperialistic nation the world has known for thousands of years. I'm speaking of Russia, of course. The same problems are being repeated there, with very little indication that anything has been learned.

Churchill: Well, I've always maintained that the people who complain the most are the ones with the most to cover up.

Leichtman: Of course.

Churchill: That's a general rule I firmly held to and used.

Leichtman: Yes. There's one other element of leadership I want to ask you about. You seemed to have an extraordinary ability for seizing opportunity and for right timing. This must be more than just luck. My own observation is that it is partly an intuitive talent to somehow sense the tides of human affairs and time your moves correctly, thereby maximizing the effect you seek.

Churchill: That's not a bad answer to your own question.

[Laughter.]

Japikse: A nicely timed comment, too. *[More laughter.]*

Churchill: Well, this is a part of leadership, as you surmise. In my case, I knew I had something important to accomplish, something I knew to be right. And so I waited for the doors to open, which they did. It's something akin to knowing that you have to dash from one building to another, but it is raining fiercely outside. You don't have to go immediately, however; you can make your trip anytime in the next hour. So you wait for the rain to lighten up or perhaps stop altogether before venturing forth. The poor leader would rush right out in the middle of the downpour and get drenched, but the intelligent one would watch out the window and wait for the rain to stop or slow down, and then make a dash for it, knowing full well that the rain will probably start up again.

In a sense, humanity is influenced by similar tides, too. There are good times and bad times to present ideas, promote programs, and take action. Theoretically, an idea can be presented almost any time, but that is not really the case: there are times when the resistance may be less and the idea will be better received. There are other times when the idea would encounter an uphill battle. It's a question of keeping your goals and ideals in the forefront of your mind, but knowing that there is an ideal time for pursuing them, and waiting for that time.

Leichtman: I'm thinking in particular that recent foreign policy decisions here in the United States have been made with incredibly poor timing, and the consequences have been obvious.

Churchill: Yes. Timing is everything.

Japikse: Suppose someone reading this interview is in a position of leadership and has some of these leadership qualities we've been discussing, but wants to bring them out more fully, in an enlightened way. What kind of advice would you give such a person?

Churchill: I can answer that only in principle.

Japikse: Sure.

Churchill: And we'll have to assume that this person already has a good capacity for organizing his time, gathering the right associates, and acting in a practical manner. If that's the case, then I think the place for such a person to begin would be to identify very clearly his long-range goals of leadership. This is important because all of the actions the leader takes, day by day, and all of the decisions he makes ought to be in harmony with these long-range goals. It is from these long-range goals that the leader draws his power to lead, and is able to see how to align himself with the people he serves. It enables him to identify his adversaries and opposition, too, so that he can be alert to everything that will affect steady progress toward attaining those goals.

My second suggestion, then, would be to learn how to compromise. There's always more we can learn about dealing with other people and bargaining, compromising, and trading favor for favor in order to achieve what you need. I suppose that will look horribly manipulative and expedient in print, but compromise is a very practical talent of leadership. It is absolutely essential for successful leadership. Leadership is not dictatorship, where the leader imposes his will. It is not fanaticism. You have to be able to compromise.

Some people may not understand this, but you also have to identify who's going to be your friend and who's going to be your enemy. You also have to understand that this population of friends and enemies keeps changing—they change the buttons on their lapels from week to week almost. Friends become enemies and enemies become friends. Some will always remain enemies, however, and the good leader must take care never to slip up in a confrontation with them. In some cases, success can only be measured in terms of how well you manage to hold down the opposition. That may sound devious and manipulative, but it's what it takes. You have to be bold and strong and courageous and resourceful, and sometimes a bit Machiavellian.

Japikse: Along that line, it may be useful to remind people that Machiavelli, after all, was a philosopher of the use of power by governments. He was not as devious as some people believe; just frank. It's always been my impression that the label "Machiavellian" has often been used fanatically to discredit certain legitimate uses of power, by making them sound evil or horrible.

Churchill: Well, let me tell you, I can speak as an authority on that. If you ever encounter someone in a large organization or government who has a reputation for being all sweetness and light, you had better believe that he has the most successful public relations people in the world working for him. You can admire him for that, but don't ever be tricked into thinking he really is all sweetness and niceness. No effective leader ever is.

Leichtman: The enlightened and intelligent use of power probably deserves a bit more discussion here. That power is not just abstract, is it? It has been my observation that it becomes quite tangible to the leader, and can have a tremendous impact on his life as well as the work he is trying to perform.

Churchill: It can be quite deceptive, too, and that poses a tremendous problem. The leader does tend to feel it at times, yes. And he sees people being overwhelmed and awed by his presence, but it doesn't occur to him that it's the power that's creating this effect. He thinks it is himself or the trappings of the office, and discounts it and forgets it.

It's easy to assume that you are not being affected by the tremendous power which comes to you. But it is a constant part of your life. Many people surrender power to you just because they are in awe of you—or because they are afraid of you or hate you. That is a form of power, too. Much power comes to you that is unwanted and unnecessary, but it comes anyway and has to be dealt with. And it's terribly deceptive to try to estimate how well you are in charge of all that power and influence. But if you are going to be a leader, you had better learn to handle the power, wanted or unwanted, because unless you are able to deal with it, it can corrupt you and bring out the very worst in you. For example, it will bring out any egotistical elements in your character. You may have been quite able to keep them in check before, but a great deal of power will bring them out and magnify them. And it does all kinds of other things as well.

To some extent, coping with power is a standard risk the leader has to assume; you just have to learn to deal with it as best you can and go on. Most people in leadership positions actually do learn to deal with the power. And you are always surrounded by people who can protect you and calm you down and tell you, not always in words, that you're out of line or overreacting to some problem. The leader tends to have lots of help in that way. *[Laughter.]*

But I suppose you can say it's never enough.

Japikse: What about the constructive side of power? Why is this power necessary?

Churchill: If you are going to have a society functioning at anything other than the caveman stage, power is going to be necessary, because you have to organize the people in the society. As soon as a community of people is formed, you begin to have community problems—a new level of problems which did not exist until you got together. They may be problems of how to handle the community garbage or how to work and live together, but they have to be resolved.

It is the evolution of society which permits the beginning of culture and civilization, but with that comes responsibilities which can only be handled by the community, whether it's maintaining a school system or building roads. There are areas of general interest which only a government can properly handle, whether it's fire and police protection, or the court system, or whatever. Society clearly has a legitimate and important need for effective government. Meeting those needs is the constructive use of power.

The power comes out of the collective needs of the community of people. In this day and age, this is hardly a new concept, but it is wise to remember that it is still an idea much of the world is getting used to. It was the Founding Fathers of the American nation who clearly identified that the right to govern came from the people. American citizens take it for granted, but it was a relatively innovative concept at the time, and is still not fully recognized.

The needs of the people are not the total basis for the power and right to govern, but they do constitute one of the most important sources of that power. It comes from the people. The proof of this statement is that if there is ever any government which for a persistent period of time fails to serve adequately the needs of its people, it will be overthrown, one way or another—voted out of office, or bombed out of office, or whatever the tradition is in that country. *[Laughter.]* The needs of the nation and community must be served. Sometimes it is just a few wealthy citizens, sometimes it is the majority of the people, but the power does come from the people.

Leichtman: I would like to go back to a comment you made a little while ago that sometimes the problems we are dealing with in civilization are really subproblems of ongoing global schemes. What would be some of the dominant patterns that concerned you in your career, and how are they being handled today? I'm referring especially to your fight against dictatorships and tyrannies, economic trends, and so on.

Churchill: The cause we fought for in the second world war has not fully triumphed. The world today is faced with essentially the same problem—the suppression of individual freedoms. Certain political schemes which seek to deny these freedoms are still trying to spread themselves throughout the world and control humanity. This has not changed for thousands of years, and once again the snake is beginning to rise.

Leichtman: What are the real roots of that problem? It is certainly not a problem of bad leadership, is it? Aren't the roots of this inherent in human nature itself and its lack of maturity, its collective pettiness, and its greed?

Churchill: In a sense, yes. The stage humanity is going through can be likened unto an eight-year-old who wants everything for himself and has very little concern for others. As long as he is provided with a candy bar every day and all other things he wants, he will be happy and satisfied. This is why the public is so easily mollified by leaders who promise and attempt to give them everything they want. And we can expect this problem to recur continually until each individual determines for himself that this is not the way it should be.

Leichtman: Is there anything else that can be done, besides waiting for conditions to get hopelessly bad and then have some saint rise out of the masses to lead us back to sanity?

Churchill: Do you have a suggestion? *[Laughter.]*

Leichtman: Actually, I do. In this day and age of easy mass communications, isn't it possible to use the free press and media to warn the world more vigorously of abuses? For instance, as we are talking here, millions of people are being killed for the sake of ideology in Cambodia, and there is a mass exodus of people from Cuba to the United States. I do not believe the propaganda value of these communist atrocities and failures is being fully exploited. There is a tremendous message in these events to warn the free people on this planet about the dangers of certain governmental practices. Shouldn't something more be done to alert the public?

Churchill: Oh, absolutely—but keep in mind the limitations inherent in human nature at this time. The public will take the attitude, "I hear the message, but let's not worry about that, because I'm okay, and until it affects me directly, I don't want to hear about it." Unfortunately, until the very existence and viability of Western civilization is physically threatened, the problems of tyranny, dictatorship, and suppression are merely problems that *other* people have, in faraway, distant countries.

Remember that my efforts to warn Europe about the threat of Germany were ignored for years and years, until it was almost too late—and those were threats which were close at hand, not remote like Cambodia.

Leichtman: Yes, we better not forget that. But it seems to me that our daily lives are more affected by international problems than once was the case. For instance, as we discuss this problem, Iran still holds fifty-two Americans hostage. We are constantly reminded of what the Iranian government has done to our citizens. And then there is the energy crisis: the constant escalation of oil prices affects us all. Whenever we buy gasoline for the car or pay our fuel bill at home, international politics are coming home to roost. So I think there may be more of an awareness of international problems than forty years ago.

Churchill: I appreciate that line of thought, but I ought to remind you that since the Arabs perpetrated the original blackmail, the prices of oil have skyrocketed and yet virtually nothing has occurred. *Virtually nothing!*

Leichtman: That's true.

Churchill: And until the economies of the West are in the throes of a major depression, caused by the inability to get oil, or the high price of oil, the West will continue to pay the price. The leaders will watch their economies get ravished by what amounts to greed and blackmail, but until it causes a major problem—until the factories are closed and the cars can no longer be driven—no major steps will be taken.

It's very clear that they have *not* been taken.

Leichtman: I'd have to say that you are right. I'd also say in the same breath that it is stupid not to appreciate the message we have been receiving now for years of what is going to happen if we fail to act.

Churchill: At the first hint of this problem, the competent leader would have seized upon it and struck the responsive chord of the citizens, saying, "Here is this major problem and here is what we have to do." The oil problem was accurately assessed years and years ago, but unfortunately no leadership emerged to solve it. In fact, what has happened is embarrassing and disgusting; the leaders of the nations being blackmailed have simply maneuvered politically to try to insure a more favorable position with those who are perpetrating the blackmail! That is indicative of a very low state of leadership.

Leichtman: Do you see a parallel between Neville Chamberlain's appeasement of Hitler in 1938 and what we have done regarding the oil crisis in the last five years?

Churchill: Of course.

Leichtman: The same thing—we've sold ourselves out?

Churchill: Absolutely.

Leichtman: Well, where does it all end?

Churchill: My deep sense of what is going to occur is that the problem will be solved. Certainly, the solutions are there—there has been no lack of analysis or consideration of various ways to resolve this particular crisis. The solutions have been vocalized; the real problem is the lack of leadership to coordinate and implement the solutions.

There will be no miracle; we should expect no avatar to come and change water into oil. *[Laughter.]* And there won't be any space ships floating in from Sirius to give us an unlimited supply of energy. *[More laughter.]*

The tide of humanity will flow in the same way it has in the past; nothing will be done until the problem reaches crisis proportions, but I do expect it to be solved.

It's interesting how the word "crisis" has been bantered around in the last twenty years. It has been overused and the public has become jaded. Many people did not believe that the oil crisis which occurred in 1973 was a crisis at all, because it didn't really appear to be one. This is a problem of ineffective communication by leaders. The true leader in 1973 would have said, "We have the potential for a crisis if we do not act now. Here are the steps we must take to prevent possible disaster." Instead, we were deluged with exercises in semantics. Now the potential crisis has become reality, but nothing has been done. Zero!

Leichtman: There are some people who have recommended rather stringent methods of dealing with the crisis, but they get shouted down on the premise that it will be too difficult to bite this particular bullet.

Churchill: That's right: the pocketbooks and well-being of the populace have not yet been pushed up against the wall. It has been difficult but not yet unmanageable.

Leichtman: I sometimes wonder if we are as defenseless against the Arabs as we seem to believe ourselves to be. There should be a little more that we could do.

Churchill: Absolutely. There are a myriad of approaches which could be taken in regards to this problem, and they have been discussed. They are no secret. However, as I said, we are suffering a dearth of leadership in the Western world; our fear and greed have overtaken our confidence in the ability to solve these problems. The only way that the tide can be shifted from fear and greed to confidence in dealing with the problems is by having the problems rammed down our throats.

Leichtman: It sounds as though you would be delighted to do the ramming if you had a physical body to express yourself through. *[Laughter.]*

Churchill: Naturally.

Leichtman: Could we be using our great wealth—our industrial supplies and our agricultural production—as economic weapons to combat the blackmail of the Arabs?

Churchill: I answered that question in a roundabout way. In world politics and in world relationships, as in any relationship, there is a civil and just way to interact with others, and then there is the ancient art of the cheap shot. *[Laughter.]*

Leichtman: We can't behave like the Arabs, can we?

Churchill: It is always preferable to deal with other nations in the proper and gentlemanly way; I infinitely prefer it. But when the other nation begins to resort to cheap shots and low blows as the primary expression of their foreign or economic policy, it is not a good idea to continue presuming that they are acting in a proper and gentlemanly way. Sometimes, the only way to counter their behavior is with a cheap shot or low blow of your own.

It's as though you were dealing with an uncouth individual who will understand you only if you speak the same language that he does. The attempt should be made not to lower your moral persuasion as to the correct way to deal with others, but when it becomes necessary, the leader must not be afraid to speak in the language which will be heard by the other party.

I believe we have reached the point where our gentlemanly conduct is going unnoticed; the normal diplomatic channels which have been used so well among civilized people for so many years are not being honored in certain areas of the world anymore. In certain instances, therefore, a more direct method of communicating should be used.

Leichtman: In other words, we cannot treat s.o.b.'s as though they are gentlemen, because they don't respond.

Churchill: No. You cannot go into the forest of the Amazon and treat the natives as you would a fine old English gentleman.

Leichtman: Parallel to what you've been saying, President Nixon makes the point in his book, *The Real War,* that the real third world war started quite some decades ago as an economic and political war waged by Russia in order to corner the world's energy and mineral resources—energy in the Middle East, minerals in Africa. Is that what is actually happening—that there is a premeditated global plan of conquest in order to bring the West to its knees, because Russia controls energy and minerals?

Churchill: In premise, it is a definite possibility, but I don't think the Russian mind is capable of such a grand scheme— a scheme that was laid out in 1950 with goals to be achieved by 1990, and everything is going according to plan. What is happening is more a step by step proposition—take an inch, then give an inch, then take an inch, and if it ever gets too hot, back off. It is a fair premise that economic interdependence is going to become more and more important. But I don't subscribe to a theory of conspiracy; it is more a case of an unsophisticated loan shark taking advantage of every opening that comes his way. It is not a question so much of having a great deal of intelligence and savvy as it is the ability to sense an opportunity and exploit it to the fullest. Until the West—and the rest of the world—realizes that it should not tempt Russia with these opportunities for the taking, this pattern will continue.

Leichtman: Aren't democracies inherently vulnerable to well-organized, dedicated dictatorships, though? For democratic societies to grow, they must often experience a period of fuzziness or mild chaos, and it seems as though these transition periods of growth are what gives Russia its opportunities.

Churchill: This is true and will always be.

Leichtman: The eternal conflict?

Churchill: Yes.

Leichtman: That's not terribly encouraging.

Churchill: Except that democracies do survive because the people have the freedom to make crucial decisions when faced with crisis. A free people is stronger in crisis than a totalitarian society.

Leichtman: Yes, this is apparent to me, that there is something deep within humanity, individually and collectively, which gets stirred up when freedom is compromised. There are hidden resources of strength that whole nations can draw upon to throw off the shackles of tyrannical despots. If you look for it, you can see signs of it already at work in Russia, Cuba, and certainly Iran. If you just look at the figures of industrial and agricultural productivity in countries run by dictatorships, they fall off tremendously as soon as governmental regimentation is imposed. That indicates to me that there is something inherently incompatible between enforced regimentation and sane, human, and spiritual living.

Churchill: That's true. You can even see that happening in free countries such as Great Britain, Germany, France, and the United States, as governmental regimentation has been imposed. As I've been saying, free peoples will let this sort of thing happen, without acting to stop it, until pushed to the limit.

It's as though you start with a beautiful statue of human individuality called "Freedom," but over a century or so vandals chip away at it, defacing it. The first few chips go relatively unnoticed: the ear is chipped and the nose, too—but it's still a beautiful statue. Our freedoms are still intact. But the chipping continues, and soon a whole finger is gone, and then a few toes and maybe the right ear. And it becomes noticeable and we say, "My, this statue has really been degraded in the last twenty-five years." But we're still busy with other problems, and before we know it, the left arm is completely gone, the statue is tottering, and then we discover that the head has been lopped off and the statue is not even recognizable anymore. That's when the public perks up and says, "Hey, what's happened to our statue? We'd better fix it up and put away the vandals who have been chipping it."

This statue of the free man has existed all throughout history and in every country, but it has continually been chipped away at. It gets repaired periodically, but then the chipping begins again. One can judge the value of the freedoms of humanity at any point in time by counting the number and size of the chips that are scattered around the base of the statue—the more chips, the less freedom.

I'd say we're rapidly approaching the point where we'll have more chips than statue again, and that fairly soon we are going to have another round of "let's fix the statue." Unfortunately, it has to come to the point where it is hard to tell what the statue represents before the need for repairs is seen.

Leichtman: That's a very good analogy—almost Churchillian in scope. *[Guffawing.]*

Churchill: Why, thank you.

Leichtman: You seem to be suggesting that it is not just despots who can tyrannize and blight the freedom of the common person, but that tyranny can arise from within—for example, in the form of a colossal bureaucracy which is determined to make sure that all wealth is shared, sends taxes sky high to support its own growth, and attempts to take over all industry and have it run by committees of bureaucrats.

Churchill: That is a much more subtle form of chipping. The mallet and chisel are put aside and replaced by very sophisticated sanders which still chip away at the statue, but so slowly and quietly that the damage is hard to detect. In fact, it is often claimed that this sanding is required in order to repair the damage done by the chippers, but it's just chipping in a different form.

Leichtman: In terms of the quality of life in England today, it might be said that the socialists and communist-dominated labor unions have succeeded in destroying something valuable that even Hitler was unable to destroy.

Churchill: That is true. Nevertheless, do not discount the will of the British people. They have a tremendous ability to throw off the shackles, as they demonstrated during World War II. It may look like the battle is lost even before they begin to fight, but the inherent desire of the people is to be free.

Leichtman: From what I hear, that is beginning to be seen again in England. At times when the labor leadership calls a strike, the people do not turn out with quite the hysterical loyalty they once demonstrated. And there is a growing rebellion against excessive bureaucratic regulation elsewhere—certainly here in the United States. But it seems as though for every set of regulations the public manages to strike down, ten others are created by bureaucrats.

Churchill: That is a problem, yes.

Japikse: This might be a good place to ask this question. We have seen the emergence of the Common Market in Europe, and we are becoming much more aware of the potential for some form of world government. What is desirable in this direction?

Churchill: It is important to move in the direction of world cooperation, but distinctly undesirable to end up with universal uniformity. Homogenizing the world community of nations is quite undesirable, because the different societies and countries of the earth are at different stages of evolution, as you well know. They serve different purposes, and therefore have different needs, resources, capacities, and cultures. For a long, long time to come, there will be a need for separate countries with distinct identities and societies.

What we are hoping for in world government is to inspire men and women of goodwill throughout the planet to be a source of leavening in their respective countries, creating a climate of goodwill and common sense so that each of these countries will better see the tremendous need for and value of intelligent cooperation. Right now, we have an international climate of selfishness, where countries are more interested in preserving their own advantages and gaining new ones than they are in cooperating with one another toward common goals. This is true even among friendly nations.

Each country will have to do a better job of identifying its national treasures and learning to invest them wisely in the world marketplace, for the benefit not just of itself but the whole planet. This is the next practical step toward world government, and it could be achieved within a couple of generations if people really set their sights on this goal. It is definitely achievable. You would still have individual nations and different groupings of nations allied with one another—and there would still be radically different philosophies of government and economic policy. Yet the cooperation I am speaking of would bind together common needs and interests of nations all over the planet.

This would not be some kind of "United States of the World," with a global parliament or senate and a super prime minister who was chief executive of it all. That kind of governmental structure for the world is out of the question for a very long time to come. In fact, it would be unwieldly and unworkable in anything but a world populated by saints—and if you had that, you wouldn't need the trappings of government.

The difficulty is that today's nations tend to behave as though they were a bunch of petulant five-year-olds playing on the school grounds. And they split up into schoolyard gangs and raid one another, to see who is the most powerful. The seeds in mass consciousness are not really conducive to the growth of this idea of cooperation; they are much more conditioned to produce issues of greed, exploitation, and antagonism. But international cooperation is becoming more and more necessary, and it is a challenge to the men and women of goodwill everywhere to sow the seeds that will enable it to grow.

A hundred years ago, perhaps even seventy-five, the nations of the world could afford to be independent of one another to a large degree; they could be isolated. We can't do that nowadays. For the economy and the technical growth of civilization to unfold properly, there must be an unselfish sharing of economic resources, natural resources, and scientific knowledge. No one can afford to remain isolated and uncooperative.

Personally, however, I am rather pessimistic about this happening. One can speak idealistically, and talk about what is possible and what is necessary—and it is practical for this generation to achieve this type of cooperation—but one must also be realistic. Do I see it happening? No.

Japikse: Many of the people who read this book will indeed be men and women of goodwill. The majority of them won't be in government, but they are citizens of this country or some other one. What can the individual man or woman of goodwill do to become this leavening factor?

Churchill: The vastness of the problem almost guarantees that anything I say will come across as simplistic. But I'll make a few suggestions.

Ideally, it is necessary to have the best possible leaders take charge of the respective governments of the world—not simply people who can smile nicely and win elections, or be devious enough to manipulate their way to the top of the heap, but the most knowledgeable, intelligent, and humanitarian people in each country. That is not something the men and women of goodwill can control or dictate, of course, but there is much that can be done in terms of fostering a climate which encourages the public to elect and appoint competent and humanitarian leaders. Of course, many of the countries which cause serious problems in the world today don't even elect their leaders, so that possible avenue of change is not available. But it is an important ideal to cherish wherever possible.

You almost have to think in terms of working to heal mass

consciousness and civilization. This is where it is up to that relatively small segment of society to recognize that it is their goodwill, their idealism, and their leadership which must be the source of this transformation. It is up to a few people to promote and foster the concepts of goodwill, brotherhood, tolerance, fairness, cooperation, and being a good neighbor. Not everyone has the opportunity to be influential on a worldwide basis, but every single man and woman of goodwill does have the opportunity to promote and foster these ideals in their neighborhoods, communities, businesses, or professions. And if the seeds can be sown at those levels, they will take root and spread on a national and international scale.

That answer may sound vague and unworkable, but it is how society evolves. I suppose some of your readers might be much happier if I were to say that you should get together one percent of the population and train them to pray for a group of saints to arrive on the scene and take over the government of every country. *[Laughter.]* That is not the way society evolves, however. But it is reasonable to challenge men and women of goodwill to work hard to foster the ideals of cooperation, tolerance, and justice as best they can, in their own circles of influence, knowing that in this way, they contribute to a much larger effort.

You must understand that the problems we have in government are really the problems of human nature itself. They are one and the same, and this soon becomes obvious to any real student of history. Just as people have difficulties with their families and neighbors and competitors, and fight and cheat and condemn and curse one another, nations also do the same thing. Nations are just human personalities blown up to the size of several million people. There is always going to be pettiness and conflict among nations, as long as human nature itself is still childish and intolerant and petty.

The ultimate solution, I'm afraid, is thousands of years in the future. But I would not be pessimistic, in spite of that statement. There is much to be done. We each bear a responsibility in contributing to the solution, no matter how many thousands of years it may take.

Leichtman: Well, to put this in perspective, so that you don't sound too pessimistic, would you care to comment a bit about the healthy signs in the world politic? Is anything going right?

Churchill: A lot of things are going right. I'm glad you asked that question because it does give me the opportunity to tell you a little bit more about how progress is made.

Many people, unfortunately, assume that progress would be something like giant beings landing in flying saucers and enforcing peace for us. That is absurd. Others look for some kind of *deus ex machina*—a new-fangled invention that will be a cheap source of energy and food, thus removing the need for international competition. But that is not how progress occurs.

A legitimate sign of progress might be an internal upheaval in a country that has abused human rights and freedom for a long time. That would be a sign that the tyrants of that country are no longer able to get away with as much as they have been. Look at what is happening in China, for example, where they are going through the embarrassment of putting some of their former leaders on trial for what might be termed crimes against their own national spirit. That's a sign that former nonsense is being decried as no longer tolerable, a sign that sanity is beginning to emerge at last.

Throughout the world, human rights are being allowed to a greater degree than before, and that's a sign of progress. The welfare of the people in general is becoming a more legitimate concern; government is operating less and less as a fiefdom of the few.

A rather amusing sign of progress is that some of the countries which have portrayed themselves as "workers' paradises" are experiencing massive strikes by their own unions—demonstrating, of course, that they have been paradises only for the politicians, not the workers. The workers have been enslaved by the system. Now, that kind of internal conflict in countries of that nature is a sign of progress. In one sense, of course, it is a deterioration of order and the systematic flow of government services. But the conflict is indicative of emerging reforms, of something good within human nature crying out for justice and for redress of sins committed by an oppressive government. That's progress. As long as the conflict can be handled in a reasonably orderly way, it is going to be all right.

Of course, some genuine signs of progress are misread by the public and the press. As you hear about violations of human rights, for example, it often sounds as though the world is going to hell, or at least some countries are, but actually conditions are much better than they used to be.

Let me add one thought to what I said earlier to your questions about what people can do to be more of a leavening agent of goodwill. I think it will give this discussion a practical focus.

I would encourage people to think about what it would mean to be a good neighbor. What would they expect of a good neighbor and how can they be more of a good neighbor themselves? They should think that through and identify the qualties it takes to be a good neighbor—such as being more tolerant and tactful and considerate. And then they should try to promote that ideal not just in their neighborhood but in their attitudes toward the people of other nations, and they should encourage others to think and act that way, too. Those are the attitudes which heal conflict between people and nations, and open up communication so that cooperation becomes more possible.

We also need to carefully eliminate from our thinking all tendencies to believe that what we really need is a strong man at the top who will handle all our problems for us and take care of all our needs. That is exactly what we do not need—and I don't just mean here in America or in Great Britain. Even an enlightened dictatorship is not the right thing—not even if the second coming of Christ Himself were the dictator. Genuine growth must come from within human nature itself. It cannot be imposed by decree.

Japikse: Is it not basically true that the only way a dictatorship can arise and survive is because the mass consciousness of the country is looking for a strong leader who will make decisions for them?

Churchill: No, that's not always true, but there is an underlying principle in what you are saying that is relevant. If this were to happen in England or Canada or the United States—which is, of course, unthinkable—yes, it would probably be because the greedy, corrupt, and aggressive elements of society finally elected one of their own. But in other countries, sometimes the political situation becomes so chaotic and confused that the wolves move in and take over. In any society, there are always a few devious, exploitative, criminal types who stand ready to take advantage of the misfortune of others. Sometimes these people rise to power even though they have no right to lead a nation—and yet, there they are. They do not serve the will of the people, they are not wanted, they have not been elected—and yet, there they are.

Nonetheless, what you are saying is basically true—that people pretty much get what they deserve. There are some countries where the people tend to be paranoid, irrational, and fanatical; they spend all their time blaming others for their problems. These countries generally put into power governments and leaders who are of their own type—often dictators. What you end up with is the equivalent of an angry, petulant child leading a whole country. Of course, you've seen this happen very recently in one particular country. The chaos they are experiencing was definitely called forth by the people.

Now that I am on this side of the veil, I can actually see mass consciousness working, and it's most interesting. The collective greed and anger and resentment and prejudice of a nation freely mingle among all the citizens of that country, creating a psychological climate which determines, in effect, what kind of leader will survive. Pollution is always democratic, whether it is chemical pollution of the air or emotional pollution of mass consciousness; it may be terribly unwanted, but it is shared. This is why I say that people tend to get what they deserve. Public attitudes set forth a common baseline of attitude and morality and philosophy which calls forth a certain quality of leader.

Of course, there are always a few nuts who believe that there are just a handful of key people who take advantage of the downtrodden masses, and that if these people could just be killed off, the rest of the world could get back to the business of living and be at peace with one another. This is absolutely untrue.

Japikse: Yes. Well, I asked the question because it seems to me that each individual can make a tremendous contribution by recognizing that to some degree, his or her attitudes help invoke the kind of government the country gets. In this country, for example, many people will rail against the government and complain about it, but at the same time are highly dependent on it. They are contributing to the bigness of government even while protesting it.

Churchill: Yes, it would be very helpful if many, many people would simply go on retreat for awhile and contemplate what they are really contributing to mass consciousness. This is one thing I admire in the Catholic church, by the way. When one of their own kind, a monk or priest or nun, criticizes the church a bit too much, they have a way of encouraging him or her to go into seclusion for meditation and reflection. It's an excellent practice. This is just a passing fantasy, but it might be nice if citizens would encourage one another to go into seclusion from time to time when they get a bit too outspoken or overly critical. It wouldn't do to have a government do this; a democracy depends upon intelligent criticism. It needs intelligent and dedicated public servants goading the government into the proper direction. I would not want to stifle that very vital function, but it is quite a temptation to quietly encourage certain angry protestors, who have a talent only for protesting and nothing else, to take a leave of absence and reflect on their idiocy. *[Laughter.]*

I'm not serious, of course; it's just a passing fantasy.

Japikse: But having suggested it, perhaps it will encourage a few people to do it voluntarily.

Churchill: That would be delightful.

Leichtman: Perhaps it can be recognized as a responsibility of the enlightened citizen, whenever he catches himself polluting mass consciousness.

Churchill: Maybe you can form a nonprofit corporation which will strike medals to be given out to "heroes of silence." *[Laughter.]*

Leichtman: If I might change the subject, I would like to ask something in reference to the British colonial system. In this day and age, of course, the concept of colonial powers and imperialism is a very tarnished one, but in retrospect I suppose there was something of a divine purpose guiding the British colonial system. It certainly provided better government in most of Africa than is the case today, for instance.

Churchill: Well, the colonial system was an excellent way to civilize certain uncivilized areas of the planet—a way of establishing order and providing direction in a number of primitive cultures.

Leichtman: Do you think that many of the developing nations in Africa would be better off if they were still governed by the French or British or Dutch?

Churchill: No. Once it became possible for these people to govern their own countries, it was best to permit them to do so.

Leichtman: Well, how many times are we going to have to watch an Idi Amin come to power?

Churchill: Ah, yes—a swell chap. *[Tittering.]* That's part of self-rule, but even that is preferable to imposing government where it is not desired.

Leichtman: Yes—it won't stick unless the people really want to sustain it.

Churchill: There's a transition period from colonial rule to enlightened self-rule, a time when mass confusion is often the order of things, and the people are trying to figure out how to do it for themselves. This transition is longer or shorter depending on the wisdom of the people and the quality of the leadership which comes to the fore.

Leichtman: Of course, there are some who equate the British colonial system with Russia's effort to "liberate" Afghanistan and the Eastern European countries after World War II.

Churchill: I would never be one to say that there were no excesses during the colonial period. Even the most beneficent of systems and ideals can be warped by greedy people. There certainly were a lot of problems due to some of the people who were placed in the colonies. A system is only as good as the people managing it. There were many instances in which the Englishmen governing a colony became rather despotic, and that was not healthy. It is a good argument against the system, obviously.

After all, even though our reasons for entering into the war with Germany in Europe were valid and correct, history will show that many mistakes were made by our people who were fighting. Many of the military personnel far exceeded the bounds of propriety, as is always the case in wartime. The soldiers of every nation committed excesses, but again, this has to be kept in the perspective of the larger issues involved. The excesses were inexcusable, but the overall effort was noble. Much the same could be said for the British colonial system.

Leichtman: There are those who would say that the colonial system, as established by France and Holland and others, as well as Britain, was really the initial experiment in world government, to be succeeded by other generations of world government.

Churchill: I think it did lay some groundwork for greater cooperation among nations.

Leichtman: How would you contrast colonialism with Soviet imperialism?

Churchill: They are *entirely* different. The growth and health of a society such as Russia cannot rely on the productivity of its own people, because the system itself denies productivity and rewards sloth and bureaucracy. Therefore, in order for the government and economy of Russia to grow, it must continually seek new sources of productivity and people to draw its vitality from. The imperialistic growth of a country such as Russia today is strictly for its own health and its continual need for more factories, more crops, more workers, and more people to exploit. Imperialistic expansion is what maintains the viability of the system.

Leichtman: It's like the Roman Empire in its heyday, then—it could not survive itself, but needed colonies to exploit.

Churchill: Yes.

Leichtman [facetiously]: Of course, Britain didn't gain any particular benefits from its colonial system.

Churchill: Of course it did—but it can also be demonstrated that Britain gave to the colonies as much or more than it took. It did not sap them of their vitality and leave them bone dry. It established thriving societies in Canada, the United States, Australia, New Zealand, and many other places where there had been none, and left them greatly enriched. Britain's motive for colonizing was not that they were necessary for Britain's survival—it was far more subtle, and I think more noble, than that. And the record showed that Britain was willing to free its colonies after a certain point—which the Soviet Union shows no signs of doing.

Japikse: As I recall it, there was a certain minor dispute over freeing the colonies in America. *[Laughter.]*

Churchill: Just a disagreement among friends.

Leichtman: I think it is fair to conclude that while Britain certainly benefited commercially from the colonies, it did bequeath to its colonies a great deal of culture and civilization, and Russia is not doing that. They may send out the Bolshoi Ballet on tour, but I don't see the cultures of Hungary or Romania or East Germany being enriched by Soviet domination.

Churchill: Of course not. And East Germany and Poland and the other Soviet satellites cannot in any way be compared with the jungles of Africa or the wilds of America three hundred years ago. East Germany doesn't need colonizing! In many ways, the cultures of these countries are richer than the culture of the Soviet Union.

Leichtman: I think this is something that the ardent materialists, who look only at health statistics or the gross national product, are missing. The fundamental basis of civilization is not measured in statistics, but in terms of the health of all institutions of civilization.

Churchill: That's very well put.

Leichtman: What I can never understand is why it seems to be the intellectuals in the West who champion Marxism. They seem totally blind to its manifold faults, when applied in actual governments.

Churchill: To the uncritical thinker, Marxism seems very appealing in many ways. In its pure, idealistic form, it is the ultimate in a cooperative and productive society. If that could be implemented, it would be a very pleasurable existence, indeed. Unfortunately, what is always forgotten is that Marxism takes the ultimate in individual freedom to make it work—not the ultimate in totalitarianism. And that has never been tried—only the totalitarian version. For Marxism in its pure form to be a viable form of government, you must have millions of people who are very productive and who feel totally free to collectivize their efforts. By that I mean that the goal of the country is put far above the goals of each individual, *but through an act of free will on the part of each individual,* not through totalitarian enforcement. That's a major distinction, but one that is usually forgotten.

Leichtman: I often notice that when Marxists champion their cause, they always discuss the theoretical aspects of Marxism, never how it is actually applied. But when they discuss capitalism, they never discuss enlightened capitalism or even the modern, democratic versions of capitalism. They talk about the robber barons of the nineteenth century and the abuses of capitalism from earlier times. It's always an unfair comparison: the worst aspects of capitalism from one hundred years ago versus the theoretical joys of Marxism.

Churchill: Yes. I might add here that there is a major difference between working very hard, making a lot of money, and deciding to turn a portion of my income over for the benefit of the whole—which is very noble—and my working very hard, making a lot of money, and having it *taken away* from me for the benefit of the whole.

Leichtman: It's the difference between generosity and theft.

Churchill: Exactly.

Leichtman: I would like to change the subject again, if we may. In reading about you, it intrigued me that you had a very fond admiration for the first Duke of Marlborough. He seemed to be something of a hero and an inspiration to you.

Churchill: He was. I wrote a biography of his life, you know.

Leichtman: Yes. There were even those who said they thought you had some kind of mystical rapport with the duke.

Churchill: I did. He was a fine gentleman and I felt very close to him.

Leichtman: I take it his spirit was around you from time to time?

Churchill: Why, of course. And still is. We're still very close, and stay in communication. He was something of a model for me. I tried to look at life as he did and emulate the ideals he stood for—the way he dealt with problems and opportunities. I spent a good deal of time learning about his life and attitudes.

Leichtman: Do you have any comments about heroism and the need of heroes and ideals in a civilization?

Churchill: Now, that sounds like a question that's just begging to be answered with a quotable quote. *[Laughter.]*

Leichtman: We have the hot line to Bartlett's on hold. *[More laughter.]*

Churchill: Well, let me say this. The concept of heroes has been tarnished and debased in this era of fatuous populism.

Leichtman: That's not bad. *[Laughter.]*

Churchill: Well, what did you expect of me?

Leichtman: I'm sorry, go on.

Churchill: Nevertheless, every society needs its heroes.

Every age needs its heroes. We need noble examples to aspire to, models of good citizenship to emulate. We need examples of kindness, honesty, dignity, and talent. The average human being is not sufficiently creative to find his or her own genius easily, but can recognize it in others, and be inspired by it. The average person does have the ability to recognize talent and nobility in others and learn from it.

Unfortunately, having recognized genius, the average person often resents it and is jealous of it. But decent people will respond well to a good example. In fact, the way in which a society treats its heroes and heroines is virtually an index to the health of that society. I'm talking about legitimate heroes now, not some rock and roll figure or sports superstar. To me, a hero is someone who makes a lasting and enduring contribution to civilization—a contribution which enriches life and helps people aspire to something better.

This should be respected and held up as a great example. These people do exist, and if they were more clearly recognized and honored in the news media and books, we would have a healthier society. We would have a better government, too. This is one of the problems of government today, after all. The common man is made to be the hero—but that doesn't give the public anything to aspire to. It strips society of one of its natural channels for regeneration and renewal.

It must be remembered that any productive society is a group of individuals who have their own motivations and talents and quirks, and these must be permitted to flourish. I might even say that they ought to be *encouraged;* it's a mistaken notion that individuality must be subjugated to the good of the whole. I would propose the exact opposite: that individuality must be emphasized and promoted for the good of the whole.

The proper recognition and appreciation of heroes is an excellent way to encourage individuality, and give it an enlightened focus.

Leichtman: But some people might think you are promoting elitism, whereas a democracy should be promoting equality.

Churchill: It should guarantee equality of opportunity—but that is a great deal different than enforcing equality of thought and attitude, where no one is permitted or encouraged to rise above a certain plateau. It is in fact a sign of decline in a society when individuality is subjugated in the name of "the good of the whole."

Leichtman: Well, in concert with your continued association with the first Duke of Marlborough, I take it there must be a large group of enlightened individuals who continue to work in spirit to oversee the evolution of the British government.

Churchill: Of course. And, I might add, that is true for most of the major governments of the world.

Leichtman: Yes, I'm certainly aware that it is true for the United States. I take it you continue to have an avid interest in the British Empire.

Churchill: Of course.

Leichtman: Since England's system is slightly different than what we have here, let me ask you this. What role do ex-monarchs play in helping the destiny of the nation unfold once they are in spirit?

Churchill: It's more of a role of helping to set the spiritual tone of the country than it is a role in giving direct governmental advice. They are involved in giving direction and definition to certain subtle energies, which influence the country, rather than in knocking the chancellor of the exchequer over the head to make him pay attention.

Leichtman: When I've looked into this psychically, I have been impressed that the ancient concept of the divine right to rule of a king or queen had a very sound basis to it. It is apparent to me that some of the spiritual power of the national spirit definitely is held by and distributed by the monarch.

Churchill: Absolutely.

Leichtman: And that this really is one of the ideal forms of government which could exist in the far, far distant future—a monarchy which literally does rule by divine right, meaning that the king or queen is an adept who is highly inspired in directing the nation.

Churchill: Yes.

Leichtman: I take it, then, that you would consider the British monarchy as an institution which deserves to continue.

Churchill: Absolutely—and I think it will. The spiritual will of the English people is focused through the monarchy. In the United States, that energy is focused through the Presidency, but there can be something of a problem there. In recent history, you have had such a rapid turnover in the Presidency that it is very difficult to maintain any sense of tradition in the focusing of the spiritual will. That is an advantage of a constitutional monarchy.

Leichtman: The monarch focuses the will of the national spirit?

Churchill: Yes.

Leichtman: Can you comment some more about the national spirit of Great Britain? How much were you influenced by this national spirit while you were leading Britain? Were you aware of it?

Churchill: That is a very complex question. Let me answer it in this way.

All major nations do have the semblance of an inner spirit, although it is a little too simplistic just to compare it to the spirit of an individual human being. The national spirit comprises, in part, the collective spiritual essence of all of its citizens, but it also consists of many other elements. There is, for example, a kind of miniature hierarchy of very enlightened people in spirit who seek to guide the government in an enlightened way. This is where the mystical fellowship of men and women of goodwill genuinely has its existence. These people are very much concerned with and committed to promoting the ideals of good government; they actually have meetings and discussions—very intense and practical reviews of the problems of the day, the trends of the future, and plans for working out the ideal course of growth for the nation.

But I don't want to leave the impression that the national spirit is just a collection of spirits which meets in council chambers. There are also aspects of the national spirit which are quite abstract, and intertwined with other national spirits. At a very high level, it could be said that there is, already, a semblance of a real world government. One might even boldly make the statement that the countries of the earth are truly "one nation under God." This is, of course, a God of light and love—not a Christian God or Moslem God or Hindu God, but the ultimate authority that we all draw our life and spirit from. And, I might add, the ultimate authority behind the ideals of any government.

The spirit of any nation therefore influences the fellowship of men and women of goodwill in spirit, who in turn seek to influence the men and women of goodwill in physical incarnation and advise the government of the country.

Was I aware of this influence during my physical lifetime? I must answer that "yes" and "no." At a very young age, I knew I had a destiny to serve in my country's government. During World War I, for example, it became clear to me that this role was going to become very important. As a student of history, I could see a polarization of national interests occurring which would once again spark a major conflict; I knew there was genuine evil lurking in human nature which would pose a constant and terrible danger to us until it was thoroughly defeated and the door shut upon it. We have made great strides toward this goal, although the battle does continue in many fronts and in new areas. But I do not think we will ever see fascism recur as it flourished in the Thirties and Forties in Western Europe.

I knew these things, and responded to them, but it would not be fair to say that I was consciously aware of the abstract and spiritual force of the national spirit while I was alive. I was aware of the power, but I never tried to identify it. I always assumed it was my own guidance and intuition. After all, at a very early age I developed a good track record for knowing when to strike, what to say, and how to get things done. By the time of the first world war, I was in full stride. I did sense guidance, but I assumed it was my own common sense and good judgment. Of course, now I know differently, but it's probably just as well that I didn't know this then. There are only a few people who can tolerate hearing voices and speaking with spirits. Most people can't be bothered with it.

Leichtman: Yes. I want to ask about your personal relationship with Marshal Stalin. You seemed to get along reasonably well for people who ordinarily would have been perpetual enemies.

Churchill: I would say that we had a deep respect for each other's talents. Stalin was a brilliant man in his own way, but he was also representative of something I totally abhorred. I respected his talent of leadership, but I abhorred the methods he chose to use to accomplish his goals. He was able to wield tremendous power, and our relationship was based on a respect for that power. I would continually remark to him that he was on the wrong side of the fence, that he was misusing his power and that some day he would regret the positions he took. He would simply laugh and proceed to tell me basically the same thing—that I would be better off working with him than in spite of him.

Leichtman: I remember reading that following the end of overt hostilities in the second world war, and even before then, you were encouraging America and France to advance as far and as deeply as possible into Eastern Europe so that the Allies would be occupying those territories, not the Russian troops. Apparently you were not terribly successful in pushing the Americans to go along with this, but you wished to maintain the Allied occupation as long as possible to keep Stalin out of those countries.

Churchill: Yes.

Leichtman: What fell apart there?

Churchill: Well, the Russians were our allies against Hitler, and a sort of camaraderie developed, which led some people to believe that this experience of fighting Hitler would bind us together in cooperation forever. There was the belief that we had trusted each other in the united effort against Germany and there was no reason why we couldn't trust Russia now. That was an emotional assessment of the situation, of course, rather than a hard cold look at the facts and what Stalin and Russia stood for. I knew what tactics they used and it seemed very logical to me that with all of our forces mobilized, as they were, we should have cleaned up the whole area right away and not fooled around trying to accommodate territorial divisions.

Instead, we were faced with the checkerboard dividing of Europe, which I found very distasteful, because we were allowing a very malignant force, however quiet at the moment, to entrench itself.

Leichtman: Would there have been a realistic chance to have had free elections and democratic governments in Poland, Czechoslovakia, Romania, and Hungary?

Churchill: I believe so. The Allied forces could have gone straight through virtually as far as they would have wanted to, but war weariness and the desire to accommodate got to such a point that everyone said, "Well, we've come this far together so let's just stop and hope that everything will work out."

Leichtman: Even today, it's not quite clear how everything was decided at the Tehran and Yalta meetings. One gets the impression that the spheres of influence of postwar Europe were pretty well worked out in advance.

Churchill: That is true.

Leichtman: And that Truman very much insisted on honoring those agreements while you attempted to persuade him to push forward and take as much territory as possible before hostilities stopped and then not give it to the Russians.

Churchill: That is right—for precisely the reasons I outlined. The Americans were very much war weary, and that is generally a very good trait in a world that can be so volatile. The Americans take an awful lot of pushing before they'll commit themselves to a war effort, and even when they do commit, it may be a half-hearted commitment until they realize they had better do something because the situation is rapidly deteriorating. This was one of my major frustrations in dealing with the Americans. As a people, they do not want to exercise or impose their will on others; they have a genuine desire to let things be. As a result, they often react too softly in counteracting those forces which would want to impose rule.

Leichtman: I'm afraid the accusation is true. Well, would you care to comment on where this all ends? Who will be pushing America in the future—the underdeveloped countries of the Third World? The Soviet Union? Are we headed for another shootout as we had in the second world war?

Churchill: It's possible, but I think the confrontation will occur in internal struggles in various countries, rather than a military shootout. It's very possible that the confrontations will continue and that the Soviet Union will continue to find the need to extract the vitality of an ever-greater number of people. And it is clear that military response to that kind of expansionism is going to be less and less viable—fortunately or unfortunately, depending on your point of view.

It is very difficult to impose freedom militarily. Philosophically, it is hard to defend the invasion of another country in the name of freedom, even if the people in that country are being suppressed by a system of government which does not permit human freedom. Over the next few centuries, therefore, the world is going to become much more aware that freedom has to be established from within. It cannot be imposed from without. Those who have free governments cannot expect to impose a democratic system on a people.

However, that is not to say that those who live in free societies do not have a duty to come to the aid of those whose freedoms are in jeopardy, because of the expansion of those who would oppress them. Freedom can be taken away by force, even if it cannot be given by force.

Leichtman: Some people, of course, seem to be eager to surrender to new tyrants. The Iranians, for example, seem to love self-destruction; as soon as they gained their freedom, they threw it away.

Churchill: It certainly does not make much sense to replace one dictator with an even more repressive one.

Leichtman: I sometimes think the ultimate tyrant is stupidity.

Churchill: Yes.

Leichtman: And that's a very difficult disease to eradicate.

Churchill: It does not take much investigation to realize that ill-informed people are often likely to vote in incompetent leaders. It takes a very intelligent populace to make correct decisions. In a sense, therefore, the best safeguard of freedom is to educate the public as fully as possible and encourage them to think for themselves, as individuals. The public must be fully versed in the issues and the problems of the day and fully capable of recognizing long-term versus short-term benefits of programs and solutions.

Of course, that's the ideal—not the reality.

Leichtman: Let me ask about another prominent individual you worked with, our American President at that time, Franklin Roosevelt. You seemed to get along together extremely well—I guess for obvious reasons. It seems that America was extremely fortunate to have such an able leader in a time of crisis. But your own personal rapport and respect for each other seemed to facilitate the cooperation of the two nations during the war. Would this have been possible with any American President, or was there something unique about Roosevelt which really made him the man of the hour, both for America and the Allied nations?

Churchill: I don't believe there would have been many individuals who could have made the decisions he made, and rallied America to support them. He had to be cajoled—as any American has to be cajoled—to support us in the days before America entered the war; I was very frustrated throughout that time by the inaction and lack of desire of America to become involved. However, once we began to understand each other and the nature of what was occurring in the world, we were able to unite and work very closely together. He was a very intelligent individual and able to grasp issues clearly. He's here with me today, in fact. Would you like to talk with him?

Leichtman: Of course. We'd be honored.

Churchill: Then I will defer to my good friend on the left here. *[The spirit of Churchill then withdrew from control of the medium, and the spirit of Franklin Delano Roosevelt entered.]*

Roosevelt: So, you've had to sit here and listen to the old goat dissertate for a couple of hours on all of his worldly wisdom, huh? *[Laughter.]*

Leichtman: Dearly so.

Roosevelt: That's fine. I love to listen myself.

Leichtman: He has a marvelous gift for conversation and writing.

Roosevelt: Yes, we had some wonderful times sitting around and—

Leichtman: I understand you both just loved to talk but neither one of you cared to listen all that much. *[Laughter.]*

Roosevelt: That's right.

Leichtman: Did you bore one another? *[More laughter.]*

Roosevelt: Of course we did. We would expound philosophically for a good many hours. Well, I don't have a statement to make. I don't even know why I am here. I thought this was Winston's show. Why am I here? *[Laughter.]*

Leichtman: We invoked you.

Roosevelt: I see. I always wondered how that worked.

Leichtman: Well, now that you are here, let me ask you a few questions. What had you hoped for as the outcome of World War II?

Roosevelt: Of course, we didn't really want to get into that war in the first place. But after Pearl Harbor, we had to.

Leichtman: In retrospect, wasn't it absolutely essential?

Roosevelt: Yes. Of course, there have been many theories advanced about why this and that happened; some people believe I secretly called up the Japanese and told them to bomb Pearl Harbor so we could get into the war.

Leichtman [sarcastically]: You mean you didn't?

[Laughter.]

Roosevelt: No, I did not. And there are those who say the war was created to pull us out of the economic nightmare of the Depression, and that is not true either. Our unwillingness to enter the war should be evidence of that.

Leichtman: Sure.

Roosevelt: It is absurd to believe that the only way to solve the economic cycles of the Western world is to create a war here and there.

Leichtman: Do I dare ask you questions about current events?

Roosevelt: Why, sure. I can always refuse to answer.

[Laughter.]

Leichtman: How do you see the current leadership in the United States? If you were to issue a report card on how well we are doing domestically and in foreign affairs here in 1980, what grade would you give?

Roosevelt [pausing]: Probably either a D or an F. I'd probably be nice and give a D but ask for some special after-school work, rather than just give an F and kick the old boys out. But I am very concerned.

One of the traditional features of the American way of government which I have always believed in is the idea that you must learn to roll with the punches and come up with new ideas. You should deal with new situations with something other than old ideas, no matter how good the old ideas were when they were new ideas.

It's being said that the economic policies of my administration have led to the economic disaster of today—that all of the programs we developed in order to deal with the economic situation of that time are the cause of today's problems. And it is said that if it were not for old FDR and the New Deal, we would have a free economy and the world would be much better off.

That's just stupidity and shortsightedness. We dealt with the problems of our time with remedies we thought would work—but that does not mean that those particular policies ought to be enshrined for all time. And it does not mean that the economic and foreign policies that we pursued in my administration are viable today. But there are those who still do believe that those policies *are* viable, and *that's the problem.*

Leichtman: Yes, there are many people who still think that you solve problems by throwing money at them and creating a new bureaucracy. Well, what would you suggest? If you could advise the leaders of America today, what would you say?

Roosevelt: Do you want me to write a whole book, or what? *[Laughter.]* Give me a subject.

Leichtman: What about—

Roosevelt: Never mind—I've got a subject. *[More laughter.]* The economic situation today demands new solutions—creative solutions. I would be the first to admit that the current situation is caused by excesses in government policy—and that these excesses began as a result of some of the policies I instituted. But that does not mean that if I were sitting in the Oval Office today I wouldn't be doing something else. I would be dismantling many of those programs—and would have done so long ago. I would not have let them go on for this long.

Leichtman: Is it really possible in this day and age, given our political climate, for someone to dismantle a governmental agency?

Roosevelt: It is not only possible, but it should be done.

Leichtman: It would be possible?

Roosevelt: Sure. You would have to be sneaky about it, but you could probably do it.

Leichtman: It's very difficult to dismantle bureaucracies and fire bureaucrats.

Roosevelt: Nonsense—you just start sending out pink slips and make no big deal about it. *[Laughter.]* I'm just kidding, of course, but there are ways of dealing with government. But I will tell you this: the person who is going to change these things is not going to ride in on a wave of election hysteria requesting that the government be dismantled.

Leichtman: No.

Roosevelt: He will be elected because of his ability to make decisions. And then, once he is in office, he will make the decision to dismantle the excesses of government.

Leichtman: That leads to another question. Do you think there is a need for reforms in the ways we elect the President? The primary system seems to lead to the selection of candidates who know how to handle the media and project a good television image as a paternalistic grandfather who smiles very sweetly, instead of someone who is competent. Is there something hideously wrong with our electoral system?

Roosevelt: No—it's the voters, not the system.

Leichtman: The blame keeps coming back to us. *[Laughter.]* Phooey.

Roosevelt: It isn't the system, it's the electorate. If the people were able to grasp the fact that they are quickening their own economic and social demise by electing such incompetents to office, they would choose better candidates.

Leichtman: I take it, then, that we are not really deficient in leadership talent—it's just that the good leaders can't get elected in this day and age.

Roosevelt: That is very true.

Leichtman: How can we turn this around?

Roosevelt: I suspect that very shortly, within the next decade or two, someone very intelligent and strong will inadvertently happen to be elected.

Leichtman: Do you mean it might be a very intelligent vice-president who succeeds the usual dummy President?

Roosevelt: Or it may be a very intelligent person who gets elected by pretending to be the usual dummy.

Leichtman: A clever disguise of mediocrity?

Roosevelt: Yes.

Leichtman: Always the perfect disguise.

Roosevelt: Well, I don't have much more to say. I just

wanted to stop by and express my admiration for Winston.

Leichtman: You were both very remarkable people. And I must say that the exuberance of both of you is still quite apparent.

Roosevelt: We'll be back, someday, somewhere.

Leichtman: Very good.

Roosevelt: You'll be strolling along somewhere, and there we'll be. *[Laughter.]*

[Roosevelt's spirit then withdrew from the body of the medium, and the spirit of Sir Winston Churchill returned.]

Churchill: Well, I thought he would never relent. *[Laughter.]* What else do you wish to speak about?

Japikse: How about the separation of church and state?

Churchill: Oh, you Americans are hysterical about that subject. *[Laughter.]*

Japikse: Is it healthy?

Churchill: Originally, it was. Your Founding Fathers were very concerned about the misuse of power which occurred during the Middle Ages and the Renaissance, when the Church got caught up in its earthly powers and authority and was too much of an influence on governments. Government needed to free itself from this kind of ecclesiastical authority. And so your Founding Fathers wanted to send all the churches a message: stick to your religious duties and leave government to us.

However, the separation of church and state is now being used to promote atheist rights, and that was not the original intent.

There's a consultation going on up here. Wait a minute.

Leichtman: All right.

Churchill: One of the problems with many governments in the world today is that they are not sufficiently spiritual. The real solution to the problem of the separation of church and state is to realize that there is a difference between our collective spiritual interests and needs versus religion itself. Governments need to be spiritual and identified with humanitarian values, but at the same time independent of religious institutions.

It would be very undesirable to have a constitutional amendment which would cut off the humanitarian influence of spiritual values in government. There is no reason to take the separation of church and state that far.

Indeed, in some countries it is probably appropriate to have one particular religion supported by the government, although obviously not in America. It depends on the people being governed. Unfortunately, when one religion is the official religion, the most fanatical and obnoxious elements of that religion tend to become too strong an influence. And whenever the religious leaders make a political statement, they hide behind God, saying: "God wants us to do this and will condemn you if you don't go along with it." They use religion to intimidate, and that is bad. Each nation and community needs to make the decision about separation of church and state for itself. There is no blanket statement I can make that would be right for all the people in all countries.

Leichtman: One thing I'm curious about: what has happened to Hitler since he died?

Churchill: I don't know where in hell he is. *[Laughter.]* I don't see him around, I can tell you that. And I'm not really interested.

Leichtman: All right. How about yourself? How do you keep yourself busy without a nation to run or books to write?

Churchill: I'm thoroughly enjoying myself. As I mentioned earlier, I continue to be involved in influencing the government of the country that was so dear to me and so very kind to me. I passionately enjoyed my work as a member of Parliament and as Prime Minister, and that line of work continues to interest me. I am still involved in it. I am still an ardent student of civilization and the history of the English-speaking peoples, too.

Leichtman: That sounds like a plug.

Churchill: I guess I did write a few volumes under that title.

Leichtman: Have you figured out a way to take your royalties with you? *[Laughter.]*

Churchill: There's a certain coin of the realm up here. Anyway, I have the opportunity to study and encourage a few people from time to time. My life and work now is in many ways an extension of those very things which interested me in my lifetime as Winston Churchill.

Japikse: I have a question to test your chauvinism. What do you think of the fact that there is now a woman filling your shoes in Number 10 Downing Street?

Churchill: I think it's wonderful. England, by the way, has often been ahead of America in its attitudes about women. We have had a number of women monarchs, after all. Some of our best monarchs were queens—Queen Elizabeth, Queen Victoria.

It's very fitting that Mrs. Thatcher should be prime minister. There are many good people who could head the government of England, but she is doing a pretty good job, considering the horrendous problems that England is facing now. I'll tell you—sometimes the woman's touch can be very effective in politics, if it's the right woman. If a woman hides behind tears and whimpering and sweetness, that is disastrous. But if she uses her natural talents for intuition and forthrightness and genuine concern for the welfare of the people, those are all attributes of a good leader. Women sometimes have extraordinary talent in those areas.

Given my concern for leadership and the welfare of the nation, it should be obvious that I don't care who the leader is, as long as the person has the talent, power, and maturity to do the job well. It doesn't matter whether it's a man, a woman, or a horse. *[Laughter.]* Leadership talent has nothing to do with sex, skin color, or physical appearance. It's the quality of mind and skill that counts.

Leichtman: I think we're about out of questions. Do you have any concluding remarks?

Churchill: A good orator always has a summation.

[Laughter.]

Leichtman: Of course.

Churchill: Let me say that the fight is not over. The war against oppression is continuing—and in fact is heating up as we move away from our last major confrontation. The fight continues; the ideals we stand for and have fought for still need to be honored and defended. To my mind, they are the only ideals worth living and fighting for, but we are still dealing with those who seek to suppress them. So the fight must go on and we must not give up. It may be a helluva fight, but in the end, the ideals are strong enough to prevail. So we must prevail in our efforts.

We cannot take this for granted. Every intelligent person has an obligation to observe human nature and study the lessons of history. It is very popular to reduce history to simplistic platitudes, but that does not serve; it leads to disaster. I would even go so far as to say that a knowledge of human nature and history is greater than the ability to read or write. Ignorance of any kind is a horrible affliction, but ignorance of human nature and history is a terrible neglect of our duties to ourself, our spirit, and our nation.

The more we are informed, the more we can participate meaningfully in our society, whether it's in our attitude toward family and work, or in the actual activity of voting for a member of Parliament or Congress.

Japikse: Can I jump in with one more question? As you were just talking about history, it occurred to me that it might be useful if you could expand on the usual definition of history. Most people think of it just in terms of memorizing dates and events and the driest of—

Churchill: Oh, that's just trivia the history teachers have become obsessed with.

Japikse: Yes. I was thinking we really have to look at the mythical traditions, the cultural traditions, and the traditions of civilization before we understand history, and there would seem to be a tremendous value to a leader or diplomat or anyone trying to be a good citizen to appreciate history in this way—as the rich tradition of any group of people.

Churchill: Well, just as individuals have personalities, countries do, too. A nation builds up a set of traditions—and traditional likes and dislikes, needs and interests—which is unique, almost like an individual personality. But the problems of national character are infinitely more complex and deeper than an individual's, and to properly understand them, they must be traced back over a period of many centuries. This is the value of history, to go back in time and discover what moved the people, what the people accomplished—artistically, scientifically, and politically—what the common people were proud of, and what they despised. And as you discover this for every epoch of a nation's history, you do learn about that nation's character. It tells you something about what that people will support or despise politically; it tells you something about their attitudes toward freedom and dictators—just about everything we've been discussing today.

I was aware of this character, and found it to be one of the sources of my power. Because I understood British history, I always had great faith in the British people and their undying loyalty to the preservation of their dignity and traditions. This was not blind faith; it was faith based on historical knowledge. It was faith based on power, and it gave me great power to act in moments of grave crisis. I never doubted that the British people would fight on the beaches if necessary to defend their island from invasion, because this is a deep, ingrained habit in the British people.

A good leader senses these deep levels of conviction in his people and draws power from them. These undercurrents of national character are really a vast reservoir of power which tempers the quick fads of interest which come and go; they form the basis for stable policy in government. Any leader who seeks to run contrary to this deeper sense of values and concerns will not survive in a democracy for very long—or even in a dictatorship, for that matter.

Japikse: Events in China would seem to confirm that idea.

Churchill: This is my point: the power to govern comes

from the will of the people—not their current opinions and desires, but their ongoing sense of what they will do. The national character, really. Anyone who does not come to grips with this and seek to understand it is not going to be a very effective leader. Unfortunately, there are far too many people who try to interpret this will at too superficial a level. They ignore history and read just the current desires and values of the people—and end up hearing only the more vocal elements of society. This can lead to serious mistakes. Much of the growth of the so-called "welfare state" is the result of this type of superficial thinking. The motives for welfare are often of the highest level of compassion, but many of the people who advocate these programs do not take the time to read the will of the people deeply enough. They do not understand that their pride will eventually be hurt by welfare programs, and that they actually do honor the will-to-achieve. The student of history would develop programs which would stimulate that will-to-achieve, not just welfare, but this lesson has usually been missed.

When one has the ability to stand back and look at the great panorama of history—something I can now do from a far more penetrating perspective than before—one can see that there *are* cycles and tides in the affairs of men and nations. These tides encourage discipline and austerity and then encourage relaxation and self-indulgence. We will always have these cycles, because they lead to healthy growth. We develop self-reliance and skill during times of austerity but tend to lose our collective sense of humor and willingness to make new, bold changes. During easy times, we release our charm and dignity and become more creative, but we also let responsibilities lapse and neglect the future.

A secret of effective leadership is to recognize these cycles in human nature and society and work realistically to harness them. This is not opportunism, but a pragmatic view of molding and focusing the patterns of destiny for a nation.

In practice, of course, the leader often has to cope with

events as they arise. He might see a nasty trend brewing but be powerless to stop it until the mood of the people allowed him to act. I certainly experienced that in my life. There are firm limits on what any leader can accomplish. At best, you can have a long-range grasp of the character of the people you lead, a sense of their traditions and destiny, and the boldness to nudge the momentum of events one way or another at the proper time.

It is folly to think that the leader of any democracy has great power in his own right. There may be the illusion that you can punch buttons and call up people, who will rush to do your bidding, but that tends to have little impact in the Parliament or the Congress—or with the people. The true leader isn't interested in telling people what to do anyway, but in cultivating a consensus which reflects the national character and helps it to flower in a civilized way, rather than in the midst of chaos and conflict. This is no simple task, because what is right for the national character is often unacceptable to the legislature. But a good leader is something like an enlightened parent to the nation.

When its mood is down, he cheers them up. When they avoid their duty, he chastizes them gently. Of course, just as indulgent parents can spoil the child, indulgent leaders can spoil the public with favors and weaken their will-to-achieve. We have seen too much of this in recent decades on both sides of the Atlantic. And just as good parents must often compromise to make headway with their children, political leaders must compromise constantly.

The good leader serves as a conscience for the people and warns them of the consequences of their demands and behavior. He must be the mouthpiece of the public will, not the tail which drags along behind everything else.

These qualities build slowly in the leader, but eventually, if he comes to grips with the power of the national character, he becomes aware of a greater sense of destiny—a greater purpose being served by this act or that veto. It is a subtle thing which wells up from deep within as an inner knowing that a certain course of action will be far more appropriate than all the others.

And that, my friends, is why I believe a study of history is of such importance to the leader. It reveals the sources of power, and eventually leads one to discover the central and unifying power that underlies all enlightened decisions of government.

And on that note, I think we can conclude.

Leichtman: Very good. Thank you for coming.

Churchill: It was my pleasure.

GLOSSARY

ADEPT: One who is skilled in a specific talent. Esoterically, an adept has mastered the skills of soul consciousness.

ANGEL: An entity belonging to the angelic or devic kingdom. Angels are not discarnate humans and have never been humans—they are part of a separate kingdom of life and have their own function and evolution. The angelic kingdom includes nature spirits, angels, and archangels.

ARCHETYPE: A basic pattern or ideal of creation. Archetypes are found at the abstract levels of the mental plane and are used by the soul as it creates the personality, its destiny, and its behavior. When Jung uses the word, however, it has a special meaning—it refers to any symbol, image, or force that is common to large numbers of people. A *Jungian archetype* is therefore a product of the collective unconscious of humanity, while a *divine archetype* is a product of the mind of God.

ASANA: A Sanskrit term meaning "posture" or "sitting quietly." In hatha yoga, the word refers to a set of complex physical postures which are taught for the purpose of integrating subtle energies into the physical body. Some people also use these asanas as part of their spiritual exercises. True asanas are not physical, however, but are a series of mental and emotional exercises designed to promote the ideal "posture" of thought and feeling as a means of developing harmony of spirit and personality.

ASHRAM: A place for learning the lessons of spiritual unfoldment. Esoterically, the word is used to refer to a group dedicated to common forms of spiritual service. Such a group would be composed of both incarnate and discarnate members.

ASPIRANT: One who actively seeks to be more attuned

to the inner life of spirit, and better able to express it in his or her daily circumstances.

ASSOCIATIVE MECHANISM: A principle of the mind, operating largely at subconscious and unconscious levels, which enables us to relate the contents of relevant memories, feelings, and speculations to our conscious focus of attention. A healthy associative mechanism is of great importance in maintaining the skills and capacities of memory and the ability to understand what we read and observe.

ASTRAL PLANE: The plane of the emotions and desires. The astral plane is an inner world made of matter that is more subtle than physical substance, yet interpenetrates all physical substance. It is teeming with life of its own.

BROTHERHOOD: The bond in consciousness that links all human beings together. Brotherhood is not an utopian fantasy, but an actual *fact*—a living presence of common purpose, shared experience, and loving potential. It is the divine ideal for all community and spiritual activity, and ought therefore to be studied and honored by all leaders, all aspirants.

BUDDHIC: Pertaining to the principle of "buddhi" or "realization." The buddhic plane is the plane of spiritual intuition, an inner world of existence which is more subtle than the physical, astral, or mental planes, yet interpenetrates the substance of those planes. A human being must be able to focus in the light of his own soul to operate consciously at the buddhic level, as the human personality is not equipped with senses able to perceive buddhic substance.

CHAKRA: A Sanskrit word meaning "wheel," a poetic allusion to the general shape of major and minor focal points of energy within the threefold human aura.

In Western occultism, chakras are often called "force centers." There are seven major chakras and scores of lesser ones in each of the subtle bodies. The science of how human energies circulate throughout these chakras—and their impact on human expression—is a complex one.

CLAIRVOYANCE: The capacity to see or know

beyond the limits of the physical senses. There are many degrees of clairvoyance, allowing the clairvoyant to comprehend forces, beings, and objects of the inner worlds normally invisible to the average person.

DESTINY: The combined plans and commitments that have been made by the innermost spirit of an individual or a group for its future. A destiny would include plans for creative fulfillment, achieving enlightenment, and the events of life. It is not imposed from without—it is formulated by spirit.

DHARMA: A Sanskrit word that can be translated as "rightness." Dharma is the right purpose of any group or individual. In simplest terms, it is our duty to express our talents and human potential, as opposed to *karma,* which is our duty to learn.

ENERGY: Conventionally, the capacity of a physical system for doing mechanical work. Occultly, however, energy is not considered to be a capacity originating in any physical system. Energy is an impulse of life which exists independently of physical matter. As it interacts with physical matter, it creates and animates and sustains physical forms. There are many different expressions of energy through form, and many different levels of quality and dimension among energies. The types of energy which have been observed and catalogued by science to date are only a tiny fraction of the energies of life.

ENLIGHTENMENT: Focused in the light of the soul.

ESOTERIC: An adjective which refers to knowledge of the inner worlds and inner life. In this book, it is used to refer to the knowledge of spirit—and to the body of teachings known as the Ancient Wisdom.

EVIL: Anything which retards the evolution of human consciousness. Contrary to public opinion, evil is not measured by likes and dislikes. Unpleasant events often help us evolve, and are therefore benevolent. The indulgences one person gives another, by contrast, may be quite pleasant, but distinctly harmful.

FAITH: The attitude that attunes the personality to the

wisdom, love, and power of the inner spirit. Enlightened faith motivates us to aspire to higher expressions of our humanity and intelligence, to serve God, and to fulfill our destiny. It creates a channel for prayer, blessing, and creativity.

FAKIR: A Moslem or Hindu holy man or ascetic.

FIFTH DIMENSION: A realm of existence in which there can be five different planes of movement from a single point, each of those planes being separated by ninety degrees or its abstract equivalent. All physical solids are part of this larger, fifth-dimensional context. The impact of the fifth dimension on third-dimensional solids can be seen as changes in the shape of a whole species or class of objects. In other words, if the growth registered in a single tree is fourth-dimensional in nature, the evolutionary growth of the species to which that tree belongs is fifth-dimensional. Archetypal ideas, from which whole species and classes of objects are produced, are part of the fifth dimension. The human soul also exists in the fifth dimension, as does heaven. Therefore, the true creative genius works in the fifth dimension. It is not, however, a common environment for the average human being.

GLAMOUR: Before the word acquired its modern meaning, it referred to "enchantments" or "magic spells." Esoterically, the word is still used in this way, to refer to any illusion or feeling that distorts our perception of reality—either by charming or frightening us.

GOD: The Creator of all that exists, visible and invisible; the life principle and creative intelligence underlying all life forms and phenomena.

GURU: A Hindu term for "teacher."

HEAVEN: The state of consciousness of the spirit. Heaven is not a place populated by those who have died; it is accessible to incarnate and discarnate humans alike. It is a state of mind. In heaven are located the archetypal patterns of all creation, as well as the ideal qualities of human expression.

HELL: A very low state of consciousness, devoid of contact with spirit. Hell is not a post mortem destination; it is a state of mind induced by strong, negative feelings such as despair, bitterness, and malice. Hell induces a state of intense emptiness in the person experiencing it.

HIGHER SELF: The animating principle in human consciousness—the inner being or soul. It is the guiding intelligence of the personality, the part of the human mind that is immortal.

INCARNATION: The period of time in which a human spirit is expressing itself through a personality.

INNER PLANES: A term used to refer to any one of several inner worlds or levels of existence, all of which interpenetrate the dense physical plane. Each physical human being exists on these inner planes as well as on the physical level, by dint of having bodies composed of matter drawn from them.

INNER SELF: The essence of the human consciousness which is the guiding intelligence of the personality. It is associated with the immortal aspect of the human mind.

INTUITION: In general usage, the capacity to know something without using the physical senses.

KARMA: A Sanskrit word meaning "reactiveness." Every one of our actions, thoughts, and emotions produces a reaction of like quality, sooner or later. Good deeds and thoughts produce beneficent reactions; cruel and selfish deeds and thoughts produce restrictive reactions. By dealing with these karmic effects, we gradually learn the lessons of maturity.

KUNDALINI: A Sanskrit term for the subtle energies that flow up the spine in the subtle bodies, connecting various force centers or chakras. As the quality of consciousness changes, various changes also occur in the quality and intensity of these energy flows.

LIGHT: Esoterically, there are many octaves of light, of which visible light is the densest. In its higher octaves, light is consciousness itself.

MAGIC: In its original sense, the acts of a Magus or wise person with conscious awareness of the inner life of spirit. Pure magic, therefore, is the focusing of creative energies for the transformation of forms.

MANTRA: A word or phrase that is silently repeated for the purpose of calming thoughts and feelings.

MASTER: An individual who has reached complete competence and perfection as a human—the epitome of genius.

MATERIALISM: The belief that the physical plane is the only plane of existence, or at least the most powerful and important. Materialism denies the importance of the soul, the existence of divine intelligence, and the invisible realms of life.

MEDITATION: An act of mental rapport in which the ideals, purposes, and intents of the inner life are discerned, interpreted, and applied by the personality. To be meaningful, meditation must be a very active state in which creative ideas, new realizations, and healing forces are discovered, harnessed, and applied to the needs of daily life. The current belief that meditation is a passive state of emptying the mind, by just sitting, is the antithesis of true meditation.

MEDIUM: A person who practices mediumship—the phenomenon of a nonphysical intelligence, usually a discarnate human, assuming some degree of control of a physical body in order to communicate something meaningful and useful.

MENTAL PLANE: The dimension of intellectual thought. One of the inner planes of existence, it also interpenetrates the dense physical plane. It teems with active life of its own, in addition to providing the substances for the mental bodies of all humanity.

METAPHYSICS: The philosophical and intellectual inquiry into the spiritual nature of all things.

MIND: The portion of the human personality that has the capacity to think. The mind is an organized field of energy which exists in invisible dimensions. It *is not* the physical brain, although it can operate through the brain.

MYSTIC: One who loves, reveres, and *finds* God and His entire Creation.

NIRVANA: A supremely refined state of consciousness

in which our individual focus of consciousness is totally directed at God.

OCCULT: The hidden secrets of nature.

PERSONALITY: The part of the human being that is used for manifestation in the earth plane. Composed of a mind, a set of emotions, and a physical body, it is the child of the soul and its experiences on earth.

PLANE: An octave in consciousness. All planes of consciousness interpenetrate the same space; they differ from one another in the quality of their substance. The human personality exists in the physical, astral, and mental planes.

PSYCHIC: A person who is able to perceive events and information without the use of the physical senses. The word is also used to refer to any event associated with the phenomena of parapsychology.

SAMADHI: An exalted state of consciousness, reached during meditation or contemplation, in which the consciousness of the meditator becomes absorbed in God and contacts divine wisdom, love, and unity. There are a number of degrees of samadhi.

SANSKRIT: An ancient language, now dead, in which many of the Hindu scriptures are written. Many Sanskrit words and phrases have been preserved in modern usage out of respect for the original form in which they appeared. In actual practice, this custom tends to obscure and distort the meaning of terms instead of clearly conveying their esoteric significance.

SENSATION: The reaction we register in our mind, emotions, or physical body in response to stimuli. Memories and ideas are mental sensations. Feelings and sentiments are emotional sensations. Sensations should never be confused with consciousness, which is our ability to be aware of the meaning, purpose, design, and creative uses of the forces, elements, and entities of our spiritual, mental, emotional, and physical environments. Detaching from mental and emotional sensations and identifying with consciousness is one of the major problems the spiritual aspirant faces.

SOUL: The individualized principle of consciousness and creativity within the human being. It is the soul that evolves and acts; it is the soul that creates the potential of the personality, vivifies it, and guides it through certain life experiences designed to increase competence in living. The soul is a pure expression of love, wisdom, and courage.

SPIRIT: In this book, a word used primarily to describe the highest immortal, divine essence within the human being. Both incarnate and discarnate humans alike possess this spirit within them. In popular usage, however, the word is used to refer to the portion of the human being which survives death.

SUBCONSCIOUS: The part of the personality that is not being consciously used at any given moment.

SUBTLE BODIES: The intangible "bodies" of thought and emotion all humans, plants, and animals have.

SUTRA: A Sanskrit term meaning "verse," as in the verses of the Holy Bible.

SWAMI: A title given to advanced members of spiritual schools or orders in India, derived from the Sanskrit for "master of one's self." Swamis are dedicated to honoring and preserving the traditions of their line of teaching and philosophy.

SYMBOL: An image, thought, feeling, or event which contains a deeper significance than what is obvious from the outer form. It points to inner dimensions of reality, force, and meaning. To discern these inner dimensions, however, the symbol must be interpreted. The study of symbolism is useful only if it leads to a discovery of the reality that the symbol veils.

THOUGHT-FORM: Literally, the form a thought takes on the plane on which it is created, usually the astral or mental. Visible only to clairvoyants, thought-forms are nonetheless created by every human being during the ordinary processes of thinking and feeling.

TRANSCENDENCE: The state of having risen above the mundane levels of consciousness and self-expression. Many people falsely assume that the mere retreat into a state of psychological quietness is enough to achieve transcendence, but that is only a withdrawal from sensation. Transcendence involves the movement of our level of awareness and perception toward spiritual consciousness; it may or may not involve significant withdrawal from outer sensation.

UNCONSCIOUS: The part of the mind not ordinarily accessible to the conscious mind. It is filled in part with repressed memories, desires, fears, and feelings. But there are other parts to the unconscious as well: the seeds of noble qualities, creative impulses, and memories of earlier lives.

VEHICLES: An occult term for the various bodies of the human personality.

VIBRATION: The movement of any energy particle, whether physical, astral, or mental in origin. The word is popularly used to refer to emanations of astral energy which are perceived by psychic sensitivity.

WILL: The force of our impulse to act and its expression. The spiritual will is the power and focused direction of our spiritual life and force. The personal will is not found in our thoughts or feelings so much as in the strength of our convictions and attitudes. It is discovered as we examine the source of our motives and sense of purpose.

YOGA: A Hindu system of personal or spiritual development. There are many kinds of yoga—the yoga of the physical body (hatha yoga), the yoga of action (karma yoga), the yoga of devotion (bhakti yoga), the yoga of wisdom (jnana yoga), and the yoga of the mind (raja yoga) are some of the better known. The word "yoga" means "union."

ZEN: A form of mysticism practiced in Japan. Although the principles of Zen are gaining some popularity in the United States, their passive nature tends to interfere with the development of the mind, rather than encourage it.

FROM HEAVEN TO EARTH

The Priests of God is one of six books in the *From Heaven to Earth* series. Each book contains four interviews between Dr. Robert R. Leichtman and the spirits of prominent psychics, geniuses, and world leaders. They may be purchased individually for $13.95 apiece (plus $2 for shipping) or as a complete set for $60, postpaid. The other five books in the series are:

The Psychic Perspective—Edgar Cayce, Eileen Garrett, Arthur Ford, and Stewart White.

The Inner Side of Life—C.W. Leadbeater, H.P. Blavatsky, Cheiro, and Carl Jung and Sigmund Freud.

The Hidden Side of Science—Nikola Tesla, Luther Burbank, Sir Oliver Lodge, and Albert Einstein.

The Dynamics of Creativity—William Shakespeare, Mark Twain, Rembrandt, and Richard Wagner.

The Destiny of America—Thomas Jefferson, Benjamin Franklin, Abraham Lincoln, and a joint interview with seven key spirits from American history—Alexander Hamilton, Franklin, Jefferson, the two Roosevelts, Harry Truman, and George Washington.

Orders can be placed by sending a check for the proper amount to Ariel Press, P.O. Box 1387, Alpharetta, GA 30239. Make checks payable to Ariel Press. Foreign checks should be payable in U.S. funds. In Georgia, please add 7% sales tax.

It is also possible to order by calling toll free 1-800-336-7769 between 8 a.m. and 6 p.m. Monday through Thursday and charging the order to VISA, MasterCard, Discover, Diners Card, or American Express.

OTHER BOOKS FROM ARIEL PRESS

Ariel Press is one of the leading publishers of fine books on the mind, psychic development, spiritual growth, healing, and creativity. Any of the following books can be ordered by writing directly to Ariel Press, P.O. Box 1387, Alpharetta, GA 30239, or calling toll free at 1-800-336-7769. Be sure to send a check in U.S. funds—or charge your order to Master Card, VISA, Discover, Diners Club, or American Express. Add $2 per book for shipping (maximum shipping charge: $5).

ACTIVE MEDITATION
by Robert R. Leichtman, M.D. and Carl Japikse
$19.95

FORCES OF THE ZODIAC
by Robert R. Leichtman, M.D. and Carl Japikse
$19.95

THE ART OF LIVING (5 VOLUMES)
by Robert R. Leichtman, M.D. and Carl Japikse
$45

THE LIFE OF SPIRIT (5 VOLUMES)
by Robert R. Leichtman, M.D. and Carl Japikse
$50

EXPLORING THE TAROT
by Carl Japikse
$14.95

THE LIGHT WITHIN US
by Carl Japikse
$9.95